The Economic Process
A Structured Approach

The Economic Process
A Structured Approach

Robert L. Darcy
Ph.D., University of Colorado

Publishing Horizons, Inc., Columbus, Ohio

Printed in the United States

2 3 4   ◀P   7 6 5 4

Library of Congress Cataloging in Publication Data

Darcy, Robert L., 1928-
  The economic process.

  Bibliography: p.
  Includes index.
  1. Economics.   2. United States—Economic conditions.
I. Title.
HB171.5.D218   1986   330   85-19412
ISBN 0-942280-16-4

for D., J., C.

Hoping these "second steps toward
economic understanding" will contribute
not only to the social virtue of *prudentia economica*
but to a higher level of individual consciousness as well.

Contents

Preface and Acknowledgments

Thomas Carlyle's description of economics as "the dismal science" turned out to be more than an apt commentary on the gloomy predictions of 19th-century economists Thomas Malthus (writing about overpopulation) and David Ricardo (analyzing class conflicts concerning the distribution of income). The description found new meaning for generations of 20th-century college students exposed to the standard two-term Principles of Economics course, complete with 900-page encyclopaedic text, "coefficients of elasticity," and esoteric "indifference curves."

Even larger numbers of Americans, however, have entirely avoided academic economics (dismal or otherwise) through lack of opportunity, intimidation, or—alas!—skepticism concerning its value. (After all, people who have never studied the economic process in a systematic manner nevertheless survive, and many prosper. As individual participants in the American economy they earn income, consume goods and services, vote on economic issues in local and national elections, and accumulate portfolios of personal investments. Nor has the economy's overall performance since the late 1960s engendered much confidence in the ability of economic theory to provide useful guidelines for public policy.)

About the Book

Why, then, might a person be interested in a book such as *The Economic Process?* First, it is designed to be cogent and readable (much more so than the five-pound, nine-by-eleven "freshman level" economics tome that arrived on my desk some time ago). While *The Economic Process* does not cover the subject as exhaustively as an encyclopaedic text, experience suggests that "small is beautiful" can apply to a book that deals with essentials accurately and in a well-organized, lucid way. (There is less risk of the reader suffering diminishing returns, and one can always read additional books.) Second, the subject matter is deeply significant. Economics, the only field in the social sciences for which a Nobel Prize is awarded, deals with a human activity that is, for millions of people, life's principal preoccupation. (In all candor, dismal jokes aside, innocence of economic science can hardly be judged a virtue in today's world.) Finally, there is a certain mystique surrounding economics—arising no doubt from the aura of power associated with great wealth—that can perhaps be penetrated by study and reflection. A clearer understanding of the social process of "getting and spending" conceivably might help put materialistic values in a more balanced perspective in the overall pattern of human life.

The Economic Process is a basic primer of (1) economics, (2) the economic process, and (3) the American economy. It reflects the author's 25 years of teaching and research experience as a professional economist. In treating a complex subject that is vital to social and individual wellbeing, the book offers economy of both substance and style, without distortional oversimplification. Its key feature is a *structured* approach emphasizing the central ideas and techniques of economics.

Points of View

Does the book express a certain point of view? The answer is a double yes. The *professional* viewpoint is that of an academic economist schooled in classical and standard neoclassical-plus-Keynesian doctrine, who moved progressively in the course of his career toward the evolutionary institutionalism of economists like Thorstein Veblen, C.E. Ayres, Gunnar Myrdal, John Kenneth Galbraith, and kindred spirits. (The appendix to Chapter 14 sketches these two streams of economic thought, along with the more radical member of the troika of economic doctrines, Marxian socialism.)

Moreover the book expresses an *ethical* point of view, clearly disclosed "up front" and throughout the various discussions of economic policy. Indeed, one tenet of the professional viewpoint is that economics, whether construed as "economic science" or "political economy," cannot possibly avoid ethical issues and value judgments. Only pretenders claim otherwise. The value position openly expressed in this book holds that economic life is enormously important not only to ensure physical survival for society's members but also to provide "the material means of human experience." And yet, even if material wellbeing may somehow be regarded as "the most important thing"—to recall football coach Vince Lombardi's famous quote—it surely is not "the only thing." The valuing of something *beyond* "the ordinary business of life" and pursuit of wealth is the philosophical point of departure for a moral perspective on such questions as the pattern of income distribution, economic power, and side effects of economic growth. The final chapters of the book specifically address value issues and the human meaning of economic progress.

Intended Readership

So, what kind of a book is this, and for whom is it written? To put it in a category, it is didactic nonfiction (to the extent that any treatise on economics can qualify as nonfiction). It focuses on economic activity as a *social* process rather than approaching the subject from the viewpoint of the individual *consumer* ("how to spend wisely") or the profit-seeking *business firm* ("how to boost revenues and cut costs") or the manager of investment portfolios ("how to get rich from dividends, interest, and capital gains while avoiding tax liability"). Despite its societal orientation, however, the book tries never to lose sight of the *individual* human being as the agent and intended beneficiary of the economic process.

The Economic Process can serve as a textbook in such college courses as "Economics and Society" and "Introduction to Economics" (but NOT the standard two-semester "Micro-Principles" and "Macro-Principles" sequence) or as independent, adult-level reading, for enlightenment and even for pleasure and profit. Author and publisher would be delighted if the book finds both types of uses and richly rewards its readers in more ways than one.

Acknowledgements

Many acknowledgements are due and most gratefully expressed. The original manuscript was reviewed by four academic economists of divergent intellectual orientations: Dr. J. Patrick Lewis of Otterbein College, Dr. Rodney D. Peterson of Colorado State University, Dr. Baldwin Ranson of Western State College of Colorado, and Dr. James A. Swaney of Wright State University. Their criticisms and suggestions were extremely helpful; of course they should not be held responsible for questionable interpretations, errors, and inadequacies that remain. Faculty colleagues at the Newark campus of Ohio State University were supportive and generous in sharing ideas from their own fields (a special thanks to classicist Joseph R. Tebben). Shirley Justice and Sue Evans helped not only by typing the manuscript but with their enthusiasm and good humor. Parts of the manuscript were read and encouragement given by Philip E. Powell, Ann E. Murphy, and Jack A. Wilson, longtime friends and colleagues from the field of economic education.

The Ameritrust Company and Love Publishing Company granted permission to use copyrighted materials. Indeed, Sections Two, Three, and Five of the 1973 Love edition of *Manpower and Economic Education,* co-authored by R.L. Darcy and P.E. Powell, will be recognized as antecedents of the present book. (An earlier edition of *Manpower and Economic Education* was published by the Joint Council on Economic Education.)

Finally, I wish to acknowledge the contributions made by my teachers and students, as well as the countless authors and numerous colleagues who in various ways have helped shape the ideas and values expressed in *The Economic Process.*

Westerville, Ohio   *Robert L. Darcy*
August, 1985

A Note to Readers
on Language and the Dictionary

Words are the vehicles upon which ideas ride.
　　　　—J. Sterling Morton

The use of language is not confined to its being the medium through which we communicate ideas to one another; it fulfills a no less important function as an instrument of thought.
　　　　—Roget's Thesaurus

Anything worth learning requires disciplined effort. The author's intent in writing this book was not to make it easy, but valuable. Some of the words used to express economic and related ideas will be unfamiliar to you. You can't understand the *ideas* if you don't know what the *words* mean. (Should an author "water down" ideas to match an arbitrarily limited vocabulary level?)

A simple yet effective solution to this problem is for the reader to make diligent use of that often-neglected learning aid, the Dictionary (any good, college-level dictionary). Don't be so rushed (or lazy?) that you fail to look up words you don't know; discovering their meaning will help clarify the particular passage you are reading and add to your overall education. (It is nice to have your own dictionary.)

For special economics terms, consult this book's *index* for page citations where you will find definitions, contexts, and applications—a better way to master the language of economics than memorizing a simplified glossary. (For additional terms, graphics, and other information beyond the scope of *The Economic Process,* or as a cross-check, refer to the index of a standard encyclopaedic Principles of Economics textbook, several of which are cited in the Suggested Readings and References. Economics glossaries and special dictionaries are generally not recommended.)

PART ONE
INTRODUCTION

In Chapter 1, the meaning of *the economic process* is explained in terms of society's productive activities directed toward the provision of material wellbeing; *economics* is identified as a field of scholarly inquiry that studies the economic process; and *the American economy* is described as the particular system of ways and means that our nation uses to carry out the economic process. Chapter 2 identifies the central ideas and skills required for basic economic literacy. It also indicates why *economic understanding* is important, even though it will always be limited and imperfect. A philosophical tone is suggested to help put the economic aspects of man's life in a balanced perspective.

The Economic Process, Economics, and The American Economy

> *The economic process* is the set of social activities directed toward the provision of material wellbeing. *Economics* is the social science discipline that studies the economic process and particular economic systems. *The American economy* is the unique blend of ways and means by which the people of our nation carry out the economic process.

An understanding of economics is an understanding of life's principal preoccupation.

    —John Kenneth Galbraith

The ideas of economists and political philosophers, both when they are right and when they are wrong, are more powerful than is commonly understood. Indeed, the world is ruled by little else. Practical men, who believe themselves to be quite exempt from an intellectual influence, are usually the slaves of some defunct economist.

    —John Maynard Keynes

This will be a short chapter. (Not as short, though, as Chapter 1 of John Maynard Keynes' 1936 treatise *The General Theory of Employment Interest and Money,* widely regarded as the most influential economics book of the 20th century; his opening chapter ran *one* paragraph occupying half a page!) The purpose here is to indicate the meaning of (1) the economic process, (2) economics, and (3) the American economy. Amplification follows in succeeding chapters. We begin with the term that is most familiar but often misused: "economics."

Economics

When politicians or journalists say (in any particular year) that "economics will determine this election," what is probably meant is that the current performance of the U.S. economy—its impact on jobs, taxes, and the prices consumers must pay for necessities and the amenities of life—will have a decisive influence on how people vote. The statement almost certainly is not referring to *economics* itself, for that term refers to a field of scholarly inquiry and professional competence. *Economics is the social science discipline that studies the economic process and the structure and functioning of particular economic systems,* such as the U.S. economy. It is "the science of material wellbeing." Economics has its own special vocabulary, distinctive values, and unique history (chronicled in books on the development of economic thought.) But economics shares with many other disciplines the basic worldview and methodologies of modern science, including heavy dependence on abstract theory and quantitative analysis.

There is an old tongue-in-cheek definition, "Economics *is* what economists *do.*" Professional economists conduct research, collect data, analyze problems, formulate proposed solutions, publish information and ideas, teach, and perform a variety of tasks (see "Economist" in the U.S. Department of Labor's *Dictionary of Occupational Titles* and *Occupational Outlook Handbook*). Among the men and women who claim the title "economist" or "economic (whatever)" are stockbrokers, journalists, business proprietors, government officials, research technicians working in incredibly narrow fields of specialization, and of course home economics teachers. There is no argument with this practice. In Chapter 9, however, an interesting test is suggested (by a renowned academic economist of an earlier generation) for categorizing the various people who "think, talk, and write about economic topics."

In Part Two, we shall present a more substantive, and therefore more useful, definition of economics than the ones reported above. However defined, economics essentially refers to a *field of inquiry and professional competence*—indeed, the only one of the social sciences in which a Nobel Prize is awarded. (Readers of this book will become acquainted with some of the great economists of modern history—Adam Smith, Karl Marx, Alfred Marshall, Thorstein Veblen, John Maynard Keynes—and such contemporary Nobel laureates as Paul Samuelson, Milton Friedman, and Gunnar Myrdal.) As practitioners of their discipline, economists at their best *(a)* study the consequences of existing economic arrangements, *(b)* suggest modified arrangements that promise better outcomes, and *(c)* try to help decision-makers understand realities of the economic process so that they can make wiser, more responsible choices.

The Economic Process

What is "the economic process" (obviously the central theme of the book since this was chosen to be the title)? *The economic process is the set of activities by which members of society produce goods and services and determine how this real income will be distributed* (or shared).

The economic process is as old as mankind. All social groups (tribes, clans, villages, feudal manors, nations) have cooperated in the production and distribution of food, clothing, shelter, etc., throughout history. Today, the world's five billion people provide for their material wellbeing by means of a wide variety of activities, some of which are technologically advanced and highly organized, while others are quite primitive—with predictably different outcomes in terms of survival rates, levels of living, and international power. This raises an interesting question: Are there some fundamental laws of economics that apply universally to *all* economic systems? To the extent that there are such universals, the lessons of *The Economic Process* (particularly Parts One, Two, Three, and Six) transcend the special case of the contemporary U.S. economy and provide globally relevant economic understanding.

The American Economy

What is meant by "the American economy"? *It is the economic system of the United States,* the particular blend of ways and means whereby the people of our nation carry out the economic process.

The U.S. economy produces $4 trillion worth of goods and services annually, making it the biggest economy in the world (most productive in terms of total output). We rank far ahead of the only other "trillionaire economies," namely Japan and the Soviet Union. Classified as an "industrial market system," the American economy has many features in common with the Japanese, Swedish, and French economies, for example, and even with the "nonmarket industrial economies" of East Germany, Czechoslovakia, and the Soviet Union. This is especially true when comparisons are made on the basis of resources, technology, and basic processes rather than particular institutional arrangements. Indeed, in terms of the *functions* that economic systems must perform and their basic dependence on *resources* and *technology,* one finds them to be essentially similar around the world. For example, the quality of resources reflects the prevailing technology; output rises as productivity increases; capital investment promotes productivity growth; and levels of living ultimately depend on total production, population size, and patterns of income distribution.

So, responding to our earlier question: Yes, there do seem to be some universal "principles" of economics. Therefore, many lessons of this book can be applied, with proper adaptation and sound judgment, to the full range of the world's economies, whether capitalist, socialist, or Third World. On the other hand, some of the book's content is "culturally limited"—because the institutions of Western civilization and special circumstances of American society create a unique setting for the interplay of economic forces. Parts Four and Five, in particular, consider some of the *institutions* and *problems* that characterize an affluent, mature, market-oriented system that in some respects has no parallel elsewhere in the world.

In summary, *the economic process* is a set of activities directed toward providing material wellbeing for the members of society. *Economics* is a field of scholarly inquiry, a social science discipline that entails specialized training and professional competence. The *U.S. economy* is a case study of the economic process, the particular ways and means employed by the American people for determining the production and distribution of income. All three subjects are interesting and important in themselves; indeed the economic process can be a matter of life or death (as periodic famines in Africa and Asia testify). But economics as a science and the analysis of any particular economic system are logically subsidiary to the basic economic process.

As for the intellectual content of economics, however, Keynes (recall his quotation at the beginning of the chapter) is not the only writer to proclaim the immense power of *economic ideas* for influencing practical affairs in the world, and even for shaping the way we view society and the nature of man himself. This is a theme that will thread its way through the entire book and receive focused attention in Part Six.

"Robinson and Marciano"

Just as Sugar Ray Robinson would not go against Rocky Marciano in the boxing ring, *The Economic Process* at 300 pages has no desire to compete with the 900-page encyclopaedic Principles of Economics textbooks. We take the opportunity here at the end of Chapter 1 to remind readers that the two types of books are different tools for different purposes (see Preface) and to identify some of the comprehensive texts that could be used for supplementary reference purposes.

As a textbook for a one-term beginning college course, *The Economic Process* offers certain advantages over longer and more traditional texts, including its perspective, conceptual structure, and analytical treatment of social values. But it would be unrealistic to expect this 300-page book to accomplish what it does and also cover the entire field of conventional economics in the same painstaking detail found in a 900-page textbook. Moreover, not everybody wants such exhaustive treatment in the very first course—certainly not the thousands of students who take only *half* the sequence (randomly either "microprinciples" or "macroprinciples"), thereby suffering bountiful feast followed by utter famine. On the other hand, there is no substitute for the comprehensive texts when it comes to covering the broad range of conventional topics in reasonable depth to meet the requirements of economics, business, and certain other majors in a two-term sequence (preferably after benefiting from the perspective of a pre-Principles introductory course).

Independent readers of *The Economic Process,* few of whom would tackle a comprehensive Principles text outside the academic setting, may find it useful to consult a library reference, e.g., to note the traditional explanation of "consumer equilibrium" and the theory of the "rational business firm." There are numerous excellent books available, five of which are listed below. Also identified is a highly readable little book (161 pages in pocket-size paperback) by Galbraith and Salinger that is both witty and wise.

Short lists of SELECTED READINGS AND REFERENCES appear at the end of chapters. They identify sources of statistical data, provide citations for many of the quotes, ideas, and works alluded to, or in some cases simply point the way toward additional study of themes introduced in the respective chapters.

Selected Readings and References

J.K. Galbraith and N. Salinger, *Almost Everyone's Guide to Economics.* Boston: Houghton Mifflin, 1978 (Bantam paperback, 1979).
J.D. Gwartney and R. Stroup, *Economics,* 3d ed. New York: Academic Press, 1982.
R.G. Lipsey and P.O. Steiner, *Economics,* 7th ed. New York: Harper & Row, 1983.
Campbell R. McConnell, *Economics,* 9th ed. New York: McGraw-Hill, 1984.
P.A. Samuelson and W.D. Nordhaus, *Economics,* 12th ed. New York: McGraw-Hill, 1985.
Milton H. Spencer, *Contemporary Economics,* 5th ed. New York: Worth, 1983.

(*Note:* Three of the last five books approach 1,000 pages; one is less than 800.)

The Elements of Economic Understanding, and A Human Perspective on the Science of Material Wellbeing

Economic understanding (what can be termed "functional economic literacy") requires knowledge of (1) the *structure of economics*, (2) *basic skills* in using three tools of economic analysis, and (3) the ability to carry out a five-step *method of economic reasoning*. Achievement of economic literacy offers practical rewards in terms of prudent individual decisionmaking, more responsible judgments as citizens of the economic community, and deeper insight concerning the proper role of economic activity in the overall life of man. Progression from lower to higher *levels of knowing* can help one make wiser decisions in many areas of human life.

I've been rich and I've been poor; rich is better.
        —(variously attributed)

If a nation expects to be ignorant and free
It expects what never was and never will be.
        —Thomas Jefferson

Man does not live by bread alone; what does it profit a man to gain the whole world if he loses his soul?
        —Holy Bible

The objective of this book is to assist readers in developing a working knowledge of economics, the economic process, and the U.S. economy—to achieve basic economic understanding, or "functional economic literacy." The book is not merely "about" these three topics, but intends to help readers move step-by-step to higher "levels of knowing" (a notion that is explained later in this chapter). This chapter outlines what people need to know as a basis for understanding the economic process.

The Structure of Economics

What are the essential "elements of economic understanding?" In keeping with the structured approach that is a distinctive feature of *The Economic Process,* we identify three broad areas in which understanding is required (see Figure 2.1.) First is the cluster of central ideas that serve as organizing themes for the entire study—what can be termed *the structure of economics.*

The first "big ideas" in the structure of economics serve to identify the basic subject matter that is studied: the interacting forces, or "variables" that are analyzed—namely resources, technology, and institutions. *Resources* are the physical inputs that can be used directly in production: land, labor, capital (and in a private enterprise system, entrepreneurship or "enterprise"). *Technology* is the sum total of tool-making and tool-using knowledge and skills available for application to society's resources. *Economic institutions* are patterns of social behavior that function as coordinating mechanisms in the use of resources and technology. These terms and others included in our outline of the elements of economic understanding are all carefully defined in the following chapters.

Thus, economists and students of economics focus their study on the *interaction of resources, technology, and institutions.* But, interaction with respect to what? For what purpose? Toward what ends? As a study of the economic process, economics must address the basic activities that determine society's material wellbeing, namely the *production* and *distribution* of goods and services ("real income"). More specifically, every economic system must determine (1) the *overall level* of economic

---

Figure 2.1 *The Elements of Economic Understanding*

I. **The Structure of Economics**
   - Interacting forces: Resources, Technology, Institutions
   - Three basic questions: How much ⎱
                            What   ⎬ to produce
                            For whom ⎰
   - Goals and values

II. **Techniques of Economic Analysis**
   - History
   - Theory
   - Statistics

III. **Five-Step Method of Economic Reasoning**
   1. Define the problem.
   2. Identify goals.
   3. Consider alternative solutions.
   4. Analyze probable consequences.
   5. Choose best solution.

activity (notably employment and production), or *how much* to produce; (2) the *composition* of output, or *what* to produce; and (3) the *distribution* of income, or *for whom* to produce. (These are variously referred to as the three basic *functions* of the economy, the three *problems* to be solved, or the three *questions* every economic system must answer.)

Consider a pizza pie. *Resources* (flour, tomatoes, cheese, human labor, kitchen implements, and an oven) are combined with *technology* (the recipe plus baking skills) and *institutions* (the restaurant, consumer addiction to fast-food, and wide-spread use of money in exchange transactions). Decisions must be made (by members of the "economic community") about the *overall size* of the pizza (large requires more resources than medium or small); its *composition* (cheese, pepperoni, green peppers); and last, but by no means least, *how to divide up* this mouth-watering delicacy among the various would-be consumers (equal shares? larger portions for the 180-pound man than the 120-pound woman? more slices for the hungriest, or for the person who paid for it?) Three *sets of interacting forces,* three *questions to be answered.*

The final member of the structure-of-economics trilogy is less definitive than the others but serves to highlight a theme of overwhelming importance in economics, namely the inevitable and controversial role of *values.* Not only does society *use* resources, technology, and institutions to determine how much, what, and for whom to produce; but through one mechanism or another, it sets *goals* specifying the *desired outcomes* of such use. These goals reflect the underlying values (criteria and standards of "goodness") of the particular society.

Economic values and goals can be stated in very explicit terms, or expressed informally. In the United States, for example, Congress has passed legislation with the declared purpose of promoting "full employment and production" and eliminating "the paradox of poverty in the midst of plenty in this Nation." By custom and public rhetoric, society also affirms the goal of producing that particular composition of goods and services that reflects "freedom of consumer choice."

Full production, freedom of choice, and *equity* in the distribution of income are not the only goals of the U.S. economy. A great deal is also said about the desirability of *stable economic growth, avoidance of inflation,* preservation of small business and the family farm, a balanced federal budget, increased productivity, lower interest rates, and numerous variations on the theme of *international balance.* What is emphasized in the present discussion is that people—workers, consumers, citizens, politicians, and economists themselves—are seldom indifferent to the particular way our economic system performs its three basic functions. *Value judgments are inherent* not only in the formulation and implementation of economic *policy* but even in the identification and analysis of economic *problems* and *issues.* Clearly, *economics is not a value-free science.* On the contrary, it was conceived out of *value conflicts* (in the 18th century, concerning efficiency and income distribution) and has developed largely as a set of rules for maximizing certain selected ends, notably output, income, and "consumer satisfaction."

Techniques of Analysis

As one develops an understanding of the basic structure of economics, glimpsing the inner workings of the economic process itself, a need arises for *tools* with which to study the identified sets of variables, questions, and social actions. This requires the acquisition of basic working skills in the areas of *statistics, history,* and *theory*—the three acknowledged *techniques of economic analysis.*

In the real world of today's U.S. economy, for example, we describe the *overall level* of production (first of the "big questions" facing every economic system) with a *statistical measure* called the *gross national product (GNP),* which is calculated and published by an agency of the federal government. In 1984, our *GNP* was $3.7 trillion (that's thirty-seven hundred *billions* of dollars!), meaning that the total output of the American economy for that year—consisting of products for consumers, investment goods, government-purchased goods and services, and net exports—had a combined market value of $3.7 trillion. Other statistical indicators that help describe the overall level of economic activity are unemployment rates, the index of industrial production, and the consumer price index (see Chapters 9 and 15).

A breakdown of *GNP* by category of spending and industrial sectors also provides insight concerning the *composition* of output. In 1984, for example, nearly two-thirds of total production consisted of goods and services for *consumers,* while about one-seventh of the *GNP* was made up of investment goods purchased by *business firms,* and one-fifth of total output was accounted for by federal-state-local *government.*

Statistics on employment, wages, government transfer payments, and the shares of personal income received by families in various income brackets help describe the actual pattern of *income distribution* in our society. Example: In 1983, half the families received incomes above $24,580 a year, while half had incomes below that median figure. Some 35 million Americans, 15% of our total population, had cash incomes below the poverty level.

Economic literacy *requires that one understand both the meaning* and *limitations of these statistical indicators,* for many of the "facts" about economic activity come to us not as tangible reality but in the form of these representational numbers.

Important as statistics is a tool of economic analysis, however, equally necessary are history and theory. *History* can be defined in a variety of ways, but for our purposes it is to be understood as more than simply "a record of past events" (e.g., details of the Western world's Industrial Revolution). History as a technique of economic analysis also requires meaningful accounts of present-day social arrangements that influence the economic process. A qualitative description of the Federal Reserve System, for example, is essential for understanding our nation's money and banking system. One of the criticisms of theory-dominated college courses in economics—"Micro Principles," "Macro Principles," and others—and of economic analysis in general, is the neglect of historical perspective and *qualitative* aspects of the economic process. In Chapters 9 and 10, and elsewhere throughout this book, the attempt is made to afford history its rightful place among the techniques of economic analysis, thereby contributing to a more realistic understanding of the economic process.

The third analytical technique is *theory.* Notwithstanding the observation made above, there can be no questioning the crucial importance of theory as a tool of economic analysis; it is economic theory that lays the groundwork for all systematic study of the economic process. Theory serves up the key questions, indicates logical ways for answering those questions, and suggests scientific "experiments" for testing hypotheses regarding cause-and-effect relationships. In the absence of theory, the tools of statistics and history lack cogent meaning. Much of Part Three and sections of Parts Four, Five, and Six deal with economic theory, though not always in the conventional terms of supply-and-demand curves and algebraic equations!

Five-Step Method of Reasoning

We have so far considered the *structure* of economics (central organizing ideas and basic themes) and the three *techniques* required for competent economic analysis. The third and final element of economic understanding is a five-step *method of reasoning* that provides a framework for applying one's knowledge of structure and basic analytical skills. Described in full detail in Chapter 16, this systematic procedure for reaching decisions on the basis of logic, evidence, and values has been called the most important component of economic understanding. And so it is, in the sense of providing a capstone framework for applying the other elements of economic competence ("to *do* something you have to *know* something"). The method requires (1) explicit definition of the problem, (2) identification of goals, (3) consideration of alternative possible ways for achieving the goals, (4) analysis of the likely consequences of each of the alternatives, and *only then* (5) choosing the best alternative in light of the stated goals. This five-step method is equally useful for solving *personal* economic problems (e.g., career choice, or whether to buy a house), *organizational* problems (wage decisions facing a business firm and labor union), and problems of *public choice* (whether to raise tax rates or cut government spending in order to reduce budget deficits).

Philosophical Perspective

The final topic to be addressed in this chapter carries us beyond the conventional boundaries of economics. It invites consideration of *philosophical* questions concerning the role of economic activity in the overall life of man and the contribution that economic understanding might possibly make to human wellbeing in areas beyond the familiar domains of consumer choice, employment and income, and responsible economic citizenship.

There is always a risk that the author of a book or instructor in a college course will over-represent his subject; it is obviously important to him, so he may exaggerate its importance for readers, students, and the world at large. Remarks in the Preface and quotations at the beginning of this chapter (suggesting, for example, that poverty and ignorance are bad while freedom and spiritual development are good) are intended to dispel this danger and invite a more *balanced perspective* on economics and the economic process. The author's own approach, in fact, is quite consistent with the views of psychologist C.G. Jung. When asked in a 1960 interview about the good life, Jung listed five contributive factors: (1) good physical and mental health; (2) personal and intimate relationships—friendship and love; (3) the ability to appreciate beauty in art and nature; (4) a reasonable level of living and satisfactory work; and (5) a philosophic or religious point of view capable of coping with the ups and downs of life.

Note that *economic* considerations on Jung's list included a good job and comfortable income. Conspicuously absent is the heavy emphasis on monetary achievement and material goods that dominates popular conceptions of the "successful" life. (Of course, Jung would be the last person to claim that all should feel exactly alike on such matters.) The question is not whether *poverty* is good or bad; genuine poverty restricts opportunities for human development and life experience. But what is the attitude toward money and material things *beyond* "a comfortable level of living"? When is enough, enough—if not a $4 trillion *GNP* and per capita consumption of $10,000, then perhaps at double those levels? Is the "insatiability of consumer wants" (euphemistic jargon for "unlimited gluttony and greed") an American characteristic of which we can honestly be proud? And what are the costs of this overvaluation of material gain, in terms of harm to the physical environment, to the men and women with whom we share this planet, and to our own psychological and spiritual wellbeing?

One of the premises of this book is that economic understanding can provide benefits that spill over into other areas of life (like the "transferable skills" that educators and job-trainers increasingly emphasize for meeting the labor requirements of our fast-changing economy). As we progress from the lowest level of under-standing—knowing "about" a subject—to higher levels, we increase our competence to make wiser judgments that can benefit (often in unforeseen ways) our own lives and the lives of people around us. (Recall the Four Cardinal Virtues of Greek philosophy and Christian tradition—Prudence, Justice, Courage, and Temperance—especially the preeminent virtue of Prudence, which requires not just good intentions but *knowledge of reality;* see Chapter 30.)

In economics, as in other fields of inquiry, one can observe a scale of understanding that we shall term the Five Levels of Knowing (this is not the same thing as the five steps in economic reasoning). The levels are: (1) awareness, or knowing *about* a subject; (2) knowing *what;* (3) knowing *how;* (4) knowing *why;* and, finally but imperfectly and tentatively, (5) judgment: knowing *the good.*

The Levels of Knowing can be clarified with an example. Nearly everyone in our culture, from age 12 up, knows "about" an automobile's carburetor (i.e., he/she has heard of it). Many people have moved to the next higher level, of knowing *what* it is, as indicated by their ability to raise the hood and point to the part of the car that goes by this name. But fewer can describe *how* a carburetor functions in an internal-combustion engine to provide power for locomotion. And how many understand the principles of physics that explain *why* it functions the way that it does? Finally, it is only after long, technically sophisticated study that it becomes possible for a very few experts to know and be able to demonstrate interpersonally "the good" concerning carburetors, i.e., to formulate certain judgements about the way they should be used to prevent pollution and conserve energy resources.

All this is not to suggest that there is always a simple and lineal progression from awareness to sound judgment, whether in automotive engineering or economics. The situation is typically far more complex, which is why economic knowledge often resembles *myth*—not in the cynical sense of distorting facts for the purpose of misleading our understanding ("lies agreed upon") but in the classical sense of conveying an image of reality that, while superficially false, in certain important respects is essentially valid ("the divine truth behind the mortal tale"). Many economic models and theories are therefore, like myths, both true and not-true.

In a future chapter we quote President John F. Kennedy: "Americans too often want the luxury of opinion without the effort of thought" (recall Thomas Jefferson's statement at the beginning of the chapter on the connection between knowledge and freedom). It is difficult to hold responsible opinions if one's level of knowing lies somewhere in the shadowy region between (1) and (2)! Yet it is obviously impossible to know the what, how, why, and "good" of everything. So in this book, and in one's general approach to economic understanding, it is necessary to adopt an attitude of *challenge* balanced with *humility.* You aren't going to find all the answers; you may be obliged to admit (to yourself and others) that you really don't know enough about certain issues (such as "cost-push" inflation and Third-World debt) to formulate a responsible judgment. Discovering what you *don't* know about economic affairs (and what the experts don't know either!) can be a valuable lesson in itself.

On the other hand, you may learn some things from your study of the economic process and economic reasoning—for example, in the areas of analytical techniques, systematic thinking, and ethical values—that will move you up the Scale of Knowing in areas that transcend economics. And this may enrich your life.

From Overview to Closer Look

This chapter previewed a number of ideas at Levels One and Two on the scale of knowing that will be examined in greater depth in the chapters that follow. The discussion provided a bird's eye view of the economic forest. In Part Two we descend to earth for a closer look at the respective elements of economic understanding.

Selected Readings and References

Economic Report of the President 1985, together with the Annual Report of the President's Council of Economic Advisers (including 130 pages of statistical tables). Washington: U.S. Government Printing Office, 1985.

C.G. Jung, *The Undiscovered Self.* New York: Mentor, 1957. (Numerous books by and about Jung are widely available. The volume containing the interview alluded to in the chapter is entitled *C.G. Jung Speaking,* edited by W. McGuire and R.F.C. Hull; Princeton, NJ: Princeton University Press, 1977.)

PART TWO
CENTRAL IDEAS IN THE
STRUCTURE OF ECONOMICS

The half-dozen chapters of Part Two focus on the trio of fundamental ideas identified in the previous chapter as the *structure of economics* (Item 1 in the Elements of Economic Understanding). Chapter 3 presents an overview of the essential *subject matter* of economics: the interacting forces of *resources, technology,* and *institutions.* Chapter 4 discusses the basic *functions* that every economic system must perform—determining *how much, what,* and *for whom* to produce. In Chapter 5, the normative orientation of economics is highlighted with a brief discussion of *goals and values,* topics that command attention throughout the book and receive special consideration in Part Six. Having presented the core themes of economics in articulated sequence, we then return to the topics of resources (Chapter 6), technology (Chapter 7), and institutions (Chapter 8) for separate treatment in greater depth.

What Economics Is All About: Resources, Technology, Institutions

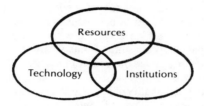

Economics is the study of how society organizes to develop, conserve, and use productive resources to provide material well-being for its members. Economics is concerned, therefore, with *resources* (labor, capital goods, and natural resources), *technology* (knowledge and skills), and *institutions* (organized patterns of human behavior)—and the way these three sets of forces interact to determine the *production* of goods and services and the *distribution* of income.

The time has come, the Walrus said, to speak of many things: Of shoes, and ships, and sealing wax, of cabbages, and kings.
    —Lewis Carroll, Through the Looking Glass

Grasping the structure of a subject is to learn how things are related; it enables a student to recognize new material as special cases of fundamental issues already mastered.
    —Jerome Bruner, The Process of Education (modified)

The whimsical verse by Lewis Carroll quoted above portrays quite accurately the broad scope and diverse content of economics. Included within the purview of this scholarly discipline are such topics as shoe production, transportation services, the communications media, agriculture, and taxation, as well as money and banking, consumer outlays, business enterprise, labor unions, the stock market, budget deficits, interest rates, international trade, inflation, jobs, and much much more.

Economics has been called the study of man in the everyday business of life...how people make a living...how society determines the material means of life and experience. Economics, as a study of the economic process and particular economic systems, obviously touches on an enormously large and important part of our lives.

But what is the basic nature of economics, the coherent theme that puts all these specific topics under a single heading? *Economics is the study of how society organizes to develop, conserve, and use productive resources to provide material wellbing for its members.*

Resources

What does this definition of economics really mean? First of all, *resources* are things that can be utilized in the production of goods and services. *Goods* are material things that can be used to satisfy consumer wants or to help produce other things. A hamburger sandwich is a "good"; a TV set is a "good"; a bulldozer is a "good." *Services* are activities that satisfy consumer wants, such as a haircut, repair of your TV set, the minister's sermon on Sunday morning, or having a tooth pulled by the dentist. (In some contexts "goods" encompasses both goods and services.) Generally speaking, it is the quantity and quality of goods and services available to a community that determine the *material wellbeing* of its members.

Economists usually divide resources—the things that can be used in production— into three categories: labor, capital, and natural resources. (A fourth type of resource, entrepreneurship, is found in private-enterprise economies.) *Production* is the use of resources to create "utility" (usefulness) in goods and services.

Labor includes all human effort—physical and mental work—used in production. Labor (sometimes called manpower) is the energy people contribute to production in their capacity as human resources; it includes digging ditches, operating machines in a factory, programming a computer, and supervising the checkers in a supermarket.

Capital includes all the buildings, tools, and equipment used in production. Note that the term "capital" is sometimes used in everyday language to mean money; but economists use the term capital in a very precise sense to mean *physical goods.* The important thing to remember about physical capital is that the goods are *produced* (they did not exist "in nature") and they are used in *further production* rather than for satisfying consumer wants directly. Examples of capital include a farm tractor, the Golden Gate Bridge, an automobile assembly plant, and a school building along with the books and classroom equipment that it contains.

Natural resources include land, air, minerals, rivers—all things that are available in nature and can be used in production. Traditionally the term *land* has been used as the label for this type of resource. This may seem strange since "land" in this broad sense includes such disparate but productively useful things as water (for river barges, for generating hydroelectric power, etc.), oil reserves still under the ground, and mountain scenery, as well as farmland and urban building sites. The usage no doubt reflects the early economists' preoccupation with *agricultural* production.

Technology

One of the most important principles of economics is that *resources are determined by technology: $R = f(T)$.* (Economists use notations such as this as a form of shorthand;

it is read: "Resources are a function of, i.e., depend on, Technology.") In what sense is this principle valid and significant?

Whether something can be used in production (*usefulness* is what makes it a resource) depends on whether people have the necessary knowledge, skills, and equipment to use it. (Back in the 1930s, there was a mining company in Colorado that was producing molybdenum—a metal similar to chromium—and throwing away another substance that happened to be found in the same rock. The substance wasn't valuable as a productive resource because industry had no important use for it. In the 1940s, however, a scientific and technological breakthrough sent the miners digging frantically to recover the "unwanted substance." It was uranium ore, and scientists had found a use for it in producing atomic energy.)

Technology simply means *society's knowledge of how to make and use tools.* Technology is one of the most important forces at work in the economy. It is the chief cause of economic change and the basic reason for the high productivity of the American economy. Technology is also a major source of economic disturbance and discomfort—as when automation and cybernation radically change the relative costs of production (e.g., in the U.S. and Japanese auto and electronics industries), reallocate market shares, and displace people from their jobs. Chapter 7 explores in greater depth the nature and influence of technology, not only as the "definer of resources" but also as a pervasive force in human culture.

Institutions

Institutions in general are patterns of social organization and behavior. *Economic institutions* are the established patterns of behavior that influence the way society develops, conserves, and uses resources.

Institutions are the *coordinating mechanisms of our economy.* They are the methods, organizations, customs, and traditions that control the use of resources. The wage system, for example, is an institution ("invented" during the Middle Ages) for having men and women exchange some of their time and effort for money—so they can then exchange the money for goods and services. Another institution is money itself, which is really not so much a "thing" as a system of behavior. We all agree to accept pieces of paper in exchange for services or goods, even though the pieces of paper have no value in themselves. They are valuable for what they can buy, and this in turn depends on the institution of market exchange.

Economics places a great deal of emphasis on the study of institutions. This is perfectly natural, for economics is a *social science.* It is social because of its concern with the *behavior of groups of people;* and it is a science because it makes use of the *scientific method* in formulating and testing its theories—making predictions and checking them against the facts. Economic science (the only one of the social sciences in which a Nobel Prize is awarded) makes extensive use of logic and quantitative analysis. As an applied policy science, economics seeks to describe the functions, structure, actual operation, and consequences of particular economic institutions and to generate knowledge that society can apply in *improving* its institutions.

Two of the most important institutions in the American economy are *the market* (or "price system") and *government.* Indeed, they are so dominant and extensive that we shall designate them *supra-institutions.* Economists devote a great deal of attention to each supra-institution separately and to the ways goverment and the market interact to form our present-day economic system, *"U.S. mixed capitalism."*

The "perceptive reader" will have noted more than a few definitions in this chapter. Terms such as *resources, production,* and *capital* are part of the technical language of economics, a scientific vocabulary (jargon in the nonpejorative sense) that is required both for *unambiguous communication* and *clarity of thinking.* Many of these terms are the verbal counterparts of concepts that are central to the intellectual structure of economics—the "big ideas" that provide a basis for organizing one's thinking about economic phenomena. *Resources, technology,* and *institutions,* for example, serve as "hooks" on which to hang additional facts and ideas about the economic process. As suggested in the quote at the beginning of this chapter, learning the structure of a subject helps one recognize the meaning of new material and see its relationship to what is already familiar. The result is a *deepening* of understanding as opposed to the feeling of bewilderment one experiences in moving to entirely new ground unconnected with what went before.

Selected Readings and References

Robert L. Darcy, *First Steps Toward Economic Understanding.* Athens: Ohio Council on Economic Education at Ohio University, 1966.

The Three Basic Problems Facing Every Economic System

Every economic system is faced with three basic questions: (1) What will be the overall level of production? (2) What particular kinds of goods and services will be produced? (3) How will the total income of the society be shared among its individual members? Answers to these questions inevitably are provided by every society in the world, whether primitive or advanced, capitalist or communist. How and how well the questions are answered will depend on the particular society's resources, technology, and institutions.

When we speak of an economic system (or "an economy") we essentially are referring to a society's productive capability and the way society is organized to use that capability in providing for the material wellbeing of its members. "The American economy" means the total economic system of the United States, including all of its institutions, technology, and resources. Later we will describe some important features of our economic system. Now, however, we turn to the question of what an economic system must *do*—the functions that every economy must perform.

How Much, What, For Whom to Produce

All systems—the planned economy of the U.S.S.R., the mixed capitalism of the U.S.A., the traditional economies of isolated villages in Africa or India—face the same basic problems and must perform three essential functions. They must:

1. Determine the overall level of economic activity, and therefore of total production.
2. Determine what particular goods and services will be produced: the composition of output.
3. Determine how the society's output will be shared among its individual members: the distribution of income.

Determining the *overall level* of economic activity answers the question of *how much* is produced. At the same time it establishes the level of employment (the extent to which available labor and other resources are currently utilized) as well as levels of income and prices. In 1984 our nation's overall level of output was by far the highest in the world; Americans produced $3.7 trillion of goods and services (the value of our gross national product/*GNP* for that year).

Determining the *composition* of the nation's output means answering the question of *what* is produced. Given the overall size of our "economic pie," what particular goods and services are produced; what *kind* of a pie is it? In recent years, U.S. production has shown a "product mix" of approximately two-thirds consumer goods, a little less than one-sixth capital goods, and a bit more than one-sixth government "collective" goods. Our *GNP* included "guns" and "butter," durable goods and nondurables, luxurious services for the well-to-do and "lower-end" goods for members of our society who are not so well off.

Perhaps the most controversial question of the three involves the *distribution* of the nation's income, determining *for whom* to produce: Who gets how much of the output and income generated by the economy? If proof is needed that economics is a value-laden subject about which most people have strong feelings, one can surely find such proof in the never-ending debates, bargaining strategies, and political maneuvers concerning the question of how the economic pie is sliced, the way income is to be *shared* among individual members (and families) in the society. Much blood has been spilled in the world and political rhetoric uttered, in America and elsewhere, over this crucial issue, not on equity grounds alone but because the answer to the distribution question generates ripple effects throughout the entire economy and society. (Widespread discontent over income shares received by working people, for example, may well have been an underlying cause of inflation in the U.S. economy during the 1970s; nor has the problem yet been truly resolved.)

Distribution affects production, influences status and power, and consigns many people to a life of poverty (currently some 35 million Americans, including 14 million children). As Parts Four, Five, and Six of this book will indicate, the dramatically unequal sharing of "the material means of life and experience" is a continuing issue both in the United States and worldwide.

Institutional Arrangements

The three basic questions facing every economic system are addressed through the *institutional arrangements* that characterize the system. In our own economy, for example, the *market system* and *government* largely determine how production and income distribution will be arranged, and how the system will initiate and adapt to *change.* (In the framework of this book it is institutions and technology that provide answers to the fundamental question of *how* to produce.)

The *overall level* of production in any particular period may be high or low (by historical standards, compared with other countries, or in relation to the economy's own potential); the *composition* of output may be balanced or skewed (too many guns, not enough butter); and the *distribution* of income may be satisfactory or unsatisfactory (too much poverty and inequality, not enough going to productive workers, too much going to the very rich or the elderly population). To the extent that society is *dissatisfied* with the actual level of production, composition of output, or distribution of income, efforts can be made to *change* the system's resources, technology, and *especially the institutions* in order to achieve results more consistent with society's goals, expectations, and values.

Comparative Economic Systems

How do the economies of today's world address the three basic economic problems? The economic system of the United States is predominantly (though not "purely") a *private-enterprise* or capitalistic market system, in which individuals and groups of people privately own most of the productive resources and make decentralized decisions as to how they should be used. Relying mainly on market institutions, the U.S. system falls into the category of "advanced industrial market economies."

The Union of Soviet Socialist Republics is a *socialist* or "communist" economy, where most of the natural resources and capital goods are owned and controlled by government. It is a "nonmarket" or "planned" economy. Great Britain has an economic system that is often described as "democratic socialism"—with some of the basic productive resources owned and operated by the government. But this birthplace of industrial capitalism is still largely a private-enterprise economy. And the same is true of France, West Germany, Sweden, and Japan, among other countries. (They too, like the United States, are considered industrial market economies; together these countries are the richest in the world.)

In some ways, the economic systems of the United States, Russia, and Britain, despite their different labels, are all very much alike. They all have well-trained, experienced industrial workers. Their methods of production are technologically advanced, and they use trillions of dollars worth of capital equipment. They are all highly productive by world standards. Where the economies differ is primarily in the way they are *organized* to use (and to develop) their productive capabilities. Their *resources* and *technology* are quite similar; it is the *institutional differences* that largely distinguish one system from another (see Chapters 8 and 29). A fascinating branch of economics that analyzes these similarities and differences is called Comparative Economic Systems, essentially focusing on how different types of economies answer the questions how much, what, and for whom to produce.

Selected Readings and References

Economic Report of the President 1985 (cited in Chapter 2; for updated statistics, see subsequent issues of the Report).

P.R. Gregory and R.C. Stuart, *Comparative Economic Systems,* 2d ed. Boston: Houghton Mifflin, 1985. (An advanced undergraduate-level college text.)

Goals and Values
of the American Economy

Few people and even fewer nations are indifferent to the way
their economic system answers the basic questions of how much,
what, and for whom to produce. They usually have preferences for
high levels of employment and production, a properly balanced
mix of the kinds of goods produced, and a functional yet equitable
distribution of income. The *goals* of economic society reflect the
underlying values of that society. These values and goals in turn
provide guidelines for economic policy.

*Unless its purpose is to provide pure entertainment or teach people to take
advantage of each other, economics must have some kind of relevance to
social policy.*
—*Frank H. Knight*

Every economic society faces the task of using its resources, technology, and
institutions to determine the overall level, composition, and distribution of *output*
(which at the same time is its real *income*). But societies, like individuals, often differ
in their notions of what constitutes *desirable* answers to these questions; they disagree
on specific *objectives, priorities,* and *methods.* In this chapter we identify six major
goals (domestic and international) of the American economy. We also consider some
difficulties encountered in operationally defining goals and dealing with goal *conflicts.*

Six Economic Goals

What goals have the American people set for their economic system—what aims,
objectives, targets ("visions of the ideal state," "ends toward which effort is exerted,"

directions identified as "better" rather than "worse")? With respect to the *overall level* of economic activity, legislation such as the Employment Act of 1946 and the Full Employment and Balanced Growth Act of 1978, as well as public statements by leaders in various fields, emphasize a commitment to *full employment, maximum production,* and *noninflationary economic growth.* Our nation wants to make full use of available labor, capital, and natural resources, moderate our recurring business cycles, prevent inflation and ensure long-term growth of productive capacity.

These macroeconomic goals ("macro" because they refer to overall aggregates) are often expressed quantitatively. "Full employment," for example, may be defined as providing jobs for all but, say, 5% of the labor force (assumed to be the irreducible minimum unemployment arising from "frictional" causes as explained later). "Maximum production" for a particular year may be identified as a Gross National Product *(GNP)* of \$4.5 trillion, reflecting estimates of the realistic production potential of the economy, given its resources, technology, and institutions. The goal of noninflationary economic growth may be interpreted to mean "reasonable" price-level stability, as measured by an annual rise of no more than 3% in the Consumer Price Index, along with an annual increase in real *GNP* (i.e., adjusted for inflation) of 4%. (Note: The percentages listed here are roughly comparable to target figures specified in the Full Employment and Balanced Growth Act.)

Goals concerning the *composition* of the nation's income are difficult to quantify. We want a "good product mix," but what is the test of goodness? Capitalist ideology stresses *freedom of choice for consumers,* not a Hobson's choice where the customer can have "any color he wants as long as it's black." Effective freedom of choice requires that a broad range of differentiated goods be produced and made available in the market. In the model of a purely competitive price system, the slogan is "consumer sovereignty" where the free choices of individual consumers ultimately determine the kinds and amounts of particular goods and services that will be produced, and the corresponding pattern of resource allocation that results. Subject to this constraint, we also want *freedom of choice for workers*—opportunities to select their own occupations and seek work in the industries and for the employers of their choice. Again subject to the pattern of resource allocation dictated by consumers, we want *free enterprise* in the sense of permitting individuals and groups to set up their own business enterprises and produce the goods of their choice. (In the real world of today's U.S. economy such freedoms unfortunately are sometimes conspicuous in their absence.)

What goals have the American people set for the *distribution* of wealth and income? Here the answer is clouded with ambiguity and controversy. Many Americans seem to want a distribution that rewards producers on the basis of their contributions ("commutative justice") while yet recognizing the principles of need and equality (sometimes termed "distributive justice" but really a blend of humaneness and political-economic functionalism). They also seem to feel that "the sky's the limit": Everyone has a right to as much income as he can appropriate. The optimum distribution of income, which we shall term *distributional justice,* must necessarily take account of equality of opportunity, provision of economic security, and indeed the total economic, political, and social consequences of how wealth and income are shared in the society.

We have so far identified the goals of:
1. *Full production* (including full employment).
2. *Noninflationary economic growth.*
3. *Reasonable stability* (of employment, production, and purchasing power).

4. *Freedom of choice* (for consumers, workers, and business firms).

5. *Distributional justice.*

Are there other economic goals that rank high in the "social value function" of the American people? Looking beyond our domestic economy, the growing recognition of interdependence among nations makes it essential to include a sixth major goal of the U.S. economy:

6. *International balance.*

This is an umbrella label meant to include harmonious relationships with other countries relative to exports, imports, investments, and international payments; a viable posture in the ongoing rivalry between capitalism and communism; and a balanced policy of trade, investment, and aid vis-a-vis the economically poor nations of the world (the less-developed "Third World" countries).

Additional goals such as environmental conservation, improving the quality of worklife, urban renovation, strengthening the agricultural sector, solving the energy problem, and perhaps even achieving zero population growth also vie for a place on the list. This illustrates once more that people are seldom indifferent on matters of economic policy. On the contrary, we seem to care a great deal about the development, conservation, and use of society's productive resources. Limitations of space prevent extensive discussion in this book of many avowedly important socio-economic issues.

Defining Economic Goals

We earlier distinguished between *macro*economic goals on the one hand (dealing with the overall level of economic activity) and *micro*economic goals (associated with the composition of output and distribution of income). Macro goals such as full employment and price-level stability seem easier to define than such micro goals as freedom and justice, not to mention the rather vague "balance" we spoke of for our international economic relations. Indeed, one of the characteristics of economic goals is that they can mean different things to different people. "Freedom for the trout," observed economist R.H. Tawney, "means death for the minnow." Distributional justice to Daddy Warbucks (Orphan Annie's affluent benefactor) means letting people keep the income they have "earned" (regardless of how much they have accumulated or how they acquired it, so long as it seems to be "legal"). For others, justice means a pattern of distribution that best ensures the present and future wellbeing of individuals in the entire society: Feeding the hungry and housing the poor, providing suitable incomes for teachers and truck drivers, as well as rewarding successful investors, popular entertainers, and lucky lottery players.

To be meaningful, goals must be expressed not as vague slogans but in operative terms. On this point, the 19th-century German social philosopher Ferdinand LaSalle resorted to verse:

Do not show the goal without the way,
For way and goal on earth are so entwined;
That each upon the other's change depends,
And different paths lead into different ends.

Indeed, defining a goal operationally often disposes of the illusion that "We all seek the same ends; our only disagreement is over the means of achieving them." Economist C.E. Ayres pointed out that "There are no ends, only means." Such a truly wise view makes it difficult for policymakers to argue that the ends justify the means, or to "cop out" by designating the ends and leaving to others the task of finding efficacious means.*

Goal clarification may disclose *conflicts,* such as those occurring among the widely espoused "slogan-goals" of freedom, progress, security, equality, and efficiency. We are painfully familiar with the conflict between full employment and price-level stability. (Not all goals clash, however: Full employment, economic security, and greater equality may be *mutually reinforcing.*) When goals do clash, tradeoffs are necessary and priorities must be set. This raises difficult problems in the area of *social values.* In Part Five we shall focus more sharply on goal-setting when we apply Chapter 2's five-step method of economic reasoning to the problem of poverty. Then, in Part Six we tackle the subject of *value analysis* and its importance for social progress and individual wellbeing.

Selected Readings and References

C.E. Ayres, *Toward a Reasonable Society: The Values of Industrial Civilization.* Austin: University of Texas, 1961. (Also see *The Industrial Economy;* Boston: Houghton Mifflin, 1952.)
Economic Report of the President 1985 (cited in Chapter 2).

----

*It may have been humorist Will Rogers who came up with the plan to end the German submarine menace in World War I. His solution was to heat the ocean to the boiling point, thus forcing all the U-boats to surface, where they could be picked off by British and American warships.

Resources: Land, Labor, Capital, and Enterprise

> Resources are all things that can be used as direct "inputs" in production. The four categories of resources, called the *factors of production*, are land, labor, capital, and enterprise. *The Law of Diminishing Returns* describes what happens to output when inputs are employed in varying proportions.

> *Two fundamental facts provide a foundation for the field of economics: (1) society's material wants are virtually unlimited, and (2) economic resources— the means for producing goods and services—are limited or scarce.*
> —Campbell R. McConnell

> *Economics is the study of how individuals and society choose to use scarce resources that could have alternative uses to better meet prescribed ends.*
> —Paul A. Samuelson

Since economics studies the *production* of goods and services (as well as income distribution), the materialistic cause-and-effect worldview of modern science suggests a very natural starting point for economic inquiry. Economists ask: What *physical resources* are available for use as direct inputs to the production process? And what is the extent of their *availability?*

The Meaning of "Scarcity"

The traditional response and orthodox chain of reasoning involves three observations. First, material *wants* in the aggregate are virtually *unlimited,* i.e., consumer

wants are insatiable. Second, *physical resources*—land, labor, capital (and enterprise)—
are inevitably *required* to produce the goods and services capable of satisfying human
wants ("there is no free lunch"). And third, at any given time, resources are available
only in *limited* quantities, i.e., they are "scarce" relative to what would be needed to
produce all the products that people would like to have. Hence, some wants must go
unsatisfied. The task of economic science, according to this reasoning, is to discover
principles for *choosing* how to maximize want satisfaction (now and in the future) in
the face of constraints imposed by the limitedness or "scarcity" of resources.
Economics thus becomes a study of the "efficient allocation of resources" either
through *(a)* the interaction of supply and demand in "free" markets, or *(b)*
institutional arrangements, market or otherwise, by which such an allocation can be
coordinated. (Economic conservatives would rely mainly on market forces while
various other groups prefer a larger role for government.)

Whether one follows the orthodox approach stressing "scarcity" and the "allocation of resources by the price system," or, as in the present book, emphasizes the social
phenomena of technology and diverse institutions, it remains true that *resources* are at
the heart of the production process and must therefore command special attention in
economic analysis. The basic laws of economics clearly focus on resources and their
employment in production.

Production and Utility

Earlier, *production* was defined as the use of resources to create *utility*, i.e., the
usefulness or want-satisfying power that characterizes goods and services. (The
distinguished neoclassical economist Alfred Marshall observed nearly a century ago
that production does not "create" goods and services; it is a process that creates utility
or usefulness in goods by altering the *form* of matter, and in the case of consumer
services, through an expenditure of human energy focused on direct want satisfaction.
It may be noted that utility can also be created in the production process by making
goods and services more conveniently available, thus generating "place utility," "time
utility," and "ownership utility" as supplements to "form utility."

Resources as Factors of Production

In Chapter 3, four types of resources were identified. *Land* (= natural resources)
was defined as all things existing in nature that can be used in production. *Labor* (=
human resources, or manpower) is human effort devoted to production. And *capital*
was carefully defined as *physical goods* (NOT money, evidences of ownership, or
claims to income) that have been produced and are available for use in further
production. A fourth "factor of production"—"enterprise," or *entrepreneurship*—
does not fit quite so neatly into a general discussion of resources because it exists only
in the special case of a capitalistic market economy. We shall define *enterprise* (=
entrepreneurship) as that factor of production in a market economy that undertakes
responsibility for (1) the basic policy decisions of the business firm (including whether
to create the firm, assemble resources, continue operation, or terminate), and (2)
bearing the firm's financial risks.

Entrepreneurship is the factor of production to which a firm's *profits* accrue (if
there *are* profits) after payment of all other resource costs: *rent* to land, *wages* to labor,

interest to capital. These are called *factor payments,* and this way of dividing up the income is termed *functional distribution* because it considers the sharing of income among the factors of production according to the respective functions they perform in the production process. Economic *theory* seeks to explain (among other things) how the four "functional shares" of income—wages, interest, rent, and profits—are determined; economic *statistics* approximates these functional shares in calculating the aggregate measure known as National Income (see Chapter 15). In this context, one can see why it is convenient to identify a fourth factor of production; otherwise, which factor would receive profits?

Quantity and Quality

As we shall emphasize in a later discussion of economic development, what makes one economic system more productive than another is not merely the *quantity* of land, labor, and capital (plus enterprise), but their *quality* (including the level of technology they embody). India has some 400 million workers (human resources), more than three times the number of American workers. Yet the total output of the Indian economy is only one-twentieth of U.S. production! Of course we have greater quantities of capital, certain kinds of natural resources, and entrepreneurship; but this does not really "explain" the fact that ours is an advanced, affluent economy while India is a "less-developed" country. The key difference in the respective "resource bases" of the two economies is the *quality* of labor and capital.

American workers as a group are more productive (more efficient) not only because they have "more tools" but because they enjoy better health; have more education, training, and work experience; are more mobile; and have acquired certain "functional work attitudes and attributes" that make them highly adaptable to the needs of an industrial economy. Our workers have acquired a very high level of what might be called "productive intelligence." Not that Indian men and women somehow lack the human capacity for becoming highly productive industrial workers; on the contrary, there is ample evidence in America and around the world that numerous Indians, Chinese, Vietnamese, Cambodians, and workers from other less-developed countries have acquired impressive levels of "productive intelligence." Education, training, and work experience generate skills; appropriate diet, housing, and medical services enhance health and vigor—all of which improve the quality of labor. Afford such workers opportunities for employment in a favorable setting (characterized by abundant capital equipment, advanced technology, effective management, and strong incentives) and the typical result is high productivity.

Capital can be viewed in similar terms, though it is perhaps even more complicated from a theoretical standpoint. There is no clearcut *measure* of the quantity of capital, or of its quality. What is apparent, however, is that machinery and equipment embody "productive intelligence" in the form of technology just as human resources embody knowledge and skills (sometimes referred to as labor's "human capital.") High-technology capital, of course, cannot by itself guarantee high productivity; its usefulness in the production process depends on the interplay of all forces in the particular economic environment.

Like labor and capital, *land* and *enterprise* also have qualitative aspects that cannot be abstracted from their quantitative dimensions. This is a reality that creates difficulties for analysts who would like to express all economic variables in mathematical and statistical terms. But recognition of the *qualitative* aspects of resources, including the influence of education and technological improvement, gives deeper insights into the nature of the economic process and of the *developmental* changes required, for example, to trigger sustained growth for the low-income nations of the world.

Natural Resources

We proceed now to a closer examination of the respective factors of production. Empirical studies of *natural resources* are often carried out by economic geographers, or by "resource economists" (a title that might seem to imply expertise concerning all categories of resources but in fact is much more specialized). They typically focus on four areas: (1) *land* resources (agricultural potential, forests, and both rural and urban patterns of land use); (2) *energy* resources (production, consumption, and reserves of various energy sources such as coal, petroleum, natural gas, and hydro as well as nuclear power); (3) *minerals* (metals and nonfuel, nonmetallic minerals); and (4) *water* resources (fresh water, including surface and underground reserves; salt water; ice caps; and fish and other marine life).

In the 1960s a prominent research organization, Resources for the Future, completed a major study of America's natural resources and published a summary of their findings in a book, *Natural Resources for U.S. Growth* (A Look Ahead to the Year 2000). The basic conclusion, self-styled as "generally optimistic," was that natural resource supplies would be adequate to support growth for the rest of the 20th century—provided that technological advances and economic adaptation continued, foreign sources remained open, and government policies along with private resource management demonstrated farsightedness, flexibility, and consistency (a demanding set of provisos, yet we are more than halfway there!).

Resources for the Future and other groups continue to investigate issues related not only to America's natural resources but world resource materials as well. Useful generalizations concerning the status of natural resources, however, are extremely hard to make in a field of such concrete and diverse content. Occasionally research findings or policy pronouncements make headlines (especially when they foretell doom!), but it takes an event like the OPEC oil embargo of the early 1970s to capture widespread public and professional attention. Since the oil shortages and dramatic rise in gasoline and other fuel prices, more economists have begun to focus on energy problems (along with environmental issues); before that time, treatment of natural resources typically was limited to "the farm problem" and the use of agricultural land to illustrate the *Law of Diminishing Returns.*

The Law of Diminishing Returns

An integral part of the "law of variable proportions" or "nonproportional returns," this famous principle of economics merits some discussion. The Law of Diminishing Returns states that *with no change in technology* the application of increasing quantities of one or more "variable" factors of production to another factor that is *fixed* in amount will, *beyond a certain point,* yield less *additional* output than resulted from adding the preceding unit of the variable factor. In other words, when you change the proportions in which land, labor, and capital are jointly used, eventually there will be diminishing returns to the non-fixed resource (often following a phase of increasing returns). Example: Keep crowding more farmers onto a fixed acreage of land and eventually (because each one now has a progressively smaller portion of land with which to work) the output attributable to each successive farmer will fall—and may become so low that it isn't sufficient to provide for his own subsistence, not to mention his dependents. Viewed on a world scale (as predicted by 19th-century economist Thomas Malthus) *overpopulation*—and a corresponding surplus of the "variable factor," labor—may lead to such low output per worker that mass starvation will occur.*

Capital

Information and analysis concerning *capital* is of particular interest to "industry economists" as well as students of economic growth and business cycles. Capital goods exist in three major forms: (1) *structures* (such as manufacturing plants, roads, bridges, dams, electric power lines, office buildings, and single- or multifamily residences; (2) producers' *durable equiment* (including manufacturing machinery, office equipment, vehicles, etc.); and (3) business *inventories* (i.e., goods that have been produced and are currently being held in the stream of the firm's business operations for eventual sale).

How much physical capital exists in the world economy, or the American economy? Attempts to answer this question encounter both conceptual and statistical problems. What common denominator can be used to express the physical stock of capital? If a decision is made to express the total capital stock in monetary terms, what method should be used to determine its value? (Estimates of the total value of all capital goods existing as of a certain date in the U.S. economy are sometimes based on the assumption of a 4:1 "capital/output ratio," which would suggest a figure of approximately $16 trillion at the present time.) Of course it is possible to describe particular forms of capital, such as electric power generating capacity, steelmaking plant, and railroad track and equipment in nonmonetary units (kilowatt-hours, metric-ton capacity, miles of track, etc.); and for purposes of international comparison such "real" indicators are often used. It is also common practice to compare industries in terms of invested capital per worker. Capital stock per hour worked in the petroleum industry, for example, in 1982 was three times the dollar value of what it was in transportation and ten times the capital/labor ratio in printing and publishing, or in trade.

An important distinction is made between the *stock* of capital (structures, equipment, and inventories that exist at a given point in time) and *changes* in the capital stock that occur over a period of time. When business firms (or government agencies) spend, say $50 million to purchase newly produced capital goods, *real investment* takes place (in contrast to "financial investments" whereby someone purchases bonds or shares of stock in a corporation). If the investment spending is for the purpose of replacing plant and equipment used up in production, there is no

---

*Technical Note: The variable factor of production is simply the resource, such as labor, whose quantity is varied while holding constant the amount of some other resource, such as land. Diminishing returns can be related to *marginal* product (i.e., the amount by which the total changes in response to adding or removing one unit of the variable factor), *average* product, or *total* product. Another application of the Law of Diminishing Returns accounts for the traditional U shape of certain cost-of-production curves and the familiar positive slope of product supply curves, as illustrated in the appendix to Chapter 17.

increase in capital; but when *net* investment occurs, the capital stock becomes larger. In practice, it is not so easy to differentiate between replacement and new capital because of the *qualitative* factor mentioned earlier. A company will often modernize its capital stock—for example, purchase equipment that embodies more advanced technology—out of funds put aside for replacement purposes. In the early 1980s, American businesses—spending more than $400 billion per year on "gross private domestic investment"—made substantial improvements in the quality of their capital goods through this updating process.

Labor: Quantity

Turning from nonhuman to *human resources,* we find that it is conceptually and statistically easier to provide both *quantitative* and *qualitative* descriptions. In the United States, for example, the total population of the country in 1984 was 237 million people, of whom 178 million were age 16 and over (and not inmates of institutions). In turn, 65% of the people in this "noninstitutional population" were active participants in the American labor force. This ratio is called the *labor force participation rate.* (The distinction between *total* labor force and *civilian* labor force is no longer of great significance; there are fewer than 2 million resident members of the armed forces, and their jobs resemble civilian employment in many respects.)

These 116 million workers made up the "supply of labor" available to the American economy at that time. Of course, a larger proportion of the noninstitutional population was *potentially* available for employment; but the *actual labor force* was just under 116 million. This labor force consisted of 107 million who were *employed* and nearly 9 million *unemployed.* Obviously there are additional millions of Americans who were *not* employed, but the only people officially counted (by the U.S. Department of Labor) as *un*employed are those who did not have jobs but were *able* and *willing* to work and *actively seeking* employment. Others such as homemakers, full-time students, and retired workers were "outside the labor force."

Note that "human resources" does not mean the same thing as "people." All human resources, of course, are people; but not all people are human resources—only the ones who are "economically active" by virtue of their labor force participation. In the U.S. economy (and many other nations of the world), the ratio of workers to total population (and therefore total number of consumers) is about 1:2, indicating a "crude labor-force participation rate" of 50%.

Labor: "Quality"

What about the qualitative aspect of America's human resources? By this is meant not "better" or "worse"—designations that would have no economic significance outside a specified functional context (is a jet pilot "better" than a coal miner for mining coal?)—but *different* in terms of characteristics that are relevant to economic questions.

Extensive data are published (e.g., in the Labor Department's *Handbook of Labor Statistics*) on educational attainment of workers, occupational skills (white-collar, blue-collar, service, or farm workers), age, and numerous other characteristics, including work experience by industry (agricultural, nonagricultural goods-production, or service industries) and whether they are "wage and salary workers" (93% of

Americans work for somebody else) or "self-employed and unpaid family workers" (the remaining 7%). Indicative of the revolutionary transformation of America's farm sector, the number of self-employed workers in agriculture declined from 4.3 million in 1950 to 1.6 million in 1980 (total employment in agriculture dropped from 10.3 million in 1930 to only 3.3 million workers in 1984, only 3% of the labor force!). Outside agriculture, the trend has been for sharply rising employment in white-collar and service occupations and in the service industries (including finance, retail trade, and state and local government), with persistent relative declines in blue-collar occupations and goods-producing industries. Correspondingly, the economic character of our human resource base is changing.

It is interesting to note that the average American worker is a high school graduate with some college ("median school years completed" = 12.7, identical for men and women; the figure is 12.4 years for black workers, while for Hispanics median schooling was 12.1 years). Two-thirds of the 116 million labor force in 1984 were in the 20-44 age category, another one-fourth were in the 45-64 age group, and fewer than 10% were in the highly publicized 16-19-year-old category (many of whom were full-time students not available for regular employment); only 3 million persons 65 and over were active labor-force participants.

Despite the impressive rise in *female* labor-force participation since the 1940s, there are still 14 million more men than women in the civilian work force (i.e., 56% male, 44% female). Note: Like yesterday's news, a lot of economic statistics—the absolute numbers themselves—tend to become *obsolete* rather quickly; Chapter 15 provides some guidelines and sources for updating basic economic indicators, especially those involving relatively stable relationships and predictable growth rates.

Extending the present discussion of human resources beyond the case-study example of the United States, it should be recognized that *wide variations* exist among nations in terms of labor force participation rates, educational attainment, worker skills, and so forth. For economic development to occur in the poorer nations of the world, *qualitative improvement* in the work force is imperative and must go hand-in-hand with the accumulation of more advanced tangible capital.

A Note on Terminology

Before closing this introduction to resources, it should be mentioned that discussions of the "factors of production" do not always employ the same terminology. We have already noted synonyms for land (natural resources) and labor (manpower, human resources). Some writers distinguish only two categories of resources: human and nonhuman or human and "property resources." Natural resources are sometimes included in a broadened category of "capital" (on grounds that most natural resources are intermingled with capital in order to be made available for production, such as the need for drilling rigs to bring oil reserves up from the ground).

There are also writers who interpret "factors of production" in an extremely broad sense, as if to ask: What are the factors or considerations that greatly influence production, whether directly or indirectly? Obvious answers include *time, money, government, technology,* even the *wants and needs* of consumers. "Resources" then becomes an all-embracing category of economic forces no longer distinguished conceptually from technology and institutions. For clarity of thinking about the economic process, it seems more useful to retain the resources-technology-institutions framework and identify land, labor, capital, and enterprise as the four categories of resources, i.e., the factors of production.

Selected Readings and References

Hans H. Landsberg, *Natural Resources for U.S. Growth* (A Look Ahead to the Year 2000). Baltimore: Johns Hopkins, 1964 (published for Resources for the Future, Washington, D.C.)

Campbell R. McConnell, *Economics,* 9th ed. (cited in Chapter 1).

P.A. Samuelson and W.D. Nordhaus, *Economics,* 12th ed. (cited in Chapter 1).

Economic Indicators (see "References," Chapter 15.)

Economic Report of the President 1985 (cited in Chapter 2).

Employment and Training Report of the President 1982. U.S. Department of Labor. Washington: U.S. Government Printing Office, 1983.

Handbook of Labor Statistics. Bulletin 2175, December 1983. Bureau of Labor Statistics, U.S. Department of Labor. Washington: U.S. Government Printing Office, 1984.

Statistical Abstract of the United States 1985 (for description of contents, see Chapter 15).

Time of Change: 1983 Handbook on Women Workers. Bulletin 298. Women's Bureau, U.S. Department of Labor. Washington: U.S. Government Printing Office, 1984.

Technology and Technological Progress

Man's ability to make and use tools is one of the major determinant's of society's material wellbeing. Technological progress makes it possible to produce new goods, better goods, and more goods. But new methods also create adjustment problems for individuals and society. Few topics in the social sciences are more vital or challenging then the phenomenon of technological progress, identified by Thorstein Veblen as central to the "economic life process of mankind."

Knowledge is power.
—Francis Bacon

Technological change—the advance in knowledge relative to the industrial arts—is an important factor responsible for economic growth and without question is one of the most important determinants of the shape and evolution of the American economy.
—Edwin Mansfield (modified)

The great paradox of automation [is seen] in Goethe's fable of the Sorcerer's Apprentice. Our civilization has cleverly found a magic formula for setting...brooms and pails of water to work by themselves, in ever-increasing quantities at an ever-increasing speed. But we have lost the Master Magician's spell for altering the tempo of the process, or halting it when it ceases to serve human functions and purposes.
—Lewis Mumford

Technology was defined in Chapter 3 as society's knowledge of how to make and use tools. The resource-creating function of technological progress was recognized as a basic principle of economics. So important has technology become in modern economic life that "low-tech" business firms have been put on the endangered species list and workers who lack sophisticated tool-using skills increasingly find themselves redundant in today's labor market. The quickening pace of technological change has thus become a Janus in disguise: The face of rising productivity and high profits is countered by the specter of business failure and unemployment.

The "Economic Life Process"

In the present chapter we consider the nature, causes, and consequences of technological progress, a phenomenon that Thorstein Veblen (1857-1929) identified with "the economic life process of man." Veblen was one of the first American economists to recognize the central importance of technology in the economic process. In his provocative books and articles in scholarly journals, Veblen urged economists to end their preoccupation with "buying and selling" and begin focusing attention on the real world of *technological progress* and *institutional change*. The founder of America's only indigenous school of economic thought, Veblen inspired an approach known as Evolutionary Institutionalism, distinctively different from both orthodox neoclassical market economics and revolutionary Marxian socialism (all three approaches are described and compared in the appendix to Chapter 14). One of Veblen's followers was C.E. Ayres (1891-1972), whose book *The Theory of Economic Progress* contributed importantly to our understanding of technology's dynamic influence on production and socioeconomic institutions.

The Importance of Technology

What makes technology so important in the economic process? First is the obvious fact that we can use things in production only if we *know how* to use them. A personal computer or deposits of uranium ore are of little value to primitive villagers on the island of Borneo. As we have emphasized, resources depend on skills and tools. Second, as society's materialistic knowledge increases, the quantity and quality of our de facto resource base expands. In terms of its size, shape, and geographic characteristics, the planet Earth is quite similar to what it was in 1500, at the end of the Middle Ages. What has grown a thousandfold is our technological ability to exploit its potentialities. Third, society has learned how to *produce* technical knowledge by applying the insights of science (as well as producing new *scientific* knowledge). Through investments in research and development (R&D), along with less formal procedures, we can enhance productive efficiency in a deliberately planned and somewhat predictable fashion. Finally, as the National Commission on Technology, Automation, and Economic Progress reported in the late 1960s, there is widespread recognition of "the deep influence of technology upon our way of life." In summary, we know that technology defines our tool-making and tool-using behavior, society has learned how to "produce" technological advance through deliberate action, and technology has a pervasive influence in modern life. For better *and* for worse, we have become a *technological* civilization.

Principles of Technological Progress

Now for a closer look at the nature, causes, and consequences of technological progress. In his writings on technology, Professor Ayres points out that all peoples have a material culture as well as a nonmaterial one; that is, they have modes of organized social behavior that relate to tool-making and tool-using as well as to other areas of activity such as religious practices. In the case of primitive people, the material culture is rather meager and perhaps therefore easier to recognize and understand than in our own case. We tend to regard our own elaborate material culture—with its skyscrapers, jetliners, automated factories, and computerized banking systems—as impersonal and external to human behavior. A *technological mystique* has developed, nowhere expressed more dramatically than with the electronic computer. Yet technology in essence is nothing more than *organized human behavior* along with accumulated artifacts such behavior has created. The causes and consequences of technological progress—past, present, and future—are therefore amenable to social analysis, and their understanding can be approached in terms of certain principles of social evolution. Drawing on the work of Ayres, three broad *principles of technological progress* can be stated:

I. THE PRINCIPLE OF TECHNOLOGICAL CONTINUITY
Technological behavior is a *cultural* phenomenon. It is that aspect of social behavior concerned with making and using tools—both tangible and conceptual (e.g., the printing press, differential calculus, and the laser). Tools exist apart from individuals. Tool behavior is *cumulative* and *continuous,* transmitted formally and informally from generation to generation as part of the cultural heritage.

II. THE TOOL-COMBINATION PRINCIPLE
The discoveries and inventions that we refer to as technological progress essentially result from *new combinations* of previously existing tools (including symbols, devices, and concepts). The "cross-fertilizing" is done by individuals who may exercise extraordinary ingenuity, but it is done under circumstances that are necessarily conditioned by the prior accumulation of tools. Such combinations occur *progressively* and at an *accelerating* rate, because the growing volume and variety of existing tools makes possible a still greater number of new combinations. (The process is analogous to a mathematical progression, according to which each new member of the series is derived from each preceding member by the same operation.) It is like a snowball gaining bulk and momentum as it rolls downhill, with, however, a path and timetable that are difficult to predict.

III. THE PRINCIPLE OF TECHNOLOGICAL IMPACT
Through its resource-creating function, technological progress is the principle source of *increased productivity* and *economic growth* (see Chapter 24). Moreover, it is a dynamic force in the *nonmaterial* culture as well, inducing changes in attitudes, institutions, and personal behavior—an effect Veblen termed "the cultural incidence of the machine process."

Technology and the Future

Given the inner logic of the tool-combination principle, one may ask: Is technological progress inevitable? And will it solve all of mankind's problems? It is easier to consider the first question from the viewpoint of historical empiricism, notably from the times of the Renaissance (14th to 17th centuries) and Enlightenment (17th and 18th centuries) than to formulate a general theory that claims validity for all times and places. Since about the 15th century, technology in the Western world has advanced at an accelerating rate. In other parts of the world, such as China, India, and Africa, *institutional resistances* at various times have operated to block technological progress. Today, technology is advancing worldwide, more rapidly than ever before. According to one government report, "as much technical knowledge will be developed in the next 30 years as has been accumulated in the entire history of mankind." The report went on to say that we produce, in America alone, approximately 25,000 technical papers every week, along with 400 books and 3,500 articles. Annual expenditure for R&D in the United States approximates $100 billion, and extensive efforts are made to increase and speed up *technology transfer* among various sectors of the economy.

"Side Effects" of Technology

Some direct economic effects of technological progress have already been noted: new products, increased productivity, economic growth. There can be enormous profits for innovative companies, career opportunities in new occupations for qualified workers, and expanding world markets for technologically sophisticated nations. But not all companies, workers, and nations prosper—as the experience of the American auto and steel industries since the 1970s demonstrates. Declining sales and profits, worker layoffs, and mushrooming trade deficits form a somber pattern for those who fall behind in the technological race. Clearly, technology has not solved quite all of mankind's problems.

Nor do the *economic* benefits and burdens listed above exhaust technology's effects. Economists from Adam Smith to Karl Marx, and countless social scientists since, have studied the dehumanizing impact of the industrial system, lamenting the personal alienation caused by machine processes and excessive specialization. One author observes that "modern technology could hardly be more ingeniously fashioned than it is for depriving men of the exercise of their character as men." All this suggests that technological progress not only *solves* problems, but *creates* them as well.

How can such human tragedies occur in "enlightened" societies? Essentially, technological innovation responds to the imperatives of cost-efficient production and largely *ignores* the impact that the *processes* of production and consumption may have on the broader human condition. The "side effects" are *accidental.* Whether a new product sells in the marketplace, or a new technique succeeds in reducing the costs of production is literally somebody's business. Not so with the impact of the new technology on lifestyles, family stability, violence, music and the arts, and personal concepts of good and bad, right and wrong. (Whether the advance of technology somehow *motivates* violent behavior may be debatable, but there is no doubt about the link between technology and man's *physical capacity* for violence—as cars, hand guns, and nuclear bombs attest.)

Cultural Incidence of the Machine Process

Veblen's widely quoted phrase citing the "cultural incidence of the machine process" is often interpreted to mean that tool behavior conditions people to think in no-nonsense terms of cause and effect, as opposed to ceremonialism and "conventional wisdom." But modern technology may inadvertently teach *additional* lessons, with unanticipated and less benign consequences. Among them: standardization, interchangeable parts, repetitive behavior, discipline of the clock, and the social power that science and technology bestow on those who control it. Technology teaches the "goodness" of these values—along with their concomitants in a market society, namely acquisitive behavior (greed?), mobility (rootlessness?), personal adaptability (repression of one's individuality?), salesmanship (hucksterism and tricksterism?), a fetishistic regard for impersonal entities like the computer (or other locuses of power, such as the company or the "system"), and an unquestioning attitude toward the objects of production such that whatever is *do-able* (and financially rewardable) becomes *acceptable.*

Not only do these "value lessons" show up in such unexpected places as intimate personal relationships, medical practice, the arts, and religion but even in the conception that individuals have of human nature itself.

The basic twofold purpose of economics, as of any positive science, is to explain *the effects of given measures* (or "causes"), and to discover *which measures will generate given effects.* Much has been learned about the causes and direct consequences of technological progress. But if economists are concerned with maximizing material wellbeing they must also acknowledge the *cultural by-products of technological change,* particularly when these side effects take on a life of their own and inflict harm on human beings.

One economist who has not ignored the multiple causes and side effects of technological progress and economic growth is Gunnar Myrdal, a Swedish exponent of Evolutionary Institutionalism who was awarded a Nobel Prize in 1974 for his "penetrating analysis of the interdependence of economic, social, and institutional phenomena." Recognition of the many-faceted, chain-reaction impact of technological progress presents a special challenge to social scientists, namely to discover institutional structures that will effectively and efficiently translate new technology into human wellbeing.

Selected Readings and References

C.E. Ayres, *The Theory of Economic Progress,* 3d ed. Kalamazoo: New Issues Press at Western Michigan University, 1978; originally published in 1944 by University of North Carolina Press. (Also see other works by Ayres cited in Chapter 5.)

Edwin Mansfield, *The Economics of Technological Change.* New York: W.W. Norton, 1968. (Mansfield is also the author of *Economics,* another of the 900-page encyclopaedic texts alluded to earlier.)

Ezra J. Mishan, "The Costs of Economic Growth," in *The Goal of Economic Growth,* Rev. ed. Edited by Edmund S. Phelps. New York: W.W. Norton, 1969.

Lewis Mumford, *The Myth of the Machine.* New York: Harcourt Brace Jovanovich, 1964. (Vol. I, *Technics and Civilization,* 1934; Vol. II, *The Pentagon of Power,* 1964.)

Gunnar Myrdal, *Asian Drama: An Inquiry into the Poverty of Nations.* New York: Twentieth Century Fund, 1968.

Thorstein Veblen, "The Cultural Incidence of the Machine Process," Chapter IX in *The Theory of Business Enterprise* (1904), excerpted as "The Discipline of the Machine," in *The Portable Veblen.* Edited by Max Lerner. New York: Viking Press, 1958.

Technology and the American Economy, Report of the National Commission on Technology, Automation, and Economic Progress, 1966.

Institutions: Their Key Role in Coordinating Economic Life

An *institution* is an established pattern of social behavior, a set way of doing things. *Economic institutions* are the habits, procedures, organizations, and behavior patterns that groups of people follow in using productive resources. Among the important institutions of the American economy are the market system, government, giant corporations, labor unions, and hundreds of structured arrangements such as the social security system. Institutions evolve over time, adapting to new technology, economic growth, and changing social values. Solutions to economic problems typically take the form of *institutional adjustments*.

Institutions are, in substance, prevalent habits of thought with respect to particular relations and particular functions of the individual and the community.

　　—Thorstein Veblen

Nothing is more conspicuous than the inordinate variability of institutional forms [including those which are] utilized to organize the economic process...[Because] institutions of whatever kind are people-made devices for organizing experience...they are always potentially modifiable by people.

　　—Marc R. Tool, The Discretionary Economy

All answers to all economic problems necessarily take the form of institutional adjustment... The fundamental principles of economics, then, must take the form of the principles of institutional adjustment.

　　—J. Fagg Foster

Economics is a study of three sets of forces—resources, technology, and institutions—and how they interact on one another. The quantity and quality of labor, capital, and natural resources along with technology together set the upper limit to what a nation can produce. However, it is the society's *institutions* that will establish the actual level and pattern of production, as well as the distribution of income, by shaping consumer wants and determining how the available resources and technology are used. Indeed, just as resources are determined by technology—$R = f(T)$—it is also true that specific consumer *wants* are largely determined by institutions, i.e., $W = f(I)$. (Prominent among such institutional determinants of wants is mass-media advertising, through which giant corporations are able to plan and create consumer demand in what John Kenneth Galbraith calls the "revised sequence" of market sovereignty.) Because of the key role that institutions play in economic life, special attention is focused on their nature, characteristics, and patterns of change.

Institutions are "Man-Made"

An important thing to remember about institutions is that these "coordinating mechanisms" reflect the beliefs and behavior of people. Most scholars agree that there are no "natural" institutions, only man-made institutions. This is not to deny, however, that some institutions may be more compatible with basic human needs than alternative ways of doing things.

John Stuart Mill, English philosopher and economist (1806-1873), pointed out more than a century ago the importance of institutions in economic life—in this particular case, the determining role they play in the distribution of wealth and income.

> The laws and conditions of the production of wealth partake of the character of physical truths. There is nothing optional or arbitrary in them... It is not so with the *distribution* of wealth. That is a matter of human institution solely. The things once there, mankind individually or collectively can do with them as they like. They can place them at the disposal of whomsoever they please, and on whatever terms. Further,...any disposal whatever of them can only take place by the consent of society... Even what a person has produced by his individual toil, unaided by anyone, he cannot keep, unless by the permission of society. Not only can society take it from him, but individuals could and would take it from him, if society only remained passive... The distribution of wealth, therefore, depends on the laws and customs of society. The rules by which it is determined are what the opinions and feelings of the ruling portion of the community make them, and are very different in different ages and countries; and might be still more different, if mankind so chose *(Principles of Political Economy,* 1848).

Of course, Mill was shrewd enough to note also that, while

> society can subject distribution of wealth to whatever rules it thinks best...what practical results will flow from the operation of those rules must be discovered, like any other physical or mental truths, by observation and reasoning.

(Today's supply-side economists, concerned with the possible harmful side effects of high tax rates, would have endorsed Mill's open-minded empiricism; and even their demand-side antagonists will acknowledge that the proper test of any institution lies in its *total* consequences, not just one or two hoped-for effects that might have motivated adoption of the institution in the first place.)

U.S. Capitalism and Soviet Communism

Another way of showing the importance of institutions is to compare alternative economic systems such as U.S. mixed capitalism and Soviet communism. As we have already noted, the two "supereconomies" are quite similar in terms of their resources and technology; it is their *institutions* that differ so strikingly. In the U.S. economy, for example, private property is not only permitted but encouraged by law and custom. Institutions and private individuals own capital goods and natural resources, and they use these "means of production" to further their own economic self-interest. (Property is not a "thing" like a factory building or oil well but is defined as a *bundle of legal rights* concerning the use of economic resources.) In Russia, the institution of private property is outlawed, with certain exceptions. The nonhuman means of production—capital and natural resources—are not owned by individuals and private business corporations. They are owned collectively by the government. Note that *physical capital* is found in both the capitalistic United States and communist Russia. The big difference between capitalism and socialism is an *institutional* difference centering on how we are organized to *use* our capital and other resources.

A second institutional difference relates to the mechanism used for allocating resources. In the U.S. economy, *prices* of most goods and services are set by market forces—supply and demand, or decisions made by private business corporations and labor unions. (Only in wartime are prices generally set and controlled by the government.) But in Russia, prices are set by government planners all the time, and consumers must adjust their buying decisions to whatever these prices may be. Thus, *"planning"* versus *"the market"* is another key institutional difference between the two systems (not to be interpreted as "coercion" versus "freedom" for it is well known that market forces can be powerfully coercive).

One further example of an economic institution is "acquisitive behavior." This is a fancy name for the desire to get ahead financially in the world. It is sometimes called "the profit motive." Many writers and businessmen speak of this desire to make a lot of money and accumulate material goods as "the American Dream." In certain other countries people are not so overwhelmingly motivated in their economic lives by the drive to accumulate money and material possessions, nor has this always been the case on the American continent. A typical villager in India, or a Pueblo Indian in New Mexico 200 years ago (or even today!), for example, would not dream of changing his job or where he lives in order to increase his wages by 15%!

The story is told of South Sea islanders who worked for the U.S. Air Force during World War II, building airfields. They worked eight or ten hours a day for as little as 25 cents. When the Air Force raised their pay to 50 cents a day out of humanitarian generosity, many of the natives decided to work only half a day. Others worked three days, then took the rest of the week off. (They went fishing, or just loafed.) Earning as much as one can get—typical American behavior—was not their way. Acquisitive behavior was not an institution of their economic system as it is in the American economy. (Note that the acquisitive "profit" motive is by no means unknown in the Soviet Union!)

Characteristics of Institutions

What are the *characteristics* of economic institutions? First of all, every institution has a *function* (or several functions) and a *history.* No matter how it came into existence, whether by deliberate decision or some other way, the institutionalized behavior may be presumed to meet or at one time to have met a human need (perhaps the institution functioned for the benefit of a particular group rather than the entire society).

Second, all institutions have a *structure*, prescribed by custom, tradition, or perhaps the authority of government and the law. Some institutional structures are highly organized, such as private property as described above and, for example, the federal tax system. Others are less formal, such as the acquisitive behavior we noted above.

Third, institutions may have an observable pattern, an actual *mode of operation*, that may or may not conform to the intended function and structure. The ideology of private property and competitive capitalism may differ from the reality of today's business system dominated by giant corporations, just as the Soviet economy of the 1980s bears little resemblance to "ideal" communism.

And finally, although institutions *tend to persist,* resisting change, they do in fact adjust to changing circumstances over time. More will be said later about the need for and process of *institutional adjustment* to guide, and in certain instances, speed up the process of institutional change to promote a more effective economy.

Information About Specific Institutions

It can be an interesting and illuminating exercise to identify some important economic institutions and consider a number of questions about each one:

1. What is the *origin* and/or known history of the institution (i.e., where did it come from, when, how, and why)?
2. What *function* does it serve (or group of functions)?
3. What is its *structure*?
4. How is it currently operating, and with what *effects*?
5. Would society, and its individual members, be better off if the institution were *modified* through deliberate action?
6. If so, what kind of action should be taken, *how,* and by whom?

Following is a sample listing of present-day economic institutions that significantly affect production and income distribution in the American economy:

- OASDI social security system.
- TV commercials and programming.
- Tax-exempt status of church property.
- Multinational corporations.
- Inheritance of wealth.
- Congressional lobbying.
- Internal labor markets.
- Federal graduated income tax.
- The nation's health-care system.
- State lotteries.

The list could be expanded 100-fold, and scores of questions posed about each one. (Historians are experts in this kind of analysis as applied to earlier eras.)

For example, when did Congress enact legislation establishing the Old Age, Survivors, and Disability Insurance system, and why? How is it financed and managed? Is it working well, or should changes be made in its structure and functions? Does TV violence, sex, and hucksterism influence the behavior of viewers? (If not, why do sponsors pay billions of dollars for TV advertising?) Should churches have the same tax liability as other social institutions? Would the world be better off without multinational corporations? Is the inheritance of wealth good for society, or does it perpetuate inequalities that are not really justified on reasonable grounds?

Should political action committees (PACs) be free to spend unlimited amounts of money to influence legislation? Are internal labor markets—promoting strictly from within—an efficient and equitable way to ration government jobs (or those in the private sector for that matter)? Should the federal graduated income tax be replaced by a flat-rate tax, and if it were, what effect would the new system have on the after-tax distribution of income? How much does the nation's health-care system cost the American people, and is the product delivered efficiently, equitably, and with appropriate quality control? (Does it make sense, for example, that a truck driver who happens to be on the payroll of General Motors or the U.S. Postal Service has a million dollars worth of hospital-medical insurance coverage, while the family of the man who drives his own truck has *none,* or half the coverage at 10 times the cost?) What are the "indirect" effects of state lotteries on social attitudes about hard work and financial prudence as opposed to gambling?

Institutions and Change

Society inherits its institutions from earlier times. Because institutionalized behavior becomes ingrained, like habits or instincts, new institutional structures are often resisted. Free public education, for example, was criticized when first proposed in the early 1800s, as were universal adult suffrage and income taxes with graduated rates. Labor unions and collective bargaining were bitterly resisted by business, the courts, and government until the 1930s. The "basic independent income" proposal (discussed in Chapter 27) continues to meet strong resistance not only because its newness seems threatening but also because it clashes with such traditional American attitudes as individual self-reliance and the belief that people should give up something (such as hours of work effort) in exchange for getting something. The *quid pro quo* principle ("something for something") is deeply ingrained in capitalist ideology.

Despite their resistance to change, institutions over a period of time do adjust to technological advances, economic growth, and evolving social values. That is not to say that the changes are all for the good; on the contrary, many institutional changes (e.g., greater permissiveness regarding drug use and pornography) are seen to have harmful effects on some or all members of society. The difficult question arises: Can society *adjust* its economic institutions smoothly and promptly enough—and in the right direction, "better" rather than "worse"—to keep pace with technological progress, economic growth, and human needs?

Take automation as an example. This form of technological change clearly is eliminating the need for certain kinds of workers. (A few years ago, there was much discussion of the claim that automation was "destroying 40,000 jobs a week" in this country and the "cybernation revolution" would leave tens of millions of workers unemployed by the 1980s.) What happens to people who lose their jobs when robots take over? From what source will they obtain the *income* they require in order to function as consumers? How will certain *social-psychological needs* be met when the individual is cut off from a traditional work setting? What replaces the job and career as a formative influence in human development?

Sometimes the disemployed can simply go out and find new jobs, using the same skills they used on the old job. But farmers, coal miners, railroad workers, firemen, manual laborers, and auto workers have not always been successful in transferring their skills or acquiring different ones. (During the past 30 years or so, 75% of the jobs in coal mining were wiped out; some 5 million jobs in agriculture disappeared; more than half the railroad jobs vanished; and, in the past decade alone, 25% of the jobs in the auto and steel industries were eliminated.) New institutions—such as manpower retraining programs, income maintenance arrangements, and different *attitudes* about sharing the burdens of change—may be required to meet the needs of people whose jobs and lives are disrupted by the new technology.

Principles of Institutional Adjustment

The title given to this chapter stresses the key role that institutions play in coordinating economic life. When institutions do not function effectively, economic *problems* are manifest—such as high rates of unemployment and inflation, persistent poverty, and abuses of economic power. As one of the opening quotations suggests, the solutions to economic problems typically take the form of *institutional adjustments;* and in effect, the "fundamental principles of economics must take the form of the principles of institutional adjustment."

There is a substantial literature on "the principles of institutional adjustment" (see the Selected Readings and References at the end of the chapter). In his long teaching career at the University of Denver, Professor J.F. Foster emphasized three fundamental principles:

1. the *Principle of Technological Determination*—recognizing that technological progress initiates socioeconomic problems and creates a need for institutional change.
2. the *Principle of Recognized Interdependence*—referring to the need for participants in the economic process to understand the roles they play in new institutional structures.
3. the *Principle of Minimal Dislocation*—a preference for limiting required changes in institutional structure to those which are most directly a part of the problem and choosing alternative structures that are least disruptive to existing nonproblematic institutions.

A truly comprehensive theory of institutional adjustment would include a theory of human nature (as Veblen emphasized) and a theory of society (articulated by C.E. Ayres). It would interface with *technology* and *psychology* (especially depth psychology), embrace both *economics* and *politics,* and above all deal head-on with what in Chapter 30 is labeled *the value question.* As Veblen so aptly described the challenge facing cultural science: "There is the economic life process still in great measure awaiting theoretical formulation." One hopes that significant advances in such knowledge will soon be forthcoming.

It bears repeating that *institutional progress* is by no means inevitable; there is no guarantee that every institutional change or deliberate institutional adjustment will prove beneficial to individuals and society. Veblen warned of this when he wrote, in *The Instinct of Workmanship:*

> History records more frequent and more spectacular instances of the triumph of imbecile institutions over life and culture than of peoples who have by force of instinctive insight saved themselves alive out of a desperately precarious institutional situation, such, for instance, as now faces the people of Christendom.

Sobering words for our current era of precipitate change and weirdly contaminated patterns of social behavior (see Chapter 31).

Resources, Technology, and Institutions

As Part Two draws to a conclusion we want to reiterate the central importance of resources, technology, and institutions in the economic process, and underscore the interrelatedness of these sets of forces in determining the production, distribution, and uses of real income. Throughout the balance of this book the following themes will find repeated application:

1. Resources are defined by technology.
2. Technological progress occurs as a social phenomenon in the course of cultural evolution.
3. Institutions change, both "autonomously" and by human discretion; institutional structures can be deliberately modified to adapt to evolving technology and recognized human needs.

Selected Readings and References

C.E. Ayres, *The Industrial Economy* (cited in Chapter 5, plus his other works cited in Chapters 5 and 7).

J. Fagg Foster, "The Papers of J. Fagg Foster" (edited by Baldwin Ranson), *Journal of Economic Issues,* Vol. XV, No. 4, December 1981.

John Kenneth Galbraith, *The New Industrial State.* Boston: Houghton Mifflin, 1967. (Also see *Almost Everyone's Guide to Economics,* cited in Chapter 1.)

John S. Gambs, *Beyond Supply and Demand: A Reappraisal of Institutional Economics.* New York: Columbia University Press, 1946. (Also see his 1952 book *Man, Money, and Goods* and subsequent revisions published under the title *Economics and Man.)*

P.R. Gregory and R.C. Stuart, *Comparative Economic Systems,* 2d ed. (cited in Chapter 4.)

Marc R. Tool, *The Discretionary Economy.* Santa Monica, CA: Goodyear, 1979.

Thorstein Veblen, *The Instinct of Workmanship.* New York: Norton, 1964; originally published in 1914 by Macmillan. (Also see *The Portable Veblen,* cited in Chapter 7.)

PART THREE
TECHNIQUES OF ANALYSIS
AND A METHOD
OF ECONOMIC REASONING

In the next eight chapters we move beyond the levels of knowing "about" and knowing "what"—to acquire *skills* in knowing "how" to use some basic concepts, techniques, and methods of economic analysis. Following a preliminary explanation of *history, theory,* and *statistics* in Chapter 9, each of the three techniques is demonstrated in the context of substantive lessons that deepen our understanding of the economic process. Chapter 10 treats the Industrial Revolution and its historic legacy for today's society. Chapters 11, 12, 13, and 14 introduce some theoretical tools that facilitate clear thinking about economic phenomena. (The appendix to Chapter 12 illustrates graphical techniques typically included in college economics courses, while the appendix to Chapter 14 sketches and compares the Standard Neoclassical, Marxist, and Evolutionary-Institutionalist schools of economic thought.) Chapter 15 on statistics describes such familiar economic indicators as Gross National Product, the Consumer Price Index, and unemployment rates. Finally, Chapter 16 outlines a five-step method of economic reasoning that makes systematic use of history, theory, and statistics to reach responsible conclusions.

History, Theory, and Statistics

To reason effectively about economic issues, one must possess basic skill in using three techniques of analysis: history, theory, and statistics. In the context of economic analysis, *history* includes not only knowledge of past events but understanding of present-day institutions as well. *Theory* provides an orderly framework for selecting, relating, and interpreting the behavior of economic facts. And many of those facts—the empirical data of economic science— appear in the form of *statistics.*

What distinguishes the "scientific" economist from all the other people who think, talk, and write about economic topics is a command of techniques that we class under three heads: history, statistics, and theory.
   —Joseph A. Schumpeter

In Part One, we identified three basic elements of economic understanding: (1) the structure of the discipline, i.e., central themes of economics; (2) techniques of analysis; and (3) a five-step method of economic reasoning that can be used to solve problems and make choices. Effective reasoning about economic issues requires *skill* in the three *analytical techniques* of *history, theory,* and *statistics.* The purpose of this chapter is to explain the meaning and importance of the respective techniques. Subsequent chapters will describe and illustrate uses of particular historical, theoretical, and statistical tools.

History

Professor Joseph A. Schumpeter (1883-1950), economist and outstanding teacher at Harvard University, argued that of the three techniques of economic analysis, the most important was *economic history*—"which issues into and includes present-day facts." History, in this sense, includes not only a study of the past but also description and careful analysis of contemporary institutions, resources, and technology. Quoting Schumpeter further,

> ...the subject matter of economics is essentially a unique process in historic time. Nobody can hope to understand the economic phenomena of any, including the present, epoch who has not an adequate command of historical facts and an adequate amount of historical sense, or of what may be described as historical experience. [Moreover]...the historical report cannot be purely economic but must inevitably reflect also institutional facts that are not purely economic: therefore, it affords the best method for understanding how economic and noneconomic facts are related to one another...

The emphasis on "historical sense" and the crucial importance of institutional facts are major themes of Evolutionary Institutionalism, the school of economic thought inspired by the work of Thorstein Veblen. (The evolutionary approach to economic analysis will be demonstrated repeatedly as we consider contributions made by institutionalists to the theories of technological progresss, valuation, and institutional adjustment, and with statistical analyses of such developments as the rise of corporate power in the U.S. economy.)

Theory

Philosopher Alfred North Whitehead once posed the rhetorical question: Which is more important, facts or ideas? His answer: Ideas *about* facts. This is what we mean by "economic theory": ideas about the facts of economic life. More specifically, *economic theory*—the second technique of economic analysis—involves the selection (abstraction), systematic arrangement, and interpretation of economic facts in such a way as to provide valid and useful generalizations about the economic process. Economic principles, laws, and theories bring order and meaning to an assortment of facts by linking these facts together in a simplified way and describing the nature of their relationship to one another. Good theory reflects an understanding of history.

Economic analysis is usually divided into two major branches, microeconomics and macroeconomics. *Microeconomic theory* deals with laws and principles concerning the behavior of particular units of the economic system, such as the decisionmaking of an individual consumer or business firm, and the determination of market price for a specific commodity. *Macroeconomic theory* focuses on laws and principles describing aggregates or totals, such as the determination of Gross National Product, the overall level of employment and unemployment, and the rate at which the purchasing power of the dollar changes from one year to the next. *Micro*economics takes the worm's eye (microscopic) view to study the detailed parts of the economy, while *macro*economics takes a bird's eye (macroscopic) view to study the performance of the total system in broader perspective.

Statistics

The third technique of economic analysis is *economic statistics*. Developments in the field of quantitative analysis (which includes statistics, econometrics, and mathematical economics) during the past 50 years are largely responsible for making economics "the queen of the social sciences," indeed the only social science in which a Nobel Prize is awarded. The great importance of economic statistics lies in the fact that so many of the facts—the empirical data—come to us in the form of statistics: Gross National Product, price indexes, wages, productivity trends, unemployment rates, foreign-exchange rates, and international payments. What the chemist can observe in a test tube, the physicist in a carefully controlled laboratory, and the biologist study under a microscope, the economist must analyze with secondhand statistical representations of economic reality. (On the other hand, economists have the advantage of working with *monetary* data, which are easily quantified.)

Because of this heavy reliance on statistical data, economic analysis sometimes suffers from a credibility gap. Among the bad jokes often heard in the vicinity of economists: "There are three kinds of lies: plain lies, damn lies, and statistics." And: "I make up my statistics; where do you get yours?" And: "You can use statistics to prove anything you want to prove." (Of course, similar derision is heaped on *history*— "fables agreed upon," "Bunk!"—and *theory*: "armchair exercises," "Fantasies to determine how many angels can dance on the head of a pin.")

Like so much else in life, there is some basis for this cynicism. But the alternative to statistics (and history) is sterility, i.e., a nonempirical "science" that ignores the facts of economic life. The alternative to *theory* is intellectual chaos. Competent economic analysts must learn how to use statistics carefully, always mindful of their limitations as well as their strengths. (Good advice, too, for journalists and politicians!) One of the hallmarks of economic literacy is the development of "statistical sense" much like the historical sense identified by Professor Schumpeter as essential if we are to avoid "fundamental errors...in economic analysis."

Extensive use will be made of history, theory, and statistics in the chapters that follow. A good test of what the reader ultimately learns from this book will be the extent to which he or she acquires skill in using the three techniques of economic analysis, and develops a critical ability to detect gaps and abuses in the use of basic economic tools by others.

Selected Readings and References

Joseph A. Schumpeter, *History of Economic Analysis*. New York: Oxford University Press, 1954.

10

Evolution of the Industrial System

Our present-day industrial system is quite different from economic life two centuries ago, or even in the early 1900s. Today's economy is the result of evolving *technology, resources,* and *institutions.* A process of continuing economic development and change is going on right now which can be expected to transform our lives in the future just as the original Industrial Revolution changed Western man's economic and social world in the 18th, 19th, and 20th centuries.

To be ignorant of history is to remain always a child.
     —Cicero

What was economic life like in Europe at the time of the Norman Conquest (1066)—or even 500 years later, say in 16th century England, where capitalism and the industrial system first developed? People worked, they produced goods and services, and they consumed. (They also paid taxes.) But *how* they worked, *what* they produced, and the quantity and quality of food, clothing, housing, and other goods and services that they were able to consume—these were all vastly different from today.

The Middle Ages

Economic life during the Middle Ages (A.D. 500 to A.D. 1500) and for roughly 250 years afterward was "pre-industrial." Most men worked as farmers; some were craftsmen; a few were merchants. Production was mainly for subsistence. There were no huge corporations or bustling factories with power-driven machinery, no armies of wage earners. Transportation and communication were primitive—without railroads, automobiles, airplanes, telephones, radios, TV. People lived and died in small isolated villages and towns, never knowing comfort, convenience, economic security, or what life was like 10 miles away. Their average life span was half that of present-day Americans.

Transition to the Modern Era

Then something happened. Over the years technology had been changing, gradually but continuously. Transportation methods were improved, productivity rose in agriculture and industry, the use of money increased, trade and commerce were expanded. The voyages of discovery, including the landing of Columbus in the New World in 1492, contributed dramatically to these changes. Like a snowball gaining force and speed as it rolls downhill, a process of revolutionary change transformed the old *feudal system* of Europe into the modern industrial world that characterizes Europe, the United States, Japan, and other parts of the world.

What happened in the mid-1700s and 1800s has come to be called the "Industrial Revolution." It started in England and Western Europe, and later spread to America and elsewhere. Some say it is still going on; others prefer to think we have commenced a *second* industrial revolution (the Computer Age). The term Industrial Revolution is used to describe a period of history when the pace of economic development was so rapid and the changes so dramatic and far-reaching that our social and economic life was "revolutionized." What are the historical facts of the Industrial Revolution? And why is the history of the Industrial Revolution significant for Americans living in the 1980s?

The Industrial Revolution

The *Industrial Revolution* was a process of technological progress and economic change that took place first in England and later in other countries of the world, in the period after about 1750 ("history turns no sharp corners"). Machines were invented; water and steam power were harnessed to operate the machines; factories were built; the use of money became more widespread; large cities mushroomed; and men, women, and children were employed as "labor" by a new class of "industrial capitalists" to produce goods for sale in expanding markets throughout Europe and around the world. The key to the Industrial Revolution was the use of new machines and new methods to produce textiles, iron, pottery and hardware, machinery, and other goods. Rapidly improving *technology* was used to expand production, and the whole pattern of social and economic arrangements was disrupted and restructured in the process.

Technological advances included inventions by John Kay, James Hargreaves, and Richard Arkwright for the spinning and weaving of cloth; Abraham Darby and Peter Onions found better ways of making iron; Thomas Newcomen and James Watt developed the steam engine. In America, Eli Whitney invented the cotton gin in 1793 and a few years later began using interchangeable parts for mass production of guns.

Before the introduction of these new machines and the factories to house them, clothing and other goods were produced primarily in workers' homes or small shops under the "domestic system." Now with the growth of factories, workers left their homes and workshops and began selling their services in the *industrial labor market.* Many books have been written describing conditions of the early factory workers in England, and later in the United States. What the *factory system* did was to bring capital equipment (machines operated by water power, then steam, and later electricity and the internal-combustion engine), under the supervision and discipline of industrial managers. One result of this was vastly increased production. There were other results, too. For example, the new system created a class of industrial workers who became completely dependent on *wage employment* for their economic survival (our own forebears!).

Significance of the Industrial Revolution

Turning to the second question that we posed about the Industrial Revolution—its significance for Americans living in the 1980s—we can answer succinctly: *the 18th-century Industrial Revolution created today's world.* The process of technological development and institutional change that accelerated after 1750 created what we now call "the industrial system" and thereby shaped the economic and social environment that we live in.

But the Industrial Revolution is also important because—as C.E. Ayres explains in *The Theory of Economic Progress*—it showed us the *process* of technological advance and economic growth (a key element in the relatively modern concept of "human progress"). This process is still going on today, at a faster rate than ever before. By looking back at the impact of industrial development in the past 200 years, we can better understand the present and even look into the future (not perfectly, of course, nor in full detail). We can see how machines affect the work that men and women do, the goods and services they consume, the kind of world they live in, and indeed, the kinds of people they are becoming. Using this knowledge of the past, we should be better able to formulate plans for adjusting our economic institutions to ensure that continuing growth and development will bring improvements in the quality of life for all members of society.

Selected Readings and References

C.E. Ayres, *The Theory of Economic Progress* (cited in Chapter 7).

Kenneth E. Boulding, *The Meaning of the 20th Century* (The Great Transition). New York: Harper & Row, 1965.

J.B. Bury, *The Idea of Progress.* New York: Dover, 1955 (originally published in 1932 by Macmillan).

Robert L. Heilbroner, *The Making of Economic Society,* 6th ed. Englewood Cliffs, NJ: Prentice-Hall, 1980.

C.H. Hession and H. Sardy, *Ascent to Affluence: A History of American Economic Development.* Boston: Allyn and Bacon, 1969.

Karl Polanyi, *The Great Transformation.* Boston: Beacon, 1957 (originally published in 1944 by Rinehart).

M.B. Schnapper, *American Labor* (A Pictorial Social History). Washington: Public Affairs Press, 1972.

Arnold Toynbee, *The Industrial Revolution.* Boston: Beacon, 1956 (first published in 1884 as *Lectures on the Industrial Revolution in England*).

Mitchell Wilson, *American Science and Invention* (A Pictorial History). New York: Bonanza Books, 1960.

Scarcity, Opportunity Costs, and Choice

One of the reasons society must organize effectively to develop, conserve, and use its productive resources is because they are limited in quantity. This *"scarcity"* of land, labor, and capital imposes on society and its individual members the need to make *choices*. And every choice involves an *opportunity cost* in terms of alternative goods foregone.

Of all sad words of tongue or pen, The saddest are these: It might have been.
—John Greenleaf Whittier

There is no free lunch.
—(conventional aphorism)

There is a child's verse that goes:
"If all the world were apple pie, and all the sea were ink,
And all the trees were bread and cheese, what would we have to drink?"
Indeed, if food and other goods and services were available just for the taking, it has been suggested (no doubt mistakenly) that there would be no economic problem and no need to study economics. Note that if it were *money* growing on trees, rather than goods and services, we would still have the same old problem of providing the material goods and services that people want. Your own private money tree might be great for you, but if everybody had a money tree, money would be worthless. You can't eat it; you can only trade it for something that has *value in use*. Even in the verse, by the way, there was still a problem of scarcity: what to drink.

"Scarcity" and Choice

Looking at the world economy as a whole, with its five billion people, we can readily see that there aren't enough goods and services available to meet mankind's basic material needs, much less to satisfy all the wants that men, women, and children can think up. In parts of the world there isn't enough *food* available to keep people from starving to death or at least suffering severe malnutrition—not so much in the United States but in Africa, India, Bangladesh, and parts of Latin America. For half the world's people, life is a desperate struggle for existence, with little comfort, convenience, progress, or hope. Income per person in the poorest countries is less than $200 per year compared to *GNP* per capita of $16,000 a year in the United States (and even higher in several other countries).

But even in our economy, most people would like to have more goods and services than they actually get. Why not simply produce more? One answer is, we don't have enough resources. We do not have sufficient land, labor, and capital to produce all of the goods and services that people would *like* to have. Goods are limited relative to our *wants*—the quantity and composition of which, you will recall, are greatly influenced by *institutions*—because the resources needed to produce the goods are "scarce" relative to the physical requirements of production. This is the conventional meaning of *scarcity*—not enough resources to produce all the goods and services we would like to have.

Because resources are "scarce," society must *economize* in their use. We must *choose* how to use our limited resources to provide the goods and services that we value most highly. Since we can't have everything we want, we must plan and make choices to get the most out of what we have. For an individual or a family, the same problem exists. Because Mr. Jones doesn't have unlimited amounts of money (i.e., command over resources), he must economize—plan how to spend his money in the most "economical" way to get maximum benefit from using the money that he does have.

Opportunity Cost

One of the facts of economic life is that resources typically are limited, and choices have to be made concerning how they should be used. (Note the words "should be"—value terms like "should" and "ought" identify economics as a *normative* science concerned with prescribing what is *good* rather than simply describing what *is*.) Are there any ideas, skills, concepts, or tools in economic science that can help people make wiser choices? So many, in fact, that economics is often referred to as the science of choice. One idea that is especially useful is the concept of *opportunity cost*. (We'll leave marginal cost/marginal benefit analysis to another book!)

Consider the case of a young consumer. To help Miss Brown decide how to spend a weekly budget of $5, first consider some possible alternative uses for the money. Given the market price of 50¢ for soda pop, $2.50 for a movie ticket, and $1 for a milkshake, she can buy 10 cans of pop, go to the movies twice, or buy five chocolate milkshakes (*or* save the $5)—or any combination that uses no more than $5. To illustrate the concept of opportunity costs, let's pose the question: What is the *real* cost of five milkshakes? With a price of $1 per milkshake, the total money cost of five shakes is $5. Thinking in terms of the *other specific goods* that must be sacrificed if the $5 is spent on milkshakes, the "opportunity cost" of the shakes was 10 cans of pop, or two movie tickets, or one ticket and five cans of pop. *The opportunity cost of buying a particular good or service is the alternative goods and services that must be sacrificed (foregone) in order to obtain the selected items.*

From society's point of view, the opportunity cost ("real cost" or simply "cost") of producing one good is *the quantity of other goods that must be foregone when resources are employed to produce the first good.* The opportunity cost of national defense to the American people is all of the houses, cars, hospitals, and schools that we *can't* have because we use so many productive resources for bombs, missiles, soldiers, and nuclear submarines. The opportunity cost of having 12 million men and women in college is the value of the goods and services they could have produced if they were employed on jobs instead of going to school. (Form the viewpoint of an individual student, the opportunity cost of spending four years in college is the amount of income he could have earned if he were employed on a full-time job during those four years. Add this to the tuition and other private and public costs in order to compute the *total costs* of a college education.)

Opportunity cost is an important theoretical concept, and a very practical one as well. By providing a basis for comparing the benefits of alternative uses of money or resources, it can help us make better decisions concerning the way we actually will use them. In the example above, if Miss Brown feels she would enjoy the benefits of five milkshakes more than 10 cans of pop—or some other attainable combination such as six cans of pop plus two milkshakes (a tradeoff ratio of 2:1, giving up four pop to gain two milkshakes)—she can be more confident that she is spending her money wisely. If we consider what specific goods and services we are sacrificing by using $10 billion worth of manpower, capital, and materials to produce *x* number of additional B-1 bombers for the Air Force, we are in a better position to choose, as citizens, whether the sacrifice is worthwhile. We not only know what we are *getting* from using our resources in a particular way, but also what we are *giving up.*

Knowing the opportunity cost of a good makes us aware of "what might have been": it reminds us that truly, "there is no free lunch." And this can help us choose more wisely how personal resources and society's resources should be allocated to obtain the greatest benefit from the limited resources available.

The appendix to Chapter 12 describes a graphical technique commonly used for illustrating opportunity costs and the proverbial tradeoff between "guns" and "butter." Independent readers of this book may find the four appendices interesting and challenging. Students using the book in a college course can expect help and elaboration from their instructors in mastering the material in the appendices.

Selected Readings and References

Statistical Abstract of the United States 1985 (cited in Chapter 15).

Division of Labor and Economic Interdependence

People learned long ago that they could produce more and better goods at lower cost by working cooperatively as a team rather than individually as a "jack of all trades." Adam Smith cited *specialization* and *division of labor* as the key strategy for increasing production and national wealth. Specialization based on comparative advantage improves *efficiency*; but it also increases *interdependence* among members of the economic community.

No man is an island, entire of itself;
Every man is a piece of the continent, a part of the main...
Therefore never send to know for whom the bell tolls;
It tolls for thee.
　　　　—John Donne

Mankind has become so much one family that we cannot insure our own prosperity except by ensuring that of everyone else. If you wish to be happy yourself, you must resign yourself to seeing others happy as well.
　　　　—Bertrand Russell

Production is the process of converting resources—labor, land, and capital—into goods and services that are capable of satisfying wants directly or can be used in further production. Resources are the *inputs* to the production process; the *outputs* are consumer goods, capital goods, and the public goods and services such as police and fire protection, schooling, and national defense, provided by agencies of government. Production can be measured in physical units (e.g., 6.3 million cars) or in terms of dollar value ($47.6 billion worth of cars).

Productivity

A related but more sophisticated concept is *productivity*, defined as the ratio of output to resource inputs. Productivity is often measured as output per man-hour, or "per hour of all persons." (Strictly speaking, output per person-hour should be termed *labor productivity*, but often the qualifying adjective is omitted.) Year-to-year changes in productivity are watched closely because they reflect the *efficiency* with which an economy is using its productive resources. Over the years, the major source of increased production is rising productivity rather than a simple increase in the quantity of labor employed.

The productivity of labor has long been a favorite subject of economists—from the times of Adam Smith (1723-1790) and Karl Marx (1818-1883) to the modern era of "human capital" theory. (*Human capital* refers to the *acquired capabilities* that make people more productive.) Improvements in the "productive Powers of Labor" was the first topic that Adam Smith covered in his famous book, *An Inquiry into the Nature and Causes of the Wealth of Nations,* published in 1776. Smith, who was a Scottish professor of philosophy, is generally considered to be the father of modern economics. Even after two centuries, many of the theories explained in *The Wealth of Nations* continue to be taught to students in the United States and all over the non-communist world. The ideas of Adam Smith mean as much to people in the capitalistic economies (whether they know it or not) as the ideas of Marx and Lenin mean in the communist countries.

Lesson number one that Smith teaches about the productive powers of labor is that *"division of labor* is the great cause" of increased productivity. His example was a pin factory that made ordinary straight pins, like those used in dressmaking, tailoring, and the packaging of clothing.

> A workman not educated to this business, nor acquainted with the use of machinery employed in it, could scarce make one pin in a day, and certainly could not make twenty. But in the way in which this business is now carried on, not only the whole work is a peculiar trade, but it is divided into a number of branches, of which the greater part are likewise peculiar trades.
>
> One man draws out the wire, another straightens it, a third cuts it, a fourth points it, a fifth grinds it at the top for receiving the head. To make the head requires two or three distinct operations; to put it on is a peculiar business; to whiten the pins is another. It is even a trade by itself to put them into the paper.
>
> The important business of making a pin is, in this manner, divided into about 18 distinct operations. I have seen a small factory of this kind where 10 men were employed, and where some of them consequently performed two or three distinct operations. But though they were very poor (and did not have the best of machinery) they could, when they exerted themselves, make among them about 12 pounds of pins in a day. There are in a pound, upwards of 4,000 pins of a middling size. Those ten persons, therefore, could make among them upwards of 48,000 pins in a day. Each person, therefore, making a tenth part of 48,000 pins, might be considered as making 4,800 pins in a day. But if they had all worked separately and independently, they certainly could not each of them have made 20, perhaps not one pin in a day—that is, not even a small part of what they are at present capable of performing, because of a proper division and combination of their labor on different questions." (From Adam Smith, *The Wealth of Nations,* pp. 4ff, with minor editorial changes)

Smith explained the reasons why division of labor resulted in greater productivity. First, being able to work at a single task helps the worker improve his *skill*. Second, there is a gain by saving *time* that would otherwise be lost in moving from one type of work to another. And third, division of labor makes it possible to develop and use specialized *machinery* (i.e., capital goods embodying improved technology) that helps workers turn out great quantities of production. In recent years, economists have extended our understanding of the sources of productivity growth, identifying *technological progress* and investments in *education and training* of workers as factors of paramount importance.

Specialization Today

The idea of specialization and division of labor is one of the basic principles of economics. It tells us first that we can get more total output of goods and services by using our brains to organize the job in order to take advantage of each worker's skills and save time as well as benefit from the use of machinery and tools. In its more sophisticated form as the *Law of Comparative Advantage,* the principle of specialization indicates that the output of the whole community, the nation, and the entire world can be increased by having particular individuals and business firms produce those goods and services for which they have cost advantages—and letting other people specialize in the goods and services that *they* can produce more efficiently.

In modern society, we "divide the labor" and carry the principle of specialization to such extremes that sometimes a worker doesn't even know what product he is producing or how his contribution fits into the overall picture! A factory worker who tightens one bolt on a truck wheel as it moves past him on the assembly line may never see what the finished truck looks like! But production managers discovered that the assembly-line method was a very efficient way to organize the job and divide the labor. And since *efficiency* stands so high in our system of values, it follows that we make widespread use of assembly lines and other fractionalized methods of mass production. (Industrial psychologists and sociologists point out that this can lend to *worker alienation.* This is one reason why robots are beginning to replace humans on the assembly line, and also why some jobs are being re-designed to improve both productivity and the quality of worklife.)

Economic Interdependence

Along with specialization of labor and increased efficiency comes greater *economic interdependence.* Just as we depend on the assembly-line worker to tighten bolts so we can have trucks, that worker in turn depends on hundreds of other people to produce food for him and his family, and to provide housing, clothing, schooling, and countless other goods and services. Indeed it can be frightening to contemplate the extent to which extreme specialization makes us dependent on the farmer to plant and harvest enough crops to feed the nation; the electric companies to produce and distribute power to light our homes and keep our refrigerators running (not to mention our furnaces in the dead of winter); the oil companies to refine gasoline and maintain adequate supplies in thousands of service stations; banks to keep our financial transactions sorted out; and state and local government to provide protective services. It takes an occasional crop loss, power outage, bank failure, trade embargo, or work stoppage in a key industry to remind us how totally dependent we are on other members of our economic society.

This high degree of *interdependence is the other side of the coin of specialization and improved productivity.* One reason why economics is such an important social science stems from the fact that we are all part of a highly interdependent economic system. Because of the roles we play as producers, consumers, and citizens we need to understand how the system is organized, how it operates, and how our personal decisions and behavior will affect other people—as well as knowing how their decisions will affect us. Inflation, foreign trade deficits, plant closings, unemployment, farm foreclosures, red ink in social security trust funds, and business failures all have ripple effects—sometimes rising to the magnitude of tidal waves—that affect virtually every member of the economic community. How apt indeed is the poet's observation: Ask not for whom the bell tolls, it tolls for all of us.

In the appendix to this chapter, the "production-possibilities diagram" is explained and applied to concepts discussed in Chapters 11 and 12. Instructions are given on how to read graphs, and some further uses are indicated for production-possibilities diagrams and transformation curves.

Selected Readings and References

Solomon Fabricant, *A Primer on Productivity.* New York: Random House, 1969.
Adam Smith, *The Wealth of Nations.* New York: Modern Library, 1937 (originally published in 1776 as *An Inquiry into the Nature and Causes of the Wealth of Nations).*
Statistical Abstract of the United States 1985 (cited in Chapter 11).

APPENDIX: Production-Possibilities and the Law of Comparative Advantage

> Economists use a graphic model called the "production-possibilities curve" to illustrate a remarkable number of concepts including the overall level of output, the composition of output, opportunity costs, output lost because of unemployment, economic growth, and the basis for specialization in international trade. The diagram, though relatively simple to understand, is one of the most versatile tools used in economic analysis.

Figure 12A.1 is a "production-possibilities" diagram that measures on the vertical axis the quantity (Q) of "guns" that can be produced by the economy when alternative amounts of land, labor, and capital are allocated to their production, while the horizontal axis measures the quantity (Q) of "butter" that can similarly be produced. (The terms guns and butter are traditionally chosen to represent any pair of alternative goods—such as public versus private goods, capital versus consumer goods, "necessities" versus "luxuries"—that might be selected for analysis in a particular context.) The production-possibilities curve itself, labeled *A, B, C, D, E,* shows the *various combinations* of guns and butter that society can produce when all available *resources are fully employed,* assuming *given conditions of technology and institutional structure.* It therefore indicates, among other things, the maximum quantity of guns that can be produced if 100% of available resources are employed in producing guns (point *A,* 10 units); and, alternatively, the maximum quantity of butter that can be produced if all resources are used to produce butter (point *E,* 4 units).

Note that if all available resources were used for producing guns, there wouldn't be any left to produce butter; hence, if the allocation of resources were that indicated by point *A,* there would be 10 guns and zero butter. Alternatively, an allocation indicated by point *E* would result in a combination of 4 butter and zero guns. These are the upper limits of production, i.e., where the curve intercepts the respective axes. No amount of "price cutting" or "profit reduction" or other imagined adjustments can

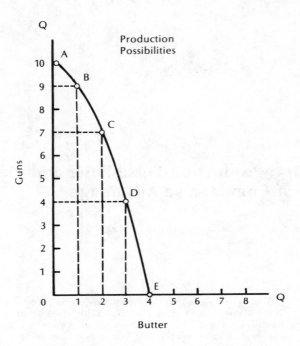

Figure 12A-1

raise these limits for the time period that is assumed in the model. Indeed, it should be clearly recognized that the production-possibilities diagram has nothing whatsoever to do with financial considerations, only *physical* output.

For the moment, let us assume that the economy is actually operating at full employment, i.e., *on* rather than below the production-possibilities "frontier." The curve therefore depicts the *overall level* of output (assuming, as we are, that these are exhaustive categories so that all production is classified as either "guns" or "butter"). Now, when a particular point is designated on the curve, the diagram also shows the *composition* of output. For example, at point *C* we are producing 7 guns and 2 butter, while at point *D* the "product mix" is 4 guns and 3 butter. (You measure from the graph's origin, O, upward on the vertical axis for guns, and from O rightward on the horizontal axis for the quantity of butter, projecting perpendicular lines from the designated point on the curve to the respective axes.)

How is the particular combination of guns and butter to be selected? Economists like to play the game of "What if—." What would it "cost" the economy to use all its resources in the production of guns? The answer is 4 butter since that is the quantity of butter lost (i.e., production opportunities sacrificed or foregone) when all the available land, labor, and capital are employed in producing guns. What would it cost the economy to produce 4 butter? The answer is 10 guns. Now what if the economy decides to produce not zero butter, but 2? The "opportunity cost" of producing 2 butter, expressed in terms of guns, would be 3 guns, because that is the reduction in output of guns resulting from employing some resources to produce butter rather than employing all resources for guns. Note that now the measuring doesn't begin at the origin of the graph, the O, but rather *at the points of intercept,* where the production-possibilities curve hits the respective axes. The reason is that we are now measuring *reductions* in output, not the quantities produced.

Economists play the "What-if" game in order to create awareness of what must be given up when resources are used in one particular way rather than another. In the real world, knowing the opportunity costs (as explained in the body of Chapter 11) can help decisionmakers arrive at wiser choices in the allocation of resources. Of course, such information does not resolve the problem; a value judgment must still be made, presumably on the basis of a wide range of considerations. Referring again to Figure 12A.1, if you are asked to pick the "best" composition of output (i.e., the "best" allocation of resources) you will recognize that there is no obviously correct ("textbook") answer. Choosing point *C* because it is "in the middle" would not be very sophisticated. Nor can one rule out point *E* (would a small, pacifist nation want to produce guns?), or point *A* (what if the consumption of dairy products is taboo in that country?)

What else can a production-possibilities diagram illustrate? Suppose an economy suffers a temporary malfunction of its institutional structure resulting in a 30% rate of unemployment (see Figure 12A.2, which is essentially identical to Figure 12A.1 except for point U). The economy cannot produce as much output with 70% of its resources as it can when it employs the entire 100%. Therefore the *actual* level of production must lie *below* the production-possibilities frontier. The actual composition can be anywhere below this frontier but cannot lie on the curve, much less beyond it. "Scarcity economics" loses some of its relevance under these conditions; the discipline of opportunity-cost reasoning is undermined. What does it cost, for

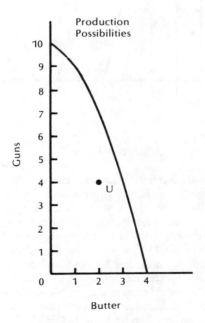

Figure 12A-2

example, to increase the production of guns from 4 to 7? It won't cost *anything* in terms of alternative products (butter) foregone if the new production comes from previously unemployed resources!

Figure 12A.3 shows a *new* production-possibilities curve that lies *above* the original, with intercepts at points more distant from the origin, indicating larger quantities of possible output. Curve G, H, J, K, L, represents the *growth* of the

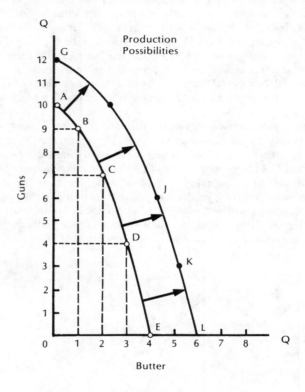

Figure 12A-3

economy, a higher level of potential output. Such economic growth results from three sources: quantitative and/or qualitative gains in *resources,* advances in *technology,* and improvements in *institutional structure.* These changes, of course, take time. Growth and development can occur only over time; but when economic growth does take place it is possible to have more butter *and* more guns at the same time ("having your cake and eating it too"). (Is it any wonder that Congress and the President, caught in the middle of national debates over national security versus income maintenance, have a strong preference for a growing economy!)

Figure 12A.4 differs from the others in that the production-possibilities curves are *linear* (straight lines rather than curves drawn concave to the origin); and there are *two* separate diagrams, though they indicate the production of the same pair of commodities. This adaptation further demonstrates the versatility of the production-possibilities model.

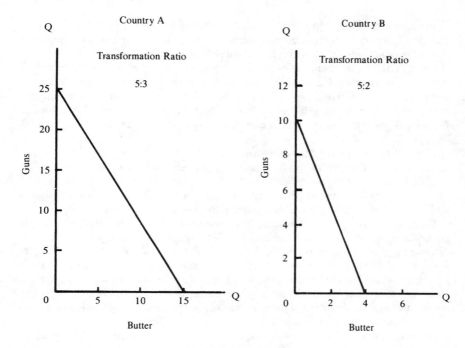

Figure 12A.4

If economics professors today placed as much emphasis on the "division of labor" as Adam Smith did two centuries ago, students would probably encounter this model earlier in the conventional "Principles" course to help them understand why individual workers, particular business firms, and sections of the country specialize in the lines of work they do. In practice, students seldom see the *linear* production-possibilities model—"transformation curves"—until late in the course, in the section on international trade. In that context it is used to demonstrate that two countries having different cost-of-production circumstances (because of dissimilar climatic conditions, labor skills, wage levels, natural resource endowment, economic traditions, etc.) can specialize in production—based on the Law of Comparative Advantage—and turn out more total output than if the countries met all of their own needs with domestic production. International specialization and trade, therefore, can result in a more efficient allocation of the world's resources and raise the world's real-income level. As suggested above, the same principle of specialization based on comparative productive efficiency applies equally to individuals, firms, and regions *within* a single country.

In Figure 12A.4, the "transformation curves" are straight lines, in part because it makes it a lot easier to use the model for teaching purposes and also because the curves purport to describe only a part of the total productive activity of the respective countries. (Technical comment: The assumption of "constant transformation ratios" is more reasonable in the international-trade context as opposed to the nonlinear transformation ratios of the whole-economy model, where opportunity costs keep changing as the proportion of *specialized* resources employed in producing a particular commodity changes).

For Country A, the opportunity cost of producing 5 guns is 3 butter (i.e., 25:15 = 5:3). For Country B (because of the dissimilar circumstances that give rise to different costs of production), the opportunity cost of producing 5 guns is 2 butter (10:4 = 5:2). If Country B uses its resources to produce guns, the "world economy" loses only 2 butter; whereas when Country A produces 5 guns the world economy gives up 3 butter. In order to maximize world output, the most efficient allocation of resources is for Country A to produce butter (gaining 3 butter at a loss of only 5 guns) while Country B specializes in the production of guns (gaining 7½ guns for a sacrifice of 3 butter).

(To follow the entire "transformation schedule" for Country A, start at the uppermost point, which shows that this economy can produce a combination of 25 guns and zero butter *or* 20 guns and 3 butter, 5 guns and 12 butter, or zero guns and 15 butter. Country B's transformation curve indicates production-possibilities of 10 guns and zero butter or 5 guns and 2 butter, or zero guns and 4 butter.)

Since the purpose of this appendix is essentially to describe the production-possibilities model and illustrate its versatility in economic analysis, substantive discussion of economic growth and international trade will be deferred until Part Four. Regarding the latter, however, some readers may find their curiosity aroused as to whether this analytical model can provide definitive answers to such questions as: How far should international specialization be carried? What prices will prevail in world markets? How will the gains from trade be divided among the trading partners? And the much-debated question: Is free trade a wise policy?

By now, many readers know that economic outcomes are rarely simple to predict, nor are policy issues so easily resolved. In the economic process, truly "everything depends on everything else;" and while abstract economic models can help clarify relationships, they cannot by themselves provide categorical answers to empirical and value-toned questions. The Law of Comparative Advantage by no means "proves" that free trade is the "correct" policy for a nation to follow.

The Circular Flow
of Economic Activity

In every economic system, decisions must be made concerning
the *amounts* and *kinds* of goods and services that are produced. In
a *market* economy, the decisions are made and communicated, for
the most part, by individual *consumers, business firms,* and *owners
of productive resources.* The decisions are expressed in a system of
markets and coordinated by flows of *money* and *goods and
services.*

Figure 13.1 is an economic model—a simplified picture of the private sector of the
economy, omitting the government "public sector," as well as market "imperfections"
that exist in the real world. The private sector accounts for about four-fifths of all
goods and services produced in the U.S. economy each year. By adding the
government sector, we could make the model more realistic (and complicated), thus
depicting our real-world mixed economy rather than the model private-enterprise
system portrayed here. Since our immediate purpose is to describe private-sector
decisionmaking in a capitalistic price system, however, we'll stick with the simpler
model (illustrated in the context of the American economy). Parts Four and Five deal
more empirically with the U.S. economy of the 1980s.

Decisionmaking Units

Our circular flow model identifies the *three units of economic decisionmaking* in a
market economy: *consumer households, business firms,* and *resource owners.* Next it
shows how the decisionmakers are linked together in markets (a *market* is defined as a
pattern of exchange relations) by means of money flows and corresponding flows of
resources, goods, or services. In the *output market* (or *product* market) consumers
spend money to purchase products desired for the satisfaction of consumer wants. The
sellers (suppliers) of the goods and services are business firms (also called companies

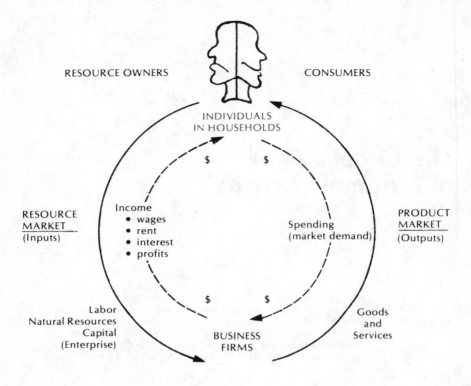

RESOURCE OWNERS   CONSUMERS

INDIVIDUALS
IN HOUSEHOLDS

$ $

RESOURCE   Income   PRODUCT
MARKET   • wages   Spending   MARKET
(Inputs)   • rent   (market demand)   (Outputs)
                  • interest
                  • profits

$ $

Labor   Goods
Natural Resources   and
Capital   Services
(Enterprise)   BUSINESS
                                   FIRMS

Figure 13.1   *The Circular Flow of Economic Activity in the Private Sector*

or enterprises). There are some 16 million separate firms in the U.S. economy, though
only a few thousand account for the bulk of business receipts. In the output market
consumers trade money for goods and *firms* trade goods for money.

Turning to the *input market* (often called the *resource* market, or "factor" market),
business *firms* spend money to purchase resource services—labor, materials,
capital—needed as inputs in the production process. These financial outlays become
the *income* of resource owners. Thus, *firms* trade money for resources, while *resource
owners* trade resource services for money.

Note that these are all voluntary transactions characterized by the presence of a
quid pro quo—something in exchange for something else. In this theoretical model
individual decisonmaking, voluntarism, and *quid pro quo* are essential features of
market transactions. (Their public sector counterparts are *collective* decisionmaking,
compulsory payments such as taxes, and *unilateral* transfers.) Note also the pivotal
role of firms: *buying* resources, converting the resources into marketable goods and
services, and *selling* the products to consumers.

How do we explain the Janus figure at the top of our diagram? The smiling face on
the right represents individuals in their capacity as consumers. Every person in our
economy is a consumer (240 million mouths to feed) and nearly all belong to
"consumer households." There are 85 million consumer households in the United
States, three-fourths of which are families. *Consumer households* make purchasing

decisions in the output market (actually, in thousands of different product markets). They decide whether to buy particular goods or services, what quantities to buy, whether to buy from one business firm or its rival across the street. Consumers spend money for goods and services in order to enjoy consuming them (and that's why the face on the right is smiling). Note that consumers *buy*; they never sell.

The face on the left shows individuals in their capacity as *resource owners.* Not all individuals own productive resources, but most of the consumer households in our economy have at least one resource owner—a person who has manpower or labor to exchange for money wages in the input market. There are some 114 million men and women in the civilian labor force, plus another two million in the armed forces—all of whom are owners of their own labor. In addition, there are people who own natural resources (such as oil wells and farmland) and people who own capital goods (factories, apartment buildings, etc.). All in all, there may be 140 million resource owners in the United States economy (without double counting). Although many people really *enjoy* their productive activity, we have drawn a frown on the left side of our two-headed individual to suggest that the input side of production is perhaps less pleasurable than consuming the output of goods and services. (Some economists say that pleasure-seeking consumption is the purpose of all economic activity, and productive effort is "a necessary evil.")

Wages, Rent, Interest, and Profits

When the owners of human resources make their services available to business firms (say, for eight hours a day, five days a week, to help produce automobiles), what do they get in return? People who contribute human effort (labor) to production receive a payment that economists call *wages.* This includes hourly wages, monthly salaries, sales commissions, tips, fringe benefits, and all the other direct and indirect payments for work.

Owners of natural resources who allow their land or other materials to be used in production are paid *rent.* Note that this isn't the same thing as the monthly rent a family pays for the house or apartment they live in. That "rental payment" really includes compensation for capital goods—the house and its fixtures—and various labor services as well as the use of land itself. (A broader concept of "economic rent" is the payment made to any factor of production that exceeds what is necessary to keep the resource committed to production, i.e., it is windfall income.)

Owners of buildings, equipment, etc., who allow their physical capital to be used in production receive a payment called *interest.* Actually, people often receive interest for letting business firms use their *money* to buy or finance production of the buildings and equipment. Money is *not* capital but can be used to purchase physical capital, hence the somewhat "versatile" concept of interest.

Finally, in addition to labor, natural resources, and capital, there is a fourth "factor of production" or type of resource that is sometimes included in a circular flow model, namely "enterprise" or *entrepreneurship*—the economic function of *making basic policy decisions* for a business and *bearing risk.* The income that accrues to enterprise is called profit. *Profit* is the residual share of income, i.e., the money that a business firm has left after paying all the costs of production. Profits belong to the owner(s) of the company (though in the real-world setting of corporate America, the "owners" do not receive their profits unless the board of directors vote to distribute them!).

"Dollar Votes"

Looking again at the circular flow diagram we can observe how *money* flows in one direction and *goods* and *services* flow in the opposite direction. Consumers spend money in the output market to buy goods and services from business firms. These expenditures are like *dollar votes* that give signals to business, telling them what to produce (more TV sets, orlon sweaters, houses, cars, and health-care services). Thus, the market is a *communication system,* linking the three units of economic decisionmaking.

When business firms receive the signals (tally the dollar votes) they can formulate plans concerning *what* and *how much* to produce. Now they can turn to the input market to obtain the *resources* needed for producing the goods and services demanded by consumers. (Sometimes business firms will also use resources to manipulate consumer demand—TV advertising, for example—thereby generating the kinds of signals they themselves want to get!)

Resource owners receive money income in payment for the labor, natural resources, and capital they provide. This income is available to be spent on consumer goods (or to be saved). Individuals take in money with the left hand as resource owners, and then spend it with the right as consumers.

The Market as a Coordinating Mechanism

Although buying and selling are not the most important kinds of economic behavior—*production* and *consumption* are surely the most basic activities—market behavior nevertheless is extremely important. The circular flow model helps us see (1) who makes the buying and selling decisions in a market system, (2) what effects these decisions have in guiding resources into particular uses, and (3) how commodities and services are "rationed" to the consumers who *want* the goods *and have the dollars to purchase them in the marketplace.*

From this model we learn that the function of business is to make profits by producing the goods and services that people effectively demand in the market. The function of resource owners is to contribute productive services in exchange for income (called *factor income* because it is paid to the factors of production). The function of consumers is to spend money to obtain goods and services for the satisfaction of their seemingly unlimited wants.

One of the economic wonders of the world is how the market mechanism manages to coordinate hundreds of millions of individual decisions made every day by the tens of millions of consumers, business firms, and resource owners that make up the private sector of a market economy. The circular flow model illustrates how this is accomplished without a system of comprehensive planning and detailed government coordination.

Selected Readings and References

Economic Indicators (see "References," Chapter 15).
Statistical Abstract of the United States 1985 (cited in Chapter 11).

Models, Theories, and the Real World

Because the economic process is so complex—involving millions of interdependent actions affecting the production and distribution of income—an understanding of its patterns and cause-effect relationships requires simplification, structuring, and generalization. To study and explain how the economy functions, scholars have developed *analytical frameworks*, simplified *models*, and economic *theories*. Many of these constructs are quite simple, yet extremely useful for explaining and predicting economic behavior.

The construction of a model consists of snatching from the enormous and complex mass of facts called reality a few simple, easily manageable key points which, when put together in some cunning way, can serve for certain purposes as a substitute for reality itself. Simplification is the heart of this process.

—*Evsey Domar*

For a person to think, talk, and write intelligently about economic matters—to be economically literate—he must develop basic competence in the use of history, theory, and statistics. In this chapter we consider the nature, necessity, and usefulness of *economic theory.*

The Nature of Theory

In the American economy there are some 60 million family households, 140 million resource owners, and 16 million business firms (broadly defined). There are approximately 250 working days in a year (52 weeks times five less 10 holidays). Most consumer households make at least one economic decision (for example, to buy a loaf of bread from the store) every working day. Multiply 60,000,000 families by 250 decisions, and that comes to 15 *billion* consumer decisions made in the U.S. economy during the year. Add the decisions made by nonfamily households, resource owners, and business firms and the total becomes incalculable!

How are all these production and consumption decisions coordinated? How can we possibly explain or predict the patterns of decisionmaking and economic behavior? The answer: by *simplifying.* And by *organizing* the important facts *systematically* in order to analyze them for the purpose of formulating *generalizations* and making *predictions.*

In considering how economists simplify and organize facts to help explain economic behavior, we can begin by recalling the basic *analytical framework* introduced in Chapter 2. We divided all the things that influence production and distribution into three groups and called them *resources, technology,* and *institutions.* This trilogy of economic forces or variables became the first element in our structuring of economics as a social science discipline. In Chapter 13 we moved beyond the basic analytical framework to develop a simple *model* called the *circular flow of economic activity,* illustrating the structure and functioning of an economic institution called "the market" (or "price system").

We know what that particular model shows; but how shall we describe the purpose and functions of models in general? Essentially a *model* is a scheme or gadget (mental or physical construct) that *represents reality,* such as the geographer's globe, which is a spherical map or model of the earth. A model enables us to see the *structure* of an entity or process and *significant relationships* among the parts. Most of the models used in economics are *mental constructs* that are illustrated graphically, pictorially, or mathematically.

What about theories? For some people "theory," "principles," and "laws" are scare words. But they really shouldn't be. An *economic theory* is just a more specific kind of model, one that purports to describe a set of cause-effect relations among economic variables. It tells something very specific about the world of facts. (Recall the Law of Comparative Advantage from Chapter 12 and the appendix.)

The supply and demand theory of market prices (described in the appendix to Chapter 17) tells us, for example, that the price of a good is determined—when pure competition prevails in the market—by the interaction of supply and demand. The theory tells us that an increase in supply, with no change in demand, will cause the market price to fall. An increase in demand, with no change in supply, will cause the market price to rise. At lower prices, larger quantities will be demanded but smaller quantities will be produced. At higher prices, smaller quantities will be demanded but larger quantities will be produced.

Operative Theories

A theory has certain *assumptions* and *definitions.* (Economists make extensive use of the *ceteris paribus* assumption—that "other things remain constant" as they focus attention on the particular variables under consideration.) A theory yields *predictions.* Operative theories show how experimental *tests* can be conducted using *facts* in the real economic world. (Many so-called theories are not really scientific-empirical theories because there is no possible way to check their validity. They are more properly thought of as speculative hypotheses.)

Good Theory and Bad

For most people interested in acquiring a working knowledge of the economic process, there is no need to master the intricacies of sophisticated economic theory. The important thing at present is to understand what a theory is (an abstract simplification describing cause-effect relationships) and what it is supposed to do (help explain the functioning of the real-world economy). This raises a couple of interesting questions.

First, when is a theory a *good* theory (and what are the characteristics of good analytical frameworks and models)? We have all heard the statement, "That's all right in theory, but it doesn't work in practice." Actually, *if a theory doesn't work in practice, then it isn't "all right."* If it doesn't work in practice, it's a *bad* theory. Theories, like all tools, are supposed to be *useful*—to help you do a job. If a theory or model is useful in describing economic behavior and generating accurate predictions, it's a good construct. On the other hand, if the theory proves unreliable as a basis for explanation, prediction, and control, then quite simply it is a bad theory.

Economics unfortunately does not have good theories to explain everything we would like to know about resources, technology, and institutions—and how we can achieve society's goals with respect to the overall level, composition, and distribution of income. During the 1970s, for example, serious questions began to be raised about the validity of the aggregate-demand theory of employment and inflation (which is described in the appendix to Chapter 22). Economic policies based on that theory were not working. As a consequence *macro*economic theory is currently undergoing extensive modification (recall the distinction made in Chapter 9 between micro and macro theory).

Economics is a fairly young science. It took physicists a long time to solve the mystery of nuclear energy. Meteorology is still not a very exact science. A social science that tries to understand and explain the behavior of *people*, in their complex and continually changing economic life, can be expected to be "inexact" and far from perfect. Nevertheless, we do have some valid theories, helpful models, and useful analytical frameworks contributing to a better understanding of the economic world in which we live.

Importance of Economic Theory

Finally, valid or otherwise, how important *are* theories anyway? Perhaps the most famous economist of our time, John Maynard Keynes (1883-1946)—the English academician and political activist primarily responsible for contemporary macroeconomic theory—wrote an answer to that question that is widely quoted (indeed, repeated in the appendix to the chapter):

> The ideas of economists and political philosophers, both when they are right and when they are wrong, are more powerful than is commonly understood. Indeed, the world is ruled by little else... Madmen in authority who hear voices in the air, are distilling their frenzy from some academic scribbler of a few years back.

In support of this claim, consider the social theories of John Locke (on democracy); Adam Smith (on market capitalism); Friedrich Nietzsche (on political elitism); and Karl Marx and Friedrich Engels (on communism). Wars and revolutions have already been fought over the ideas of these "academic-scribblers" and today the threat of world annihilation may well turn on the issue of which economic ideology— Smith's or Marx's—is to prevail.

Finally, it should be emphasized that *all* economists make use of theory— analytical frameworks, models, principles, and "laws". But their particular theories are not always the same. Economists can differ in their basic worldview, their values, and the way they experience the world (e.g., an attitude of extraversion or intro- version, and reliance on thinking, sensation, feeling, or intuition as the dominant "data-processing" function, in the terminology of psychologist C.G. Jung). Accordingly, they ask different questions, select different facts to study, and spin different kinds of theories.

The appendix to this chapter sketches three distinct streams of economic thought: standard neoclassical, Marxist, and evolutionary-institutional. Intellectual contribu- tions of Adam Smith, Alfred Marshall, John Maynard Keynes, Karl Marx, and Thorstein Veblen are duly noted.

Selected Readings and References

C.G. Jung, "A Psychological Theory of Types," Chapter 4 in *Modern Man in Search of a Soul.* New York: Harcourt Brace Jovanovich (first published 1933).

John Maynard Keynes, "Concluding Notes on the Social Philosophy Towards Which the General Theory Might Lead," Chapter 24 in *The General Theory of Employment, Interest, and Money.* New York: Harcourt Brace, 1936.

Statistical Abstract of the United States 1985 (cited in Chapter 11).

Note: Also see citations in the appendix to this chapter.

APPENDIX: Streams of Economic Thought

The chronicles of Western intellectual history describe numerous and varied *schools of economic thought* and particular *economic doctrines*, from Plato and Aquinas to such 19th-century social reformers as Henry George. In the 20th century, however, the three major streams of economic thought have been: (1) the standard *classical-neoclassical tradition* of Adam Smith, as modified by Keynesian macroeconomic theory; (2) *Marxism*; and (3) the *evolutionary institutionalism* of Thorstein Veblen and his followers. All three schools are represented in America today by professional economists who are competent and articulate.

The ideas of economists and political philosophers, both when they are right and when they are wrong, are more powerful than is commonly understood. Indeed, the world is ruled by little else. Practical men, who believe themselves to be quite exempt from any intellectual influences, are usually the slaves of some defunct economist.
— *John Maynard Keynes*

Modern economics stands the truth on its head by considering goods as more important than people and consumption as more important than creative activity. It [shifts] the emphasis from the worker to the product of work, that is, from the human to the subhuman.
— *E.F. Schumacher*

Economists disagree so often on details of theory and policy that some people believe there are as many brands of economics as there are economists. (They also say that if you laid all the world's economists end-to-end, they would never come to a conclusion, but laying them end-to-end would still be a good idea.) Although this view is not entirely without substance, it understates the vast areas of fundamental agreement among most Western-world economists, for whom such labels as "neo-classical," "standard," "orthodox," or "conventional" are willingly accepted. The overwhelming majority of American economists are well within the mainstream. On the other hand, there are two bona fide alternative "brands" of economic theory which are so clearly differentiated from the mainstream, and which have significant numbers of adherents in America today, that separate descriptions are warranted.

In this appendix we first recapitulate the mainstream classical-neoclassical tradition of economic thought, the essence of which is known today as post-Keynesian neoclassical economics ("brand X"). This tradition dates back to Adam Smith (1723-1790) and his famous book *The Wealth of Nations,* published in 1776. (Smith's view of what *is,* and what *ought to be* in economic life has so dominated thinking in the Western world that we sometimes forget that not everyone agrees with the assumptions, values, and "scientific truths" of market economics.)

We then consider two dissenting schools of economics. Prominent among the "heretics," of course, are the Marxists ("brand Y")—scattered throughout the world including the United States, but concentrated in communist Russia, Eastern Europe, and China. (In those countries, Marxism is mainstream economics; advocates of market principles are the heretics.) In addition, there are *non*-Marxist dissenters, including the only distinctive American school of economic thought, the evolutionary institutionalists ("brand Z"). Neoclassical and dissenting economists alike take the ideas of Adam Smith as their point of departure and also share Keynes's conviction that economic ideas can change the world. (Indeed, who can doubt that traditional capitalism, radical Marxism, and democratic welfarism—conceived successively in the 18th, 19th, and 20th centuries—are among the most powerful ideological forces at work in the world today?) We therefore begin with the market economics of Adam Smith and his 20th-century intellectual descendants.

Classical/Neoclassical Economics

What today is known as the neoclassical system (or post-Keynesian neoclassical economics) began with Adam Smith's book *An Inquiry Into the Nature and Causes of The Wealth of Nations.* In this classic of world literature, the renowned Scottish professor of moral philosophy expounded the theory of a self-regulating market society. Under a system of private property and competitive markets, if individuals were allowed to pursue their own economic self-interest—as workers, consumers, resource owners, and entrepreneurs—the economic interests of society as a whole would be served automatically. Resources would be properly allocated (according to the principle of "consumer sovereignty"), production would be efficient, and income would be equitably distributed. Not only was selfish behavior assumed to be consistent with human nature, Smith also believed that consumers had a natural propensity to "truck and barter" and knew instinctively which goods and services would best satisfy their true needs. Under these conditions, detailed government regulations and controls (the norm under 18th-century mercantilism) were not only unnecessary but inevitably harmful. Hence the policy should be "laissez faire": let the market alone. As if guided by an "invisible hand," self-regulating capitalism would promote efficiency, social stability, and—through increased specialization of labor and accumulation of capital equipment—economic progress. Not that Smith was unmindful of such dangers as extreme specialization of labor (which could make workers "as stupid and ignorant as it is possible for a human creature to become") and tendencies for businessmen "to [conspire] against the public... to raise prices." But risks notwithstanding, laissez faire capitalism was judged to be the system most conducive to expanding the nation's wealth and furthering the goal of material progress for all members of society. (Many of Smith's ideas, such as natural order and equilibrium, were borrowed from Newtonian physics.)

By the middle of the 19th century the Classical School had profited from theoretical contributions by Thomas Malthus, David Ricardo, and others, reaching its highest stage of development with the publication of John Stuart Mill's *Principles of Political Economy* in 1848. Further refinements in the 1870s produced the now-familiar microeconomic theories of supply and demand, "marginal analysis" (guidelines for maximizing consumer satisfaction and business profits), and the marginal productivity theory of income distribution ("to each according to his contribution")—theoretical innovations that earned mainstream doctrine the designation Neoclassical economics. In 1890 a new definitive text, *Principles of Economics,* was published by English economist Alfred Marshall (1842-1924). Reflecting the "marginal utility" doctrines of the Austrians as well as advances in British mathematical economics, Marshall's *Principles* dominated the field for 40 years (hence the term "Marshallian economics").

After the turn of the century, the rise of big business led to new *micro*economic theories of market structure and business behavior ("monopolistic competition" and "oligopoly"); and in the 1930s the distinguished neoclassical economist John Maynard Keynes *(The General Theory of Employment, Interest, and Money,* 1936) introduced the theoretical tools of "Keynesianism" that eventually were absorbed into the mainstream as standard *macro*economics. Despite subsequent developments in quantitative analysis (notably "econometrics") and monetary theory (including works by Nobel laureate Milton Friedman), the ideas of Smith, Marshall, and Keynes continue as of the 1980s to define the content of conventional economics. The essence of the neoclassical system today is a belief in private ownership and operation of the means of production, resource allocation on the basis of utilitarian consumer preferences, and a distribution of income consistent with the principles of marginal productivity (i.e., "to each according to his contributions," not his needs). Key values are "maximizing," profit-making, and efficiency. Government is seen as having a place in the economic system—primarily to enforce rules and stabilize the overall functioning of the economy—but in the interest of efficiency and freedom, government's role should be carefully defined and narrowly limited.

Marxism

When classical economics reached its peak in 1848, Britain and the rest of Western Europe could look back on a full century of economic life under conditions of the Industrial Revolution. (In America, industrial capitalism predictably lagged a few decades behind.) Generations of eager scholars had refined and elaborated Adam Smith's pathbreaking insights to crystallize the science and ideology of market capitalism (though not without passionate dissent from an assortment of British, French, and German "utopian" socialists).

Then "came the revolution"—the intellectual revolution that we know today as Marxism. It was this same year, 1848, that Karl Marx (1818-1883) and his lifelong collaborator Friedrich Engels (1820-1895) issued their famous *Communist Manifesto*, a 38-page tract outlining their materialistic, class-struggle theory of history and prognosticating the doom of capitalist society. Nineteen years later, Marx published Volume I of *Das Kapital*, a scholarly and prodigious critique of capitalism, appearing in English as *Capital* only in 1887. Today one-third of the world—the Soviet Union, China, East Germany, Cuba, and elsewhere—pays homage to the theories of Karl Marx in much the same way that many Americans and Europeans venerate the ideas of Adam Smith. (Nations of "the Third World," plagued by low incomes and rising expectations, are so designated because they face the quandary of choosing between these two traditions, or finding a viable new alternative.)

What are the essentials of Marxist thought, and what place does Marxism occupy in the evolution of economic ideas? Marxism means different things to different people; not just to Marxists as opposed to non-Marxists, but also within the respective camps. In an often-cited quote, Marx himself is reported to have said, "I am not a Marxist." (Perhaps Adam Smith would similarly have disavowed classical economics if he had seen what it would become in the hands of *his* interpreters.) Two aspects of Marxist thought will be described briefly in this appendix: the dialectical materialism/ class struggle theory of history, and Marx's critique of capitalism.

In *The Communist Manifesto* and elsewhere, Marx and Engels outlined a theory of social relations and historical change. At the foundation of every society is an economic base, or mode of production. This consists of *(a)* the "forces of production," notably people, skills, technology, and equipment; and *(b)* the "relations of production," i.e., institutions of hierarchy and power, social classes, and control of the means of production. According to Marx, this "mode of production" influences the superstructure of ideas and sociopolitical arrangements that help define the overall character of the particular society. Inherent in the relations of production are class antagonisms concerning the distribution of income, wealth, and privilege. In capitalistic society, a "class struggle" goes on between the elite owners of the means of production and the masses of wage workers (the proletariat). Economic considerations, though they may not be the only factor in history, were seen by Marx and Engels as the "ultimately determining element."

To this materialistic, class-struggle view of history, Marx added the concept of the *dialectic* which he borrowed from the German philosopher G. W. F. Hegel (1770-1831). According to the dialectical perspective, everything in the universe contains within it tensions and contradictions that inevitably generate change. The capitalist mode of production is no exception. Dominated by a technology that requires cooperation between capital and labor, capitalism nevertheless is founded on a production relationship that is highly individualistic, namely the institution of private property. Add to this contradiction the dynamic forces of a constantly changing technology, and the potential for class struggle and eventual disruption of the system becomes "inevitable."

In *Capital* (subtitled "Critique of Political Economy"), Marx showed how dialectical materialism and class struggle found expression in the "laws of motion of capitalism," leading to collapse of the system and its replacement first by socialism and eventually by communism. The starting point of Marx's critique is his concept of surplus value. This is the difference between the *exchange value of commodities* produced by labor and the *price of labor power* (i.e., the wage rate). Because the capitalist owns the means of production, he can limit the worker's claims to an agreed-upon wage and appropriate the surplus value for his own private gain. Market competition, however, threatens to squeeze the capitalist's profits and forces him to adopt labor-saving technology, which does not yield surplus value. Hence, profits decline; smaller firms fail, and in the course of recurrent business cycles, increasingly larger shares of the market are taken over by a few giant firms. Meanwhile, recessions and mechanization create an "industrial reserve army of the unemployed," swollen by the addition of women and children to the work force. The growing exploitation and misery of the working class eventually leads to revolution, in which "the [capitalist] expropriators are [themselves] expropriated." Trained, disciplined, and organized by industrial capitalism, the proletariat seizes control of the means of production (with its economic surplus) and establishes a transitional socialist regime, to be replaced eventually by a classless society of pure communism. Thus, the capitalistic system contains the seeds of its own displacement.

The villain in the capitalistic system, in Marx's view, is not a class of people but a legal institution that distorts production and deprives workers of the human dignity and freedom which society's level of technology would otherwise permit. The institution of private property entails a "mystification" of production—what Marx termed "the fetishism of commodities"—that alienates workers and perpetuates class antagonism, thereby hindering human creativity and individuation. The passing of the capitalist stage of history—in which, to its credit, material insufficiency has been overcome—removes unnecessary and artificial barriers to human freedom; another phase of social evolution runs its course.

In sum, Marxism as described here is essentially a theory of history and a critique of capitalism, not a blueprint for socialism. While Marx did have a vision of such a system, his life's work focused on a method of social analysis (i.e., dialectical materialism) and its use in revealing the beneath-the-surface nature and human consequences of capitalism. (As for the relation of Marxism to present-day governmental systems, one may ponder whether it is any more appropriate to credit or blame Marx for the legacy of Leninist-Stalinist Russia than to attribute to Adam Smith the likes of Hitler's Germany or certain other capitalist regimes of dubious merit that have evolved in both the Eastern and Western hemispheres.) Whether seen from the perspective of radical American economists of the New Left, or Soviet communists, the essence of Marxism is (1) a repudiation of (the elitist institution of) private ownership of the means of production, (2) advocacy of public ownership with comprehensive economic planning, and (3) the eventual elimination of material poverty and worker alienation for all members of society.

Evolutionary Institutionalism

"Brand Z" of economic theory has fewer avowed adherents than either conservative capitalism or radical Marxism. Inspired by the ideas of Thorstein Veblen (1857-1929), American Institutionalism is a 20th-century phenomenon. Less doctrinaire than neoclassical economics or Marxism, its theories have scored quiet victories in such varied fields as labor and social security legislation in the United States, empirical studies of the large corporation, Fabianism in Britain (the intellectual source of the Labor Party's platform), and the economic development work of Swedish Nobel laureate Gunnar Myrdal.

The first and most famous of Veblen's 11 books, *The Theory of the Leisure Class,* was published in 1899 when this American-born son of Norwegian immigrants was on the faculty of the University of Chicago. (Later Veblen taught at Stanford, the University of Missouri, and the New School for Social Research in New York City.) Other works, including *The Instinct of Workmanship and the State of the Industrial Arts,* stressed the importance of technological progress in determining economic wellbeing. Like Marx, Veblen was critical of orthodox economic theory; but unlike his socialist predecessor, Veblen offered no revolutionary theory of historical change. Instead, he and his followers urged the adoption of a more *evolutionary* ("Darwinian") and *holistic* approach to socioeconomic analysis and structural economic change.

Veblen differed sharply from mainstream and Marxist theories of human nature and argued that capitalism "contaminated" positive human instincts (such as workmanship, creative curiosity, and a desire for social progress)—in part because of its preoccupation with pecuniary values (e.g., maximizing income and making invidious comparisons based on personal wealth) as opposed to efficiency-oriented "instrumental" values. Production for profit rather than for use was seen as a tragic flaw in the institutional structure of 20th-century capitalism.

Three variants of post-Veblenian evolutionary institutionalism developed: (1) the social-reform strategy of John R. Commons (1862-1945); (2) the statistical methodology of Wesley Clair Mitchell (1874-1948); and (3) the "critical genetic" approach of Clarence E. Ayres (1891-1972). Key ideas shared by all institutionalists include a focus on group behavior and choice as opposed to individual hedonistic decisionmaking; emphasis on technological progress as the chief determinant of a society's productivity; a search for social values as guidelines to economic policy; and the continuing need for adjusting the structure of institutions. Institutional methodology emphasizes the use of history and statistics in economic analysis in contrast to the neoclassical preoccupation with deductive logic and abstract mathematical models; and it acknowledges the interdependence of political, social, and economic behavior. Although contemporary "neoinstitutionalists" lack consensus on a theory of human nature (tending toward extreme behaviorism), all agree that the hedonistic psychology of neoclassical economics is outmoded and inadequate. Most institutionalists follow Veblen's lead in placing as much distance as possible between themselves and the politically unpopular ideas of Marxism.

In summary, evolutionary institutionalism rejects utilitarianism and reliance on the market as the ultimate mechanism of economic value, while emphasizing the "instrumental values" of scientific-technological progress and political democracy. The fundamental principles of economics, from the evolutionary perspective, are not the laws of supply and demand but the social principles of technological progress and institutional adjustment.

Synchronistic Postscript on Economics and Psychology

Hedonistic (pleasure/pain) utilitarianism has long provided the psychological basis for the neoclassical theory of consumption, and by extension all rational economic decisionmaking. And, of course, the neoclassical school is proudly materialistic in its scientific orientation. It requires no great leap to connect neoclassical economics with Freudian psychology.

Sigmund Freud's surname is German for "pleasure; satisfaction." Freud was an extravert, oriented outward toward objects in the material world. In the Freudian scheme, sexual libido (again, like "winning" for football coach Vince Lombardi, not just the most important thing, but the *only* thing) serves to drive the individual toward *pleasurable gratification of wants.* In *neoclassical economics* (which also leans toward oversimplification) hedonistic rationality leads consumers to *maximize the satisfaction of wants* (total utility), and resource owners to minimize the "pain" of work and sacrifice (disutility). Freud's psychology meshes symbiotically with market economics in an extraverted world of consumerism, money, and commercialized sex, where unconscious wish fulfillment is acted out through the "rational" satisfaction of material wants.

The second member of depth psychology's founding troika (all from Central Europe, writing at the turn of the century) was Alfred Adler, an introvert whose orientation was inward toward the subject. The word "Adler" in German means "eagle," a familiar symbol of strength and power. The core of Adler's school of Individual Psychology was not sexual libido but the *power drive*—to compensate the individual for his own feelings of inferiority or weakness. It may not be too far-fetched to associate Adler's power orientation with the totalitarian regime of *Marxist* Russia (but admittedly also with the fascism of Nazi Germany, and certain contemporary dictatorships which lack distinctive economic "isms"). The power drive is, of course, also highly relevant to the capitalistic quest for great wealth.

C.G. Jung (whose ideas are reflected throughout this book) was the third pioneer of depth psychology. He is the one who *formulated* the theory of extraversion and introversion—in the context of trying to explain why Freud and his former associate Adler viewed the same reality in such totally different light! The word "Jung" in German means "young; youthful," the symbol of *potential for growth.* The central focus of Jung's Analytical Psychology is the process of *individuation,* in which the individual human being—whose psyche is an infinite complex of archetypal pre-dispositions and potentialities—is impelled teleologically to fulfill himself in the same sense in which (according to the doctrine of entelechy) the proverbial acorn seeks to achieve its full potential as a mighty oak. Of course, not all acorns make it, just as men and women differ in the degree to which they achieve balanced growth and human fulfillment.

Does *Jungian psychology* harmonize with *evolutionary-institutional economics* the way Freudian psychology does with the economics of capitalism and Adlerian psychology with Marxism? As expressed by Thorstein Veblen—Jung and Veblen were contemporaries, their lives overlapping for 54 years—there can be little doubt that American Institutionalism and Analytical Psychology have much in common, beginning with their *instinctual/archetypal premises* and consistent orientation to *evolutionary growth.* (The hard-line behaviorist orientation of many *neo*institutionalists, based on the ideas of John B. Watson and B.F. Skinner, seems to be an unfortunate aberration.) It may not be too much to hope that the interface of Veblen's evolutionary-institutionalism with Jung's analytical psychology (a la C. E. Ayres' tool-combination principle) can yet trigger significant advances in the science of human behavior.

As for the *literal meaning* of the Germanic surnames—Freud, Adler, and Jung—could there be for psychologists themselves a more confirmatory, if whimsical, example of Jung's concept of synchronicity (meaningful acausal coincidence)!

Selected Readings and References

Robert L. Heilbroner, *The Worldly Philosophers,* 5th ed. New York: Simon & Schuster, 1980.

E.F. Schumacher, *Small Is Beautiful: Economics as if People Mattered.* New York: Harper & Row, 1973. (Of particular interest is Chapter 4, "Buddhist Economics," which is not as exotic or esoteric as the title may suggest.)

Standard Classical-Neoclassical Tradition

Adam Smith, *The Wealth of Nations.* New York: Modern Library, 1937 (originally published in 1776).

Alfred Marshall, *Principles of Economics,* 8th ed. New York: Macmillan, 1949 (1st edition, 1890).

John Maynard Keynes, *The General Theory of Employment Interest and Money.* New York: Harcourt Brace, 1936.

American Economic Review. Published quarterly by the American Economic Association (AEA).

Journal of Economic Literature. Published quarterly by the AEA.

Marxist Tradition

Karl Marx and Friedrich Engels, *The Communist Manifesto,* 1848 (various editions).

Karl Marx, *Capital.* New York: Modern Library, no date (Vol. I of *Das Kapital* first published in 1867).

The Monthly Review. Published by The Monthly Review Press.

Review of Radical Political Economics. Published quarterly by the Union for Radical Political Economics.

Evolutionary-Institutionalist Tradition

Thorstein Veblen, *The Theory of the Leisure Class.* New York: Modern Library, 1934 (originally published in 1899 by Macmillan). Other major works by Veblen include *The Theory of Business Enterprise* (1904), *The Instinct of Workmanship* (1914), *The Engineers and the Price System* (1921); *The Portable Veblen* was published by Viking in 1958.

Journal of Economic Issues. Published quarterly by the Association for Evolutionary Economics.

Review of Institutional Thought. Published annually by the Association for Institutional Thought.

Gross National Product and Some Fundamentals of Economic Statistics

The gross national product *(GNP)* of any nation measures the total value of all the goods and services that its people produce in a particular year. *GNP statistics* are useful because they provide important facts about the *overall level* and *composition* of our current production and help us understand how our economy is behaving. In addition to *GNP*, other "economic indicators" such as the *consumer price index (CPI)* and the *unemployment rate (TUR)* are widely used in measuring the performance of our economy.

Statistics are indispensable, but...they must be interpreted with greater skill and discretion. [The American public is] prone to take statistics too literally, to ignore their limitations, and to confuse partial truths with the whole truth about complex realities.
—Arthur Ross, former U.S. Commissioner of Labor Statistics

Economics is a social science. This means that scientific methods, including extensive reliance on *measurement* and *quantitative analysis,* are used in studying the subject matter. As indicated in Chapter 9, people who want to read, think, and talk intelligently about economic questions have to become competent in using the techniques of history, theory, and statistics. The first two types of skills were discussed in the five preceding chapters. Now we consider *economic statistics* and, specifically, the use of gross national product *(GNP)* data, indexes of price-level changes, and unemployment rates—to measure the overall performance of our economy.

Attitude toward Statistics

Earlier we noted the skeptical attitude that many people have toward statistics. "Figures don't lie," they say, "but liars figure." There is even a highly successful book with the tongue-in-cheek title *How to Lie with Statistics.* The book performs a very useful function: It teaches us how to detect and avoid the *misuse* of statistics. Skepticism can be a healthy attitude when it alerts people to be careful about the way they use statistics. Unfortunately some people go beyond caution—they refuse to believe any statistics at all! And since most of the facts about economic affairs come to us in the form of statistics, this comes close to saying, "Don't bother me with the facts; I'll make up my mind without them."

What *are* economic statistics? We use the term here to mean numbers (often based on sample surveys and reports) that describe what is happening in the economy regarding production, spending, employment, price movements, and other activities. The numbers come from business, labor, farm groups, private research organizations, and state and federal government agencies. *GNP* and other *national income statistics* are calculated and published by the U.S. Department of Commerce. Studies of government statistics have repeatedly been made by unbiased experts, and their judgment over and over again is that the data generally are as accurate, honest, and complete as anyone could reasonably expect though by no means perfect, either conceptually or in terms of data collection. To the extent that "liars figure" the problem is more serious with users than with producers of the data.

Gross National Product and Its "Cousins"

Let's look at one set of economic statistics: the gross national product *(GNP)* accounts of the U.S. economy for 1984.

Table 15.1

Gross National Product of the United States by Sectors, 1984

	Billions of dollars	Per cent distribution
Personal consumption expenditures *(C)*	$2,342	64%
Gross private domestic investment *(I)*	637	17%
Government purchases of goods and services *(G)*	748	20%
Net exports of goods and services *(X$_n$)* (i.e., total exports minus total imports)	-62	-2%
Total *GNP*	$3,664 bil.	100%

Source: *Economic Indicators,* February 1985

What do these figures tell us? The "bottom line" is that the *market value of the total output of final goods and services* produced by the U.S. economy in 1984 amounted to $3.7 trillion (rounded). The *dollar value* of all the thousands of different goods and services that we produced that year—cars, breakfast cereal, missiles, TV sets, haircuts—totaled $3.7 trillion. How do we compute the total? We simply add up all of the money that *consumers* spent to buy goods (durable and nondurable) and services during the year ($2.3 trillion); plus the investment spending by *business firms* on equipment and buildings, etc. ($637 billion); plus the money spent by local, state, and federal *government* agencies to purchase goods and services including the labor of government workers ($748 billion); plus the *net exports* of goods and services we produced in this country and sold to foreigners above what other countries produced and sent to the United States (- $62 billion, i.e., net exports were a *negative* value because our *imports* exceeded our exports). The formula for calculating GNP therefore is: $GNP = C + I + G + X_n$.

GNP is the effective aggregate market demand or *total spending* for newly produced goods and services during the year, eliminating the double counting of "intermediate" goods that are bought and sold by businesses in the process of production (e.g., wheat milled into flour and used in baking bread). Another way to look at *GNP* is to see that it is the total money *value* of the final goods that our nation produces. *GNP* equals the quantity *(Q)* of goods and services produced, multiplied by the average price *(P)* at which the goods and services were sold. Conceptually, $GNP = P \times Q$. It is *output,* measured in terms of its dollar value. Note that gross national product is *not* gross national *wellbeing.* Greater output often can enhance the wellbeing of the nation's people, but as we shall suggest in Part Six, "more" does not always equate with "better."

The four components of the *GNP* formula show that *four major spenders—*consumers, business, government, and foreigners—purchase and absorb the entire output of our economic system.

There is no need for the beginning student of economics to become an expert in national income accounting. The important thing to remember is that *GNP* is a measure of the total *output* of the economy. When *GNP* goes up, after adjusting for changes in the value of money (i.e., the general level of prices), then we know that production has increased. If *GNP* remains constant year after year, then the economy is not experiencing growth. If the *GNP* goes down, we are in a "recession." But note the importance of *adjusting for changes in the price level.* Without this adjustment, we would not know whether a change in money *GNP* resulted from a change in output *(Q)* or in the *measuring stick* we use to calculate the value of output *(P).* This is why economists distinguish between "money *GNP*" and *real GNP* (adjusted for inflation). For certain purposes such as making international comparisons and calculating rates of economic growth, economists also calculate *per capita GNP,* which is simply *GNP* divided by the total population of the country. In 1984, our per capita *GNP* was $15,460 (i.e., $3,664 billion $\div$ 237 million people = $15,460). In *total GNP* we ranked *first* in the world; in per capita *GNP* we ranked about 10th (for 1982 comparisons, see Table 29.1 in Chapter 29).

GNP is not the only measure of the nation's income. The U.S. Department of Commerce publishes estimates of *five* aggregates reflecting different concepts of income: (1) *GNP,* already defined as the market value of the total output of *final* goods and services produced during the year; (2) *Net National Product,* i.e., the market value of the *net* output of final goods and services, after deducting for the capital used up in production; (3) *National Income,* defined as the net output of final goods and services valued not at market prices but *factor costs* (conceptually, $NI =$ Wages + Rent + Interest + Profit); (4) *Personal Income,* which measures the flow of money income received by persons from all sources during the year; and (5) *Disposable Income,* equal to Personal Income minus personal taxes.

For our purposes in this book, it is enough to be aware of the five different national income measures (settling for a place somewhere between Level 1 and Level 2 on the scale of knowing) and to know that *GNP* is a measure of *output,* while Personal Income (the basic referent for money income received by families and individuals) reflects not output but simply the *dollars received by persons* during the year, whether in the form of factor payments (defined in Chapter 6) or funds transferred from government.

Consumer Price Index

Two other statistical indicators are widely used to measure the economy's performance: the consumer price index *(CPI)* and the unemployment rate *(TUR).* The consumer price index *(CPI)* or "cost of living" index is a statistical indicator that measures *changes* in the buying power of the dollar. (It is the most familiar of the various price indexes that economists use; others include indexes of producer prices and implicit price deflators for *GNP.*) When the *CPI* goes up it means the general level of prices is rising for the goods and services that consumers typically buy. *As prices go up, the value or purchasing power of the dollar goes down.* This is why inflation is considered to be a distressing condition—because people with a given number of dollars (such as older people living on savings or fixed-income pensions) are unable to buy as many goods and services as they could before price inflation occurred.

At the present time, the consumer price index—calculated by the U.S. Bureau of Labor Statistics (BLS) with survey data collected each month—uses 1967 as the base year (1967 = 100). By 1975 the *CPI* stood at 161.2 (the average of monthly figures for that year); and by December 1981, after averaging more than a 10% increase per year since 1978 ("double-digit inflation"), the index reached 281.5. This meant it took $2.82 to buy the same "package" of goods and services that could have been purchased in 1967 for $1.00. Prices had nearly *tripled* since the base year. Because of inflation—as measured by the 181.5% rise in the *CPI*—the value of the dollar had declined to *36¢* (compared to its 1967 purchasing power, i.e., 100 ÷ 281.5 = 0.36).

That 14-year episode of accelerating inflation created a national economic crisis, with the latest *CPI* making front-page news as it was announced each month. Why? Because inflation alters the distribution of real income and wealth in arbitrary and inequitable ways (prices, interest rates, and incomes do not all change in the same proportions!) and triggers disruptive changes in the structure and functioning of the economy. People behave differently during inflationary times, and their *expectations* concerning *future* levels of prices, incomes, and interest rates further distort decisions and behavior.

Only through a tightly restrictive monetary policy (explained in Chapter 26) was the federal government finally able, in 1982, to bring inflation under control. By the end of 1982 the index stood at 292.4—up only 3.9% during the year, for the smallest December-to-December increase in a decade. (Unfortunately it was one of the very few favorable economic indicators for that deeply troublesome recession year.) Consumer prices remained remarkably stable throughout 1983 and 1984, averaging less than a 4% annual rate of inflation.

Using a Price Index to Adjust for Inflation

Earlier in the chapter we distinguished between "money *GNP*" and "real *GNP*," the latter being adjusted for inflation. We then saw that the rate of inflation is measured by movements in price indexes (such as the *CPI*). We are now ready to perform the important operation of converting money *GNP* (actually, *GNP* expressed in current prices) into real *GNP* (expressed in *constant* prices).

The general formula for "deflating" magnitudes expressed in current prices—whether the measure is *GNP*, money wages, Personal Income, or whatever—is as follows:

$$\frac{PN_b}{PN_c} \times \$M_c = \$M^*$$

where PN_b is the appropriate price index in the *base* year,
PN_c is the same price index in the *current* year,
$\$M_c$ is the measure or magnitude to be deflated (e.g., *GNP*), and
$\$M^*$ is the magnitude expressed in *real* terms, after adjustment for changes in the value of the dollar.

We can illustrate with hypothetical data. Assume that the price index in the base year is 100, but by Year 5 it has risen to 200. Assume that *GNP* in Year 5 is $3.4 trillion (expressed in current Year-5 prices), whereas in Year 1 *GNP* was $2.2 trillion. The question is, has *real GNP* gone up, or down, and by how much? Using the deflating formula, we find that

$$\frac{PN_b}{PN_5} \times GNP_5 = GNP^* \text{ or } \frac{100}{200} \times \$3.4 \text{ trillion} = \$1.7 \text{ trillion}$$

What had appeared to be a huge *increase* in *GNP* (from $2.2 to $3.4 trillion, or a rise of 55%) turns out to be a sharp *decrease* in *real GNP* (from $2.2 to $1.7 trillion, expressed in terms of constant Year-1 prices), a drop of 23% over the five-year period.

Repeating the illustration with *actual* data, using 1983 *GNP* (taken from the Statistical Appendix to the *1985 Economic Report of the President/ERP)* and the *GNP* implicit price deflator (1972 = 100) as the appropriate price index, we see that

$$\frac{PN_b}{PN_{83}} \times GNP_{83} = GNP^* \text{ or} \frac{100}{215.34} \times \$3,304 \text{ billion} = \underline{\$1,534.7 \text{ billion}}$$

(To confirm this result, see Tables B.1, B.3, and B.2 in the ERP, or note the *GNP* figures for 1983 in the Statistical Reference Table at the end of this chapter.)

Note what is required to adjust economic statistics for price-level changes: (1) data expressed in current prices/dollars and (2) the *appropriate price index*. The construction of a price index entails conceptual as well as statistical problems, and maintaining the series of index numbers is a tricky and costly task. In the statement from which this chapter's opening quotation was taken, Arthur Ross lamented the false economy of starving the government's statistical agencies in terms of money and personnel, pointing out that better data "could provide information potentially worth billions of dollars in terms of more intelligent policy choices." The fact is that we have become terribly dependent on economic statistics but, as in the case of other forms of technology, have not yet learned to avoid abuses that range "from the comical to the tragic."

Unemployment Rates

GNP measures the overall level of *production,* and the *CPI* measures changes in the *general level of prices* (i.e., the rate of inflation). The third statistical indicator considered in this chapter measures the quantity of unused manpower in the economy—the rate of *involuntary unemployment,* which we shall label *"TUR"* for *total* unemployment rate. The *TUR* is a measure of the number of men and women who are able to work and actively seeking employment but do not have a job, expressed as a percentage of the labor force. Let's examine some statistics on employment and unemployment.

As explained in Chapter 6, the U.S. labor force is made up of persons 16 years and over who are "economically active," meaning that they meet certain BLS requirements for inclusion in either of two categories: *employed (E),* or *unemployed (U).* In 1984, the labor force ($LF = E + U$) totaled 115.2 million workers, of which 113.5 million were civilian and nearly 1.7 million were resident armed forces. On average during the year 8.5 million of these workers were jobless. The nation's *unemployment rate (TUR)* therefore was 7.4%

(i.e., $TUR = \dfrac{U}{LF}; \dfrac{8.5}{115.2} = 7.4\%$).

This was 2.1 percentage points below the *TUR* of 9.5% which prevailed in 1983 and 1984—the highest rate of unemployment in the United States since the Great Depression. (The *civilian* unemployment rate in 1984 was 7.5%, down from 9.7% in 1982.)

As we have indicated (compare the not-quite-equal 1984 *TUR* of 7.4% with the civilian unemployment rate of 7.5%), there is not just *one* unemployment rate; indeed there are as many rates as we care to compute—to reflect the percentage of any particular category of labor that currently is involuntarily unemployed, e.g., total, civilian, black, female, teenage, high school dropout, etc. (Unemployment rates illustrate dramatically that general statistics can *conceal* as well as *reveal.*)

If one observes only the *total* unemployment rate—a gross average for the entire labor force—a great deal of vital information about the *structure* of unemployment will be overlooked. In the recession year of 1982, for example, when the *TUR* was 9.5%, the unemployment rate for *black* workers of all ages was 17%, for *teenage* workers (all races and both sexes) 23%; and for *married men* (all races) only 6.5%. The highly publicized *UR* for *black male teenage* workers (who account for less than 1% of the labor force) was 41%. If one were to adjust the official *TUR* to include "discouraged workers" (people who have dropped out of the labor force because they have given up looking for work), the rate would *increase* by one to two percentage points. Adjustments in the opposite direction, to reflect more accurately the true availability of people for work (e.g., full-time students who can only work certain hours, and seasonal workers) would probably *lower* the *TUR* by similar amounts.

There is no single *UR* that can provide a satisfactory picture of how much involuntary unemployment exists in the economy at any given time. But a *TUR* of 9.5% clearly represents a great deal more idle (wasted) manpower than the 5.8% rate of the nonrecession year of 1979. (Note, however, that the 1982 average rate of 9.5% did not mean fewer people were working; the absolute number of persons employed was actually 773,000 *higher* in 1982 than in 1979. *UR*s reflect changes in the *size of the work force* as well as the number of jobs in the economy.)

Statistics on employment and unemployment are valuable indicators of the use our economy is making of available resources. When the *TUR* rises substantially we can assume that utilization rates are declining for *capital goods* and *natural resources.* In effect their "unemployment rates" are also rising. When this happens, our economy is wasting resources, losing goods and services that could be produced but are not. *Actual GNP* is below *potential GNP.* Equally important, unemployment of human resources means failing to provide wages and salaries for people who are dependent on the labor market for both their livelihood and their sense of participation as productive members of society.

Statistical "Tips"

We conclude this chapter with two statistical "tips." The first is a generalization: Always use common sense when working with statistics; don't be awed by numbers as if they were some sort of god. The concluding chapter of *How to Lie with Statistics* serves up a banquet of good advice in the title and subheadings themselves: "How to talk back to a statistic. Who says so? How does he know? What's missing? Did somebody change the subject? Does it make sense?"

In some contexts, painstaking detail is called for (e.g., to demonstrate the accuracy of a procedure such as adjusting 1983 *GNP* using the implicit price deflator); in other cases, approximations and round numbers are perfectly adequate. In fact excessive detail is sometimes ridiculous, as when the press reports in shrieking headlines "Rise in the Poverty Rate"—from 14.7 to 14.9%! The truth is that *error factors* will account for much bigger differences than two-tenths of 1%. These are just *estimates,* based on sample surveys!

Regarding the *timeliness* of statistics, always ask "as of *when*?"—and exercise sound judgment on *updating* such statistics as *GNP,* Personal Income, the poverty standard, etc., reflecting your general knowledge of rates of growth, inflation, etc. Most important, know *where to find* up-to-date statistics so that you will not be dependent on somebody else's data ("pulled from the sky," "made up," or blindly passed along). Several convenient *sources* of economic statistics are listed at the end of the chapter, some of which include descriptions of how certain data were collected and how they should be interpreted.

The second tip is one of those little gems that circulates from classroom to classroom and book to book. It is called the "Rule of 70" (described in Campbell McConnell's *Economics,* which we cite among our references in Chapter 1). To calculate the number of *years* it takes for some particular magnitude to *double,* simply divide the *percentage growth rate* of that magnitude into 70. Thus, at an inflation rate of 7% per year, the price level will *double* (and the value of a dollar be cut in half) in just *10 years.* With inflation at 10%, it takes only *seven* years. If an economy's annual growth rate is 5% (as Japan's was during the 1970s), *GNP* doubles in 14 years. If world population was 4.5 billion in 1980 (as indeed it was estimated to be) and grows at the rate of 2% per year, by 2015 there will be 9.0 billion people on the earth.

A Statistical Reference Table

Following is a Statistical Reference Table (SRT) that can be perused now for general familiarity (beware of the irresistible fascination of economic statistics!) and

Table 15.2

Statistical Reference Table: Economic Indicators for the U.S. Economy in Selected Years, 1929-1984[1]

Year	GNP (Current Dollars) billions	GNP (Constant 1972 Dollars) billions	Civilian Employment millions	Unemployment Rate %	CPI (1967 = 100) index no.	Inflation Rate (CPI) Dec. to Dec. %	Output per hr. (Year-to-Year Change) %	Median Family Income (1983 Dollars rounded)	Average Weekly Earnings (1977 dollars)	Poverty Rate (Poor Persons ÷ Population) %	Population millions
1929	$103	$316	48	3.2	73[2]	.2	n.a.	n.a.	n.a.	n.a.	122
1930	91	[287]	45	8.7	[71]p	[-2.6]	n.a.	n.a.	n.a.	n.a.	123
1933	56	221	39	24.9	[55]p	.5	n.a.	n.a.	n.a.	n.a.	126
1939	91	320	46	17.2	[59]p	-.5	n.a.	n.a.	n.a.	n.a.	131
1944	211	569	54	1.2	[75]p	2.1	n.a.	n.a.	n.a.	n.a.	138
1946	210	478	55	3.9	59	18.2	n.a.	n.a.	n.a.	n.a.	141
1948	260	490	58	3.8	72	2.7	5.3	n.a.	n.a.	n.a.	147
1950	286	535	59	5.2 (ch)	72	5.8	7.9	$13,700	$123	[32][3]	152
1953	367	624	61	2.8	80	.6	3.2	n.a.	134	[26][3]	160
1955	400	658	62	4.3	80	.4	4.0	16,400	145	[25][3]	166
1960	506	737	66 (ch)	5.4	89	1.5	1.5	18,900	153	22.2	181
1965	691	929	71	4.4	94	1.9	3.5	22,000	165	17.3	194
1968	873	1,058	76	3.5	104	4.7	3.3	24,700	183	12.8	201
1970	993	1,085	79	4.8	116	5.5	.8	25,300	188	12.6	205
1971	1,078	1,122	79	5.8	121	3.4	3.6	25,300	187	12.5	208
1972	1,186	1,186	82	5.5	125	3.4	3.5	26,500	191	11.9	210
1973	1,326	1,254	85	4.8	133	8.8	2.6	27,000	198	11.1	212
1974	1,434	1,246	86	5.5	148	12.2	-2.4	26,100	198	11.2	214
1975	1,549	1,232	87	8.3	161	7.0	2.2	25,400	190	12.3	216
1976	1,718	1,298	89	7.6	170	4.8	3.3	26,200	184	11.8	218
1977	1,918	1,370	92	6.9	182	6.8	2.4	26,300	187	11.6	220
1978	2,164	1,439	96	6.0	195	9.0	.5	26,900	189	11.4	223
1979	2,418	1,475	99	5.8	217	13.3	-1.2	26,900	183	11.7	225
1980	2,632	1,479	99	7.0	247	12.4	-.5	25,400	173	13.0	228
1981	2,958	1,512	100	7.5	272	8.9	1.9	24,500	170	14.0	230
1982	3,069	1,480	100	9.5	289	3.9	.2	24,200	168	15.0	232
1983	3,305	1,535	101	9.5	294	3.8	2.7	24,600	171	15.2	234
1984	3,664	1,640	105	7.4	311	4.0	3.2	n.a.	173	n.a.	237
1985											
1986											
1987											
1988											

Source: *Economic Report of the President* (1960, 1985); *Economic Indicators* (Feb. 1985)

[1] For technical details, see footnotes in original tables. Boxes around years indicate wartime; brackets and "ch" indicate series that are not strictly comparable or estimates; "n.a." means not available.

[2] Base period 1947-49 = 100.

[3] Percent of *families*.

consulted later in the context of particular problems. People who think, read, and talk about economic topics are well advised to *check the facts,* and study relationships among key variables (such as production, employment, rates of unemployment and inflation, and trends in earnings and poverty). Data in the SRT provide only a small sample of the richly informative statistical series found in sources listed in the Selected Readings and References.

Suggested Readings and References

Elizabeth W. Angle, *Keys for Business Forecasting,* 5th ed. Richmond, VA: Federal Reserve Bank of Richmond, 1980. (Available from the bank's Public Services Department.)

Darrell Huff, *How to Lie with Statistics.* New York: W.W. Norton, 1954.

Arthur M. Ross, "The Use and Misuse of Statistics," *Washington Post,* June 30, 1968.

Mark Twain, "Sixth-Century Political Economy," Chapter 33 in *A Connecticut Yankee in King Arthur's Court,* (various editions)

Economic Indicators. Prepared by the President's Council of Economic Advisers for the Joint Economic Committee, U.S. Congress. Washington: U.S. Government Printing Office, *monthly.* (An excellent brief compendium of current and recent-year statistics.)

Economic Report of the President. Together with the Annual Report of the Council of Economic Advisers. Washington: U.S. Government Printing Office, *yearly.* (Issued in January or February, the Report contains 130 pages of statistical tables, with preliminary data for the year just ended.)

Federal Reserve Bulletin. Washington: Board of Governors of the Federal Reserve System, *monthly.* (Contains 70-page statistical section, including monetary, international, and domestic nonfinancial data.)

Statistical Abstract of the United States. National Data Book and Guide to Sources. Bureau of the Census, U.S. Department of Commerce. Washington: U.S. Government Printing Office, *yearly.* (The most complete statistical compendium of annual data, with references to publications containing monthly and quarterly statistics; nearly 1,000 pages of tables, charts, definitions, and technical notes.)

Historical Statistics of the United States, Colonial Times to 1970. Bureau of the Census, U.S. Department of Commerce. Washington: U.S. Government Printing Office, 1976.

Current Population Reports. U.S. Bureau of the Census. (Various series, based on Current Population Survey.)

Employment and Earnings. Bureau of Labor Statistics, U.S. Department of Labor. Washington: U.S. Government Printing Office, *monthly.* (Also *Monthly Labor Review* and the annual *Handbook of Labor Statistics.)*

Survey of Current Business. Bureau of Economic Analysis, U.S. Department of Commerce. Washington: U.S. Government Printing Office, *monthly.* (Authoritative source of GNP and other national income statistics as well as data on the international balance of payments.)

Information Please Almanac. Boston: Houghton Mifflin, *yearly.*

A Five-Step Method
of Economic Reasoning

Economic problems are like many other kinds of human problems. If you want to find good solutions, it helps to organize your thinking and use a *systematic, step-by-step approach.* This involves developing a clear understanding of the problem, thinking about desirable goals, considering different possible solutions, anticipating the probable consequences of the alternative solutions, and then choosing the best solution.

Americans too often want the luxury of opinion without the effort of thought.
    —John F. Kennedy

Finding the right way is not sentimental work; it is scientific work requiring observation, reasoning, and intellectual conscientiousness.
    —George Bernard Shaw

We have seen that every economic system must answer three basic questions: how much, what, and for whom to produce. There are times when members of the economic community do not like the answers they're getting. They perceive certain *problems,* such as inflation, unemployment, economic insecurity, environmental pollution, poverty, urban blight, and international imbalance. How are the problems to be solved? For an answer we make use of Point III in our earlier outline of the elements of economic understanding (Figure 2.1).

Five Steps in Reasoning

In seeking ways to improve the economy's performance, society can make use of a method of analysis so popular with economists it has been termed "the steps in economic reasoning." The procedure involves five steps:

1. *Define the problem* by carefully examining facts and clarifying causes, effects, and key issues—making effective use of history, statistics, and theory.
2. *Identify goals,* i.e., state clearly what you would like to accomplish and what *underlying values* should be adhered to regarding both the *ends* and the *means* of policy.
3. *Consider alternative methods* for pursuing the goals (usually there are more ways than one to get the job done and the imaginative use of *theory* and *history* can suggest a variety of possible strategies).
4. *Analyze the probable consequences* that might result from *each* of the different methods that might be used for achieving the goals—including the anticipated *benefits, costs,* and *other effects.*
5. Finally, after studying the likely consequences of the alternative solutions, *choose the best solution* in light of the stated goals and underlying values.

Note that one does not leap from Step 2 directly to Step 5. The distinctive feature of this rational-empirical-comprehensive method of policy analysis (to use its more sophisticated label) is that judgments are based on careful *reasoning* and the examination of *evidence* as well as the explicit recognition of *goals and values.* This procedure enables decisionmakers to know the *how* and *why* of their actions along with the what.

It is also important to note that the Five-Step Method of Economic Reasoning is a *continuous* process (see Figure 16.1). Choosing the best course of action in Step 5 is by no means the end of the road. Seldom do individuals, organizations, or nations solve their problems on a once-and-for-all basis. Having arrived at a responsible decision, it is then necessary to *implement* the decision with a program of action in the real world. Experience will generate *actual* data on benefits, costs, and other effects and (recalling the Levels-of-Knowing scheme) may very well suggest *changes* not only in policies and programs but *goals* as well.

Uses of the Method

As suggested, the five-step method of economic reasoning can be used in *personal* as well as *organizational* and *societal* decisonmaking. Planning one's education, choosing an occupation, or buying a home can all benefit from the conscious setting of goals, consideration of alternative courses of action, and careful analysis of costs, benefits, and possible side effects. Many a business firm and civic organization has rescued itself from disaster with a self-analysis proceeding along these lines. So important is the ability to use the tools of analysis in systematic economic reasoning that the decisionmaking method described here has been called *the most valuable element of a person's economic understanding.*

In Chapter 27, the Five-Step Method of Economic Reasoning will be illustrated in the context of America's problem of poverty amid affluence; and the method can readily be applied to other problems discussed in Part Five, including unemployment,

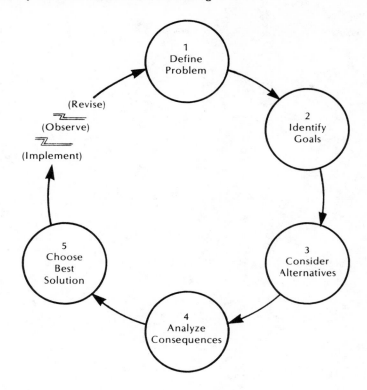

Figure 16.1   *A Five-Step Method of Economic Reasoning*

inflation, threats to the environment, concentrations of economic power, and strains in international economic relations. Because of the central importance of goals and values, both in the five-step method of reasoning and in the study of American economic ideology, institutions, and problems (the subjects of Parts Four and Five), readers may want to turn immediately to Chapter 30. The chapter can then be read a second time after finishing Part Five.

Selected Readings and References

Robert L. Darcy, "The Nature of Economic Enterprise," Chapter 5 in *Vocational Guidance and Human Development.* Edited by Edwin L. Herr. Boston: Houghton Mifflin, 1974.

M.A. Robinson, H. Morton, and J. Calderwood, *An Introduction to Economic Reasoning.* Washington: Brookings Institution, 1956 (and later editions).

Phillip Saunders et al, *Master Curriculum Guide in Economics: A Framework for Teaching the Basic Concepts,* 2d ed. New York: Joint Council on Economic Education, 1984.

Economic Education in the Schools. Report of the National Task Force on Economic Education. New York: Committee for Economic Development, 1961.

PART FOUR
THE AMERICAN ECONOMY: IDEOLOGY AND INSTITUTIONS

In the first 16 chapters, the reader has been introduced step-by-step to the essential elements of economic understanding. While learning some general principles of the economic process, there has also been a gradual exposure to a core of concepts and analytical tools that constitute the scholarly discipline called economics. Now it is time to add flesh-and-blood details and apply these economic lessons to the particular setting of *the American economy.* We begin in Chapter 17 with a description of the distinctive institutions and ideology of "model capitalism" (including an appendix that summarizes the supply-and-demand theory of market price). Recognizing that the economic system as it exists in the United States today is a *mixed economy* rather than a pure market system, we explore the real-world institutions of *business* (Chapter 18), *the household sector* (Chapter 19), *labor unions* (Chapter 20), the *money and banking* system (Chapter 21), and (in Chapter 22) the supra-institution of *government* (along with an appendix explaining the theoretical basis for macro-economic stabilization policies). Finally, we use the American experience as a case study to glimpse the general processes of *international trade* (Chapter 23) and *economic growth* (Chapter 24).

Model Capitalism: Anatomy of a Competitive Market System

The economic system of the United States is a *mixture* of private enterprise and government, competition and "monopoly" power, market calculation and "irrational" behavior. But even though it is a complex blend of many things, it still remains basically a *capitalistic system* built on the foundations of private property, the profit motive, free enterprise, competition, and market-determined prices.

The basic problem of social organization is how to coordinate the economic activities of large groups of people. Fundamentally there are only two ways of [accomplishing this]. One is central direction involving the use of coercion; the other is voluntary cooperation—a free private enterprise market exchange economy...the system of competitive capitalism.

—Milton Friedman

The U.S. economic system is known by many different names: industrial market economy, free-enterprise system, competitive capitalism, profit system, price system, private enterprise, market system, mixed capitalism, and other labels less neutral or complimentary. Each of these terms tells us something about the way our economy is organized and how people believe it operates. What is the correct name for our system? What kind of economy do we really have?

Of course, the answer is that we have a very complex system, and there is no "right" name for it. Most economists would probably agree on a term like "mixed capitalism," or "mixed economy," or "basically private-enterprise market system." Where do all the labels come from and what do they mean? If our economy is a mixed system, what are its ingredients?

In essence, the American economy is a blend of two "umbrella" institutions, or *supra-institutions,* each of which encompasses numerous "sub-institutions." One supra-institution is "the market": a comprehensive system of voluntary exchange for private gain. Its *sub-institutions* include product markets, "the" labor market, stock exchanges, etc. Our other supra-institution is democratic government: a political system which entails group choice and compulsory compliance. Its numerous sub-instititutions include the federal tax system, public education, arrangements for local police and fire protection, the Federal Reserve System, and the armed forces.

Viewing the U.S. economy from a less neutral perspective (as neoclassical market-biased economists tend to do), it is a mixture of (1) model capitalism—"pure" or "ideal" capitalism and (2) those real-world factors such as market power and government "intervention" that inject variations or "impurities" into the system. (These "impurities" are not necessarily bad; sometimes they are exactly what society wants and needs.) First, let's consider the anatomy of model capitalism, the theoretically "ideal" free-enterprise system.

Features of Model Capitalism

Model capitalism has five distinctive *institutional* features, first explained in 1776 by the celebrated author of *The Wealth of Nations* (in Kenneth Boulding's description, both the "Adam" and the "smith" of systematic economics). The five basic institutions of capitalism are: (1) private property, (2) the profit motive, (3) free enterprise, (4) competition, and (5) market-determined prices.

Private property is the fundamental institution of capitalism, the core and foundation of the entire system. Without the legal institution of private property, capitalism could not exist. What, then, is meant by "private property"? It is the *legal right to own capital goods and natural resources,* and the right to use and dispose of these "means of production" essentially as the owner wishes. Private property is not a thing, like a factory or coal mine. It is "a bundle of legal rights" that indicates how the factory or coal mine may be used. Because we have the institution of private property in the United States, individuals and private groups are allowed (and encouraged) to own coal mines and other resources and decide how they are to be used in production.

How *are* coal mines used under the institution of private property? This is where the second feature of capitalism comes in: *the profit motive.* In a capitalistic system, with the institution of private property, resources are presumed to be used by their owners in such a way as to yield them the largest possible "profits." The profit motive is identified as the driving force that both activates and allocates resources for use in production. The *desire for monetary gain* is the heart of the incentive system in a capitalistic economy. Not only the owners of natural resources and capital but also workers and consumers are presumed to be motivated to do as well as they can in the economy *and* to be sufficiently well informed so their choices and decisions are appropriately directed. Economists refer to behavior that is aimed at maximizing some economic magnitude as *rational behavior.* Materialistic rationality—the "late and soon, getting and spending" behavior that poet William Wordsworth said was "too much with us"—stands out as a major institution of market capitalism.

Free enterprise is another feature of model capitalism. This means that an individual or private group is free to start a business, i.e., to bring a producing unit into existence. Entrepreneurship (undertaking the responsibility to establish a business enterprise) is a logical outcome of the institutions of private property and the profit motive. It is a good way to take advantage of money-getting opportunities in a capitalistic economy.

A fourth characteristic of pure capitalism is *competition,* the critical importance of which was so strongly emphasized by Adam Smith. Without perfect competition in the market, business firms might take advantage of consumers, charging high prices and selling shoddy merchandise. But "perfect competition" requires that all buyers and sellers be extremely well informed, highly adaptable, and economically rational. It also requires that there be so *many* producers of a good that no single firm will account for a large enough portion of total market supply to have any perceptible influence on market price (and, further, that *new* firms are free to enter the industry). Competition and price-cutting *force* producers to be efficient and responsive to consumers. *Competition* is the great *regulator* of a market economy. It drives consumer prices down near the cost of production. Without this kind of competition "ideal" capitalism cannot exist. Note that the economist's concept of *pure* competition (less demanding than "perfect" competition) is *not* the same as "rivalry" or "trying harder"; it is the *absence of market power* (see Appendix).

Finally, under model capitalism, *prices are determined by the forces of supply and demand in competitive markets* and these *market prices are relied upon to allocate resources and "ration" final goods and services.* Large numbers of independent buyers and sellers interact in free markets, none with sufficient power to influence price perceptibly, and prices are established *impersonally* rather than through the exercise of market power or government fiat. It is characteristic of competitive pricing in the long run that (1) business firms are forced to produce at optimal efficiency, i.e., lowest costs per unit; (2) resources are allocated according to consumer preferences, i.e., price equals "marginal" cost; and (3) firms earn "normal" profits, i.e., total revenues will just equal total costs, including an appropriate return on investment and entrepreneurial services. Thus, there is no arbitrary restriction of output, no mis-allocation of resources, and no excess or monopoly profits. Thanks to competition, the pursuit of private gain results in public benefits—as if the system were guided by "an *invisible hand*" (to use Adam Smith's often-quoted metaphor.) Note that in model capitalism competitive supply-and-demand determine *resource* prices as well as product prices.

Comparison with the U.S. Economy

Does today's American economy conform to the requirements of model capitalism? To answer this question, check each of the five institutional features listed above. Do we permit private ownership of the means of production? Are Americans driven by the profit motive? Is there free enterprise in the sense that people can start up and continue operating their own businesses? Is there pure competition in the market for consumer goods, and in resource markets? Finally, are prices and wages determined by the impersonal forces of supply and demand operating in competitive markets?

Your answers probably suggest several reasons why the U.S. economy today resembles but does not fully exemplify *model* capitalism. There are many *non-competitive* markets. Big corporations and labor unions often exert monopoly influence in setting the prices of goods and services. Government steps in to regulate prices and production in certain areas like public utilities, labor markets, and agriculture. People aren't always well informed and highly adaptable. Nor do they always behave in an economically rational way; perhaps we would not be human if we always functioned as the "lightning calculators of pleasure and pain" assumed in economic theory. Yet, without enlightened rationality on the part of consumers and other economic decisionmakers, the system cannot work *efficiently* according to the model. Finally, the institution of private property hardly operates in today's world of billion-dollar corporations the way it would under conditions of small-scale, free-enterprise entrepreneurship. For one thing there is wholesale separation of *ownership* from *control* (i.e., stockholders own shares in giant corporations but seldom have any control over how the corporations are run).

Actually, pure capitalism has never really existed—except as an ideology (i.e., a body of doctrine, myth, symbol, and values), a standard for comparison, or a theoretical model in people's minds and economics textbooks. But something approximating model capitalism did exist (in many, if not all, sectors of the economy) in Britain, the United States, and other European and English-speaking countries of the world during the 1800s. It was widely praised for its enormous productivity but at the same time criticized as a harsh, elitist system incapable of dealing with "social costs" and community needs. Some critics of raw capitalism went so far as to suggest that it was the institutional incarnation of the Seven Deadly Sins: Avarice (greed), Envy, Gluttony and Lust (the staples of present-day TV advertising), Anger, Sloth, and Hubris (the arrogance of power).

Today, however, most countries of the world have *mixed* economies. Our own economy probably retains as many features of capitalism as can be found anywhere in the world. The system continues to grow and change; we can predict that 50 years from now it will be quite different from what it is in 1986. But, as today, the name "mixed capitalism" half a century from now will probably fit our economy pretty well. That's why a basic understanding of *model* capitalism—its ideology and institutions—is so helpful in comprehending the structure and functioning of America's real-world economy.

Selected Readings and References

Kenneth E. Boulding, *Economic Analysis,* 4th ed. New York: Harper & Row, 1966. Volume I,
    Microeconomics; Volume II, *Macroeconomics.*
Kenneth E. Boulding, *Economics as a Science.* New York: McGraw-Hill, 1970.
Milton Friedman, *Capitalism and Freedom.* Chicago: University of Chicago Press, 1962.
Milton and Rose Friedman, *Free to Choose.* New York: Harcourt Brace Jovanovich, 1979.
Gardiner C. Means, *The Corporate Revolution in America* (Economic Reality versus
    Economic Theory). New York: Collier, 1964.
Adam Smith, *The Wealth of Nations* (cited in Chapter 12).

APPENDIX: Microeconomics—The Supply and Demand Theory of Market Price

Supply, demand, and equilibrium price are among the most familiar concepts in economics. They form the core of *micro-economic* theory. Economists teach that market prices in pure competition are determined by the interacting forces of supply and demand. Moreover, the concepts of supply and demand find wide application as general analytical tools in many areas of economics, including international trade, taxation, and even *macro*economic theory. The concept of *elasticity* carries supply and demand beyond basic generalization to permit more precise quantitative predictions about the effects of price changes.

In seeking to explain the patterns of economic behavior that determine resource allocation in a system of "model capitalism," standard theory makes three basic assumptions about conditions in the economy. First, resources are scarce. Second, markets are perfectly competitive. And, third, all economic decisionmakers—consumers, resource owners, and business firms—behave "rationally," i.e., they try to maximize some particular magnitude keyed to their own economic self-interest. The logical implications of these assumptions constitute the core of microeconomic analysis.

In a market system, goods and services—as well as the resources used to produce them—are rationed or allocated by *relative prices*. Higher prices encourage greater production (and larger quantities of resources). Lower prices encourage greater consumption but discourage production (and resource use). *Price* is the basic *criterion* for making *market* choices.

But what determines price? The answer given by mainstream economists for the past century (since Alfred Marshall's 1890 text, *Principles of Economics*) has been "supply and demand." Supply and demand are analytical concepts—categories of market forces—which are used to organize the numerous specific variables in the economy that interact to determine prices. In the following discussion, the context is the supply and demand for a particular consumer product (such as oranges).

Demand is defined as a schedule of the various quantities of a good that consumers will buy at a series of alternative prices. Demand is a conditional ("iffy") concept: *If* the price is $10, *then* the quantity demanded will be 17; but if the price is $8, then the quantity demanded will be 23 (hypothetical data). Economists use the notation $Q_D = f(P)$ meaning quantity demanded is a function of price.

The *Law of Demand* states that the quantity of a good that a consumer will buy varies *inversely* with the price of the good. That is, the higher the price, the smaller the quantity purchased and vice versa. This law is valid for individual consumers and for consumers as a group. When demand is shown graphically (see Figure 17A.1), the *demand* curve has a negative slope, slanting from upper left to lower right—with the independent variable, price, plotted on the vertical axis and the dependent variable, quantity, on the horizontal. (Note: For help in reading graphs see the appendix to Chapter 12).

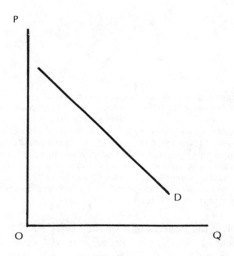

Figure 17A.1

Validity of the Law of Demand is explained on the basis of *(a)* empirical observation, *(b)* the *income and substitution effects* of price changes, or *(c)* the *Law of Diminishing Marginal Utility.* This law states that in the continuous consumption of a good, as more units are consumed, beyond a certain point each additional unit provides the consumer with less extra utility or satisfaction than the preceding unit. (After eating a piece of coconut cream pie your desire for yet another helping will be somewhat less intense than it was at the start. In the case of White Castle hamburgers, diminishing marginal utility might not begin until the third or fourth or fifth units, depending on individual taste and capacity.) Since you are now deriving less utility per dollar of outlay, you will not be willing to purchase additional units unless the price is reduced (e.g., first pizza is full price, buy a second pizza and get it for half-price). This law presumes that, while wants in general may be unlimited, wants for particular goods can be satiated. (Note that this principle is NOT the same thing as the Law of Diminishing Returns, which refers to physical output rather than psychological gratification.)

The major determinants of an individual's demand for a particular good are: (1) purchasing power (mainly income); (2) tastes (wants, needs, desires, preferences), (3) prices of related goods; and (4) expectations about the future availability of the product, future prices, and other conditions. (Goods can be "related" in either of two ways: as substitutes for each other or as "complementary" goods consumed together.) Using notation, $d = f(Y,T,P_{xy},X)$ where Y is income, T is tastes, P_{xy} are the prices of related goods, and X is expectations. *Total market demand* is the sum of all the individual demand functions, $D = f(Y,T,P_{xy},X,N)$ where N is the number of consumers.

The demand for a particular product will *change* when there is a change in any of the determinants listed above (Y,T,P_{xy},X,N), such as increased personal income during a period of national economic expansion, diminished popularity of the good because of adverse publicity concerning its nutritional value, price cuts in complementary or substitute goods, anticipation of future shortages, and expansion of sales into new market regions. When demand changes, the entire demand curve *shifts* (see Figure 17A.2). Note, however, that a change in the price of the product itself can NEVER change *demand* (price is already included in demand!) it can only change the *quantity* demanded (i.e., at higher prices smaller quantities are demanded, and vice versa).

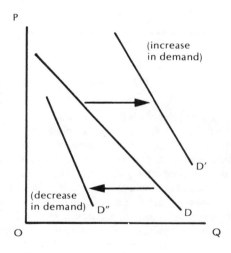

Figure 17A.2

Elasticity of demand refers to the degree of responsiveness of quantity demanded to price changes. If the relative change in quantity exceeds the relative change in price, demand is said to be "elastic." If the relative change in quantity is less than the relative change in price, demand is "inelastic." Expressed as a formula,

$E = \dfrac{\% \text{ change in } Q}{\% \text{ change in } P}$. (The minus sign is ignored.)

Supply is defined as a schedule of the various quantities of a good that producers will offer for sale at a series of alternative prices: $Q_S = f(P)$. The *Law of Supply* states that the quantity of a good that producers will offer for sale varies *directly* with the price of the good. That is, the higher the price, the larger the quantity offered and vice versa. (*Note:* "Directly" doesn't mean proportionately.) When supply is shown graphically (Figure 17A.3), the supply curve has a positive slope, slanting from lower left to upper right.

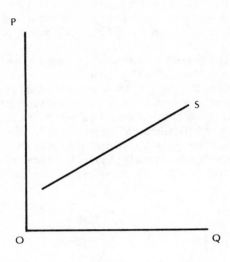

Figure 17A.3

The validity of the Law of Supply is based on empirical observation as well as on the *Law of Diminishing Returns.* As explained in Chapter 6, this law states that, with a given technology, if more units of a variable factor of production (such as labor) are added to one or more fixed factors (such as a given acreage of land), beyond a certain point the marginal physical product will diminish. Note: "Marginal physical product" is the *extra* amount of *output* that results from adding one more unit of the variable factor of production. Also note that the *Law of Diminishing Returns* is a technological principle concerning *physical* inputs and outputs; by itself it says nothing about money or profits and can be applied to a psychological experience only metaphorically. The primary determinant of the supply of a particular reproducible good is the *cost of production.* Because of diminishing returns, beyond a certain level of output, production costs per unit tend to rise for each succeeding unit; hence, sellers require a higher price before they are willing to incur the extra costs involved in expanding output any further. Note once again that different market prices for the product will change the *quantity* supplied, but the only things that can change *supply* (i.e., the schedule of prices and quantities) would be increases or decreases in production costs or a change in the number of producers. (see Figure 17A.4).

Elasticity of supply refers to the degree of responsiveness of quantity supplied to price charges (same formula as for elasticity of demand). An important determinant of supply elasticity is the time available for adjusting output. Economists distinguish three time periods: the *market period, short run,* and *long run.* Supply is most elastic in the long run because time permits more adjustments to be made in the production process.

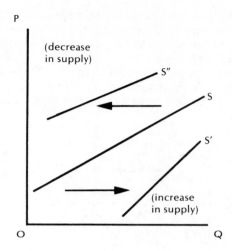

Figure 17A.4

The forces of supply and demand, interacting in a free, competitive market, determine *equilibrium price,* i.e., the price at which *quantity supplied and quantity demanded are equal.* It is the price that tends to be established in the market and the one from which there is no tendency to depart so long as supply and demand remain the same. When shown graphically, the supply curve and demand curve intersect at the equilibrium price and quantity (P_e and Q_e in Figure 17A.5). *Only when one or both curves shift their positions will equilibrium price change.* Note: When economists

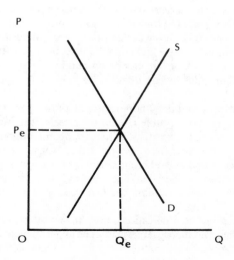

Figure 17A.5

wish to study the effects on price of a change in one particular market variable (e.g., productive efficiency or consumer preferences) that will trigger a shift in supply or demand, respectively, they make the heroic assumption of *ceteris paribus* that "everything else remains the same."

There are two kinds of *disequilibrium prices* (shown in Figure 17A.6). If the actual price prevailing in the market at a given time is above the equilibrium price (P_a higher than P_e), producers will be offering larger quantities than consumers are willing to

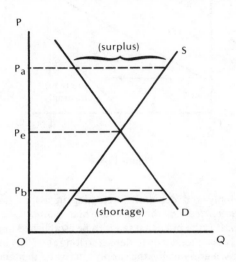

Figure 17A.6

buy at that price; hence, unwanted inventories (surpluses) accumulate, and sellers predictably will cut price to increase sales. If the actual price prevailing in the market is below the equilibrium price (P_b lower than P_e) consumers will want to buy more of the good than producers are offering at that price; hence *shortages* will occur. Some consumers will be willing to pay a higher price rather than go without. In either type of disequilibrium, forces are set in motion to eliminate the disparities and move toward the equilibrium price, where quantity demanded and quantity supplied are equal.

Economists use supply and demand analysis to clarify a host of microeconomic issues ranging from "the farm problem" and the effects of minimum wage laws to foreign exchange rates and tax burdens. When applied in different contexts, such as markets for labor or borrowed funds as opposed to consumer products, particular supply and demand curves have different *meanings* because they represent different circumstances and kinds of behavior. The "curves," by the way, can be *linear or nonlinear,* and under certain conditions can be perfectly perpendicular or parallel to the axes rather than slanting.

Thus, because of all these applications, even if market power in the real world makes supply-and-demand theory largely obsolete and irrelevant *as a comprehensive explanation of resource allocation,* the concepts of supply, demand, elasticity, and equilibrium price and quantity remain useful techniques for analysis and explanation. (Besides, failure to understand the mechanics of supply and demand tends to mark one as an "economic illiterate.") Like the production-possibilities diagram of Chapter 12 (Appendix), supply-and-demand is an extremely versatile tool of economic theory. In recent years economists have begun using superficially conventional demand and supply curves to explain the *macroeconomic* problem of "stagflation."

Business Enterprise in the Real World: The Dominance of Large Corporations

Business firms and households are the principal institutions of the private sector of our mixed economy. Together they account for four-fifths of total production and spending (government purchases of goods and services accounting for the remaining one-fifth). Profit-seeking *business firms* make many of the decisions that influence the overall level, composition, and distribution of output and income in the economy. *Corporations* receive nine out of every ten dollars of business receipts in the U.S. economy and play a dominant role in national and international economic life.

The business of America is business.
  —*Calvin Coolidge*

Business firms play a pivotal role in a market economy, as illustrated by the circular flow model of Figure 18.1 (adapted from the diagram in Chapter 13). Correspondingly, the *business sector* occupies a central role in the real-world setting of the American economy. To understand the structure and functions of this powerful institution in today's economy, we begin with a lexicon of business terms.

What Business Firms Do

A business firm (also called an *enterprise* or *company*) purchases or hires productive resources—land, labor, and capital—in the *input* market. The firm combines various types and quantities of these resources and uses them to produce

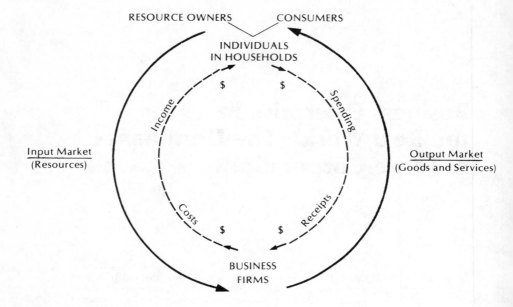

Figure 18.1   *The Circular Flow of Economic Activity in the Private Sector*

goods and services, which are then offered for sale in the *output* market.

Why are business enterprises willing to incur the costs and bear the risks and responsibilities of production? The answer is that *they hope* to *make a profit.* (That is why capitalism is sometimes called "the profit system.") Firms expect to be able to sell their finished products for prices high enough to cover all costs of operating the business and still generate a financial surplus. *Economic profits* are defined as the *excess* of total business receipts, or revenues, over total costs: *Total profits equal total receipts minus total costs.* (Contrast "economic" profit with the "normal" profit of Chapter 17).

Thus, business firms produce commodities and services not specifically to satisfy consumers' *wants* but to sell the goods at a *profit.* Generally speaking, in order to make profits the company must produce items that *do* satisfy consumer wants. This system of production not only provides *goods for consumers* and *profits for entrepreneurs*—the people who undertake the operation of business firms—but also *jobs* and *incomes* for workers and investment opportunities for owners of other resources. Sometimes, of course, the expectation of profit proves disappointing and firms incur *losses.* In a private-enterprise system the sword cuts both ways. (There are always important exceptions to generalized descriptions. In America's current era of "paper entrepreneurialism," to use Robert Reich's term, there has been a dramatic rise in the influence of business firms that acquire their profits by *manipulating assets* rather than producing goods and services, e.g., through corporate mergers, takeovers, and the creation of conglomerates.)

Forms of Business Organization

How many business firms are there in the U.S. economy? It is not easy to provide a meaningful answer. If we include self-employed professionals like doctors and lawyers, "Mom and Pop" stores, family farms, and similar small enterprises along with larger proprietorships, partnerships, and corporations, the total is over 16 million (see Table 18.1).

But only three million of these firms have business receipts of $100,000 or more; and only a few hundred thousand have sales revenues of $1 million or more. In 1981, the 440,000 largest corporations—3% of all business firms in the United States— accounted for 83% of all business receipts, while the other 97% of the companies shared the remaining 13%. (Businesses organized as producer or consumer *cooperatives* are not included in the table.)

Table 18.1

Business Firms and Business Receipts in 1981

	No. of Firms	Percent Distribution	Receipts	Percent Distribution
Sole proprietorships	12,185,000	74%	$ 523 bil.	7%
Partnerships	1,461,000	9%	272 bil.	3%
Corporations	2,812,000	17%	7,026 bil.	90%
Totals	16,458,000	100%	$7,821 bil.	100%

Source: *Statistical Abstract of the United States 1985* (p. 516).

As Table 18.1 indicates, the vast majority of businesses are small *proprietorships* (companies owned by an individual, called a proprietor or entrepreneur); most employ fewer than four workers. Many of these small firms make no economic profits or even normal profits (which is really an "implicit cost"); and thousands of them "go broke" every year. They are continually replaced by other venturesome entrepreneurs who want to get rich, or at least be their own bosses. The average life of a business firm in the United States is about seven years. A *partnership* is an unincorporated business firm owned by two or more persons.

In addition to being classified by size and type of legal organization, firms are grouped into *industries* on the basis of the particular kinds of goods and services they produce. Often a firm has two or more *plants,* which are physical establishments where fabrication or other specific functions are performed. The Ford Motor Company, for example, is a *firm* operating in the automobile *industry*, with *plants* located in Dearborn, Michigan, and Los Angeles, California, among other places. (Note: Ford is not "an industry.")

The Dominant Role of the Large Corporation

The dominant form of business organization, and perhaps the preeminent institution in our economic system, is the *corporation.* (There is strong justification for identifying the giant corporation as a supra-institution, along with the market and government!) Corporations have a separate legal existence from their owners and managers. Money to set up and operate the business comes from people who buy newly issued shares of stock in the corporation. These shareholders (stockholders) are thought of as the "owners" of the business. If they choose, they can sell their shares to other people, often through a highly organized institution called a stock exchange (such as the New York Stock Exchange, located on Wall Street in New York City). Stockholders are willing to risk the money they "invest" in the corporation because they hope to receive *dividends* (periodic payments of money on each share of stock they hold) and also to realize *capital gains* ("profits" from increases in the market value of the stock) when they sell their shares. Under the corporate form of business organization, basic policies are set by the *board of directors,* whose members are elected by the stockholders. The board hires a president, treasurer, and other members of *management* as officers to run the corporation. (Once in control, the management in very large corporations tends to perpetuate its own power by hand-picking future board members. The shareowners seldom have a real voice in running the corporation; hence the de facto separation of ownership from control.)

The power and influence of corporations in American life—not only economic life, but *politics, education,* the *arts,* and virtually every other area of society—is suggested by statistics on the tiny fraction of 1% of the nation's business firms known as the "Fortune 500." Each year *Fortune* magazine lists the 500 largest industrial corporations in the United States and reports their sales, assets, and profits, along with other data. In 1984 this elite group of American business firms had combined assets worth $1.4 trillion, employed over 14 million workers, generated sales of $1.8 trillion, and enjoyed profits of $86 billion. One company alone, Exxon Corporation, had receipts of $91 billion—down from the 1981 figure of $108 billion but still more than the combined *GNPs* of Bangladesh, Egypt, Ethiopia, Pakistan, and Peru, countries which together have a population of a quarter of a billion people!

Some economists who have studied the giant quasi-public corporation feel it is a unique institution, bearing little resemblance to the business firm assumed in the model of competitive capitalism. Ownership of corporate shares is not quite the same as private property in the context of a sole proprietorship; as noted above, stockholders typically have little or no power to influence the business. Similarly, the profit motive, competition, free enterprise, and market-determined prices have different characteristics in the world of giant corporations. Market power replaces atomistic competition. Hence, unlike the predicted outcomes of pure competition—where firms are obliged by market forces to produce at lowest unit costs, allocate resources in the socially optimal manner, and receive only normal profits—oligopolistic corporations can flourish for decades in spite of production and pricing practices judged inefficient by competitive standards. (*Oligopoly* means "few sellers" in the industry.)

In some respects, the large corporations—with their tenured employment systems, diverse constituencies, multibillion-dollar budgets, long-range development plans, and "administered prices"—bear a closer resemblance to government agencies (or Ministries, as they are called in some foreign countries) than to the innovative entrepreneurships of competitive capitalism. Yet these superpowerful corporations are operated for *private* gain.

To the extent that the large quasi-public corporations differ in nature from the competitive business firms of economic theory, capitalism no longer exists. New concepts of *efficiency, equity,* and *social responsibility* are needed to replace the traditional ideology of competitive capitalism.

Economists point out, however, that in certain areas, such as research and development, corporate giants may perform *better* than competitive firms. They also offer consumers a wider variety of products in the marketplace (not always a blessing!) and they provide more fringe benefits and job security to their employees (through the operation of their own "internal labor markets") than competitive firms can provide. Economists note that giant corporations—whether national or multi-national—are neither good nor bad in themselves. Their dominance in the economy, however, has created a new and powerful *institutional structure* quite different from model capitalism. (The theme of corporate power in American society is taken up in Chapter 28.)

Selected Readings and References

John Kenneth Galbraith, *The New Industrial State* (cited in Chapter 8).

C.H. Hession and H. Sardy, *Ascent to Affluence: A History of American Economic Development* (cited in Chapter 10).

Gardiner C. Means, *The Corporate Revolution in America* (cited in Chapter 17).

Robert B. Reich, *The Next American Frontier.* New York: Times Books, 1983.

"The Fortune 500: The Largest U.S. Industrial Corporations," *Fortune,* April 29, 1985.

The Household Sector: Consumers, Resource Owners, Citizens

Nearly every person in the country is a member of a *household*, which is the basic unit of personal decisionmaking in our economy. Three-fourths of our 85 million households are *family households*. Members of households play three roles in economic life—as *consumers, resource owners*, and *citizens*. In the U.S. economy, the two major sources of income are *factor payments*, made to reward productive contributions, and *transfer payments* received from government. A majority of households now have two or more income earners. The unequal distribution of income among households gives rise to vast differences in consumption, saving, and lifestyle. In their civic-political role as citizens, household members can influence "the rules of the economic game" by participating in processes of institutional adjustment.

Like the previous chapter on business enterprise, this chapter relates to the basic circular flow model of a market system (see Figure 13.1), applying it to the real-world setting of contemporary America. Together, business firms and households constitute the core of the *private sector* of our mixed economy.

Households

Every one of America's 240 million people is a *consumer*, but a large share of consumer decisionmaking is more "collective" than individual. In recognition of this fact, the U.S. Bureau of the Census reports an enormous amount of information on the status of "households," of which there were 85 million in 1984. A *household* consists of all persons (related family members as well as unrelated persons) who occupy a housing unit, i.e., house, apartment, or even a single room used as separate living quarters. There are about 60 million *family households* and some 25 million *nonfamily households* (we shall not go into the complex details of all the census categories such as "unrelated individual" and types of "subfamilies"). About 2½% of the total population live in "group quarters" such as college dormitories, homes for the aged and correctional institutions, and therefore are not included among the population living in households. The average size of a family household in 1984 was 3.24 members.

In describing the household sector of the U.S. economy, we identify three *economic functions* performed by households: (1) consumption, (2) ownership of resources, and (3) citizenship. One can also think of these as the *roles that individuals play in economic life.* (As for the logic of this schema, it should be noted that all individuals are consumers, but infants, for example, do not make consumer decisions in the marketplace. *Most* households contain at least one individual who is a resource owner, but not all do; some households have nobody who is an active participant in the labor force nor anyone who owns natural resources or capital. The citizenship function is seldom performed in a significant way until individuals reach voting age. In describing rational consumer behavior, economic *theory* centers on the *individual,* whereas in the real world much of the *empirical* analysis focuses on *households.*)

Consumer Activities

The first function of the household to be considered is *consumption,* defined dualistically as the *spending* of money and the *physical gratification* derived from using goods and services to satisfy wants. American consumers as a group are well fed, housed, clothed, transported, entertained, and cared-for medically. They spend more than $2 trillion annually on goods and services ($10,000 for each man, woman and child in the country), pay nearly half a trillion in personal taxes, and save a modest $150 billion. The millions of decisions they make in thousands of different markets throughout the country interact with business firms to help determine the composition of the nation's output. If their "dollar votes" do not make consumers "sovereign," realistically speaking, neither are they entirely without influence. Consumer preferences—shaped by a multitude of conscious and unconscious factors ranging from basic physical needs to fads and high-powered advertising—contribute to the product mix summarized in Table 19.1 and to the lifestyle that it reflects. Note the relative importance of the burgeoning *services* sector, which today accounts for 50% of all consumer spending (up from 42% in 1965).

Personal Income and Its Distribution

Where does all the money come from that households spend so lavishly on goods and services? Most of it comes from "wage and salary disbursements" (60%) and other *factor payments*—in the form of interest income (14%), proprietor's income (5%), dividends (3%), and rental income (2%). An increasing amount, however, comes from *transfer payments* (14%) such as social insurance benefits, public assistance, and veterans payments. (These percentages are based on 1984 Personal Income of $3.0 trillion and will, of course, change from year to year because of inflation, growth, and phases of the business cycle.)

Dividing Personal Income by total population yields a *per capita income* of some $13,000 per year before taxes ($11,000 *after* taxes), which means that there is enough income flowing through the economy to provide every three-person family with an

Table 19.1

Composition of Consumer Expenditures, 1983

	Billions of dollars	Percent distribution
Durable goods		$280	13%
Motor vehicles and parts	$129		
Household equipment and furniture	104		
Other	47		
Nondurable goods		802	37%
Food	365		
Alcoholic beverages	51		
Tobacco products	28		
Clothing and accessories	150		
Gasoline and oil	90		
Other	118		
Services		1,074	50%
Housing	363		
Household operation	154		
Transportation	73		
Other (includes health services, entertainment, etc.)	484		
Totals		$2,156	100%

Source: *Statistical Abstract of the United States 1985* (p. 435). (For additional details and updates, see *Survey of Current Business,* especially the July issue.)

income of about $40,000 per year—if income were distributed equally. In actuality, of course, there is substantial *in*equality in the distribution of income (a topic to be emphasized in Chapter 27). Table 19.2 shows the distribution of cash income (including transfer payments but before taxes) among families in 1983, based on sample surveys conducted by the U.S. Bureau of the Census. Note that the poorest 20% of families get only about 5% of the nation's income, while the richest 20% receive nine times that amount. (Among black Americans, the distribution of money income is even *more* unequal than among whites.) Income distribution *after* taxes is only slightly more equal than the figures reported in Table 19.2, but when *noncash income* such as food stamps, public housing, and government-financed medical care is added to money income the share of *real* income rises for the lowest quintile.

Median family income in 1983 was $24,580, which means that half of all families in the United States had income *above* this figure, while half had *lower* incomes. Four-person families had the highest median ($29,184) with larger families trending lower (to $23,177 for families with seven or more persons). Median income for the nation's 6.7 million *black* families was $14,506 in 1983; while for the 3.6 million *Hispanic* families the median was $16,956. For families headed by a *college graduate,* regardless of race or ethnicity, the median income was $40,520.

Even before the impact of higher taxes (notably Social Security payroll contributions) median family income was actually *lower* in 1983 than the levels of 15 years earlier (see the Statistical Reference Table, Chapter 15). Rising more or less steadily after World War II, the figure stood at $24,720 in 1968 and then peaked at $27,107 in 1973 (both in constant 1983 dollars). The absolute decline in family income was seen

Table 19.2

Money Income of Families, 1983

Quintile	Income Rank of Families	No. of Families (millions)	Percent of Total Income	Upper Limit of Income for Each Quintile
I	Lowest 20% of families	12.4	4.7%	$11,629
II	Second-lowest 20%	12.4	11.1%	20,060
III	Middle 20%	12.4	17.1%	29,204
IV	Second-highest 20%	12.4	24.4%	41,824
V	Highest 20%	12.4	42.7%	NA
	(Top 5% of families)	(3.1)	(15.8%)	(67,236) lower limit
	Totals	62.0	100%	
	Median family income			$24,580

Note: 1987 income figures will predictably be about 20% higher; "NA" means not applicable.

Source: *Statistical Abstract of the United States 1985* (p. 448).

by many as another symptom of America's economic slide during the "stagflation" era of the 1970s.

The distribution of income is an enormously complex subject, becoming even more so as a result of changes in family structure and personal lifestyles that are occurring in American society. Of great significance is the rise in *female-headed family households* with no husband present. From 1950 to 1984, when the total number of family households was rising by 58% (from 39 to 62 million), the number of families headed by a woman rose 168% from 3.7 million to 9.9 million (containing 21 million children!). As the divorce rate more than doubled between 1960 and 1980, incomes of the affected family members had to be spread over a larger number of households. To be sure, many "displaced homemakers" entered the labor force and became wage earners; but seldom does total income in such cases increase the required 100% to match the doubling of the number of post-divorce households. As we shall see in Chapter 27, the decline of median family income and increase in the poverty rate among U.S. families may be more directly attributable to *disintegration of families* than poor performance of the economic system per se.

During the 1960s and 1970s, the number of one-person households in the United States nearly tripled to just under 20 million, with women accounting for well over half (the number of *nonfamily* households of *more* than one person is also growing). Whether on balance this represents socioeconomic progress or the opposite, it certainly reduces the "cost efficiency" of consumption in American society.

The distribution of income among households, as we shall emphasize in Part Five, has an enormous effect on consumption patterns, personal saving, lifestyles, the allocation of society's resources, and both the composition and overall level of the nation's income. The reason is that the *market* operates quite differently from the one-person, one-vote principle of democratic government, following instead the rule of one *dollar*, one vote. If Consumer A has 100 times as many dollars as B, his voting power in the marketplace can be 100 times as great!

Resource Ownership

Turning to the second of the three functions performed by households in the U.S. economy, *resource ownership,* only about 10 million families have *no* income earners (9.3 million in 1983, averaging $10,438 of income, mainly from government transfer payments, alimony and child support, and investment income). All of the other families, and many nonfamily households, have at least one member actively participating in the labor force, in effect owning and selling their own *labor resources.* In total there are some 120 million workers in the economy plus 20 million or so individuals who are not active labor-force participants but do own *capital* and/or *natural resources.* Each of these 140 million resource owners (members of the 85 million households) makes decisions that influence the overall level of employment, allocation of resources, and distribution of factor income. (A qualitative-quantitative sketch of the U.S. labor force, i.e., human resources, and the other three types of resources was provided in Chapter 6.)

In what is surely one of the most remarkable socioeconomic changes in the post-World War II era, the *average American family* now has *two* income earners (typically husband and wife) instead of only one. Indeed, only 18 million families have just one earner while 25 million have two, 5½ million have three, and 2½ million have four (data for 1983). One implication of the rise in the number of working wives is that unemployment no longer has quite the same devastating effect on family income that it once had. Today if a married worker loses his or her job, the spouse may continue as a breadwinner (with earnings supplemented temporarily by unemployment compensation paid to the jobless member of the family.) Another year the situations might be reversed. (This "cushion" arrangement, of course, also works in the case of multiperson nonfamily households.)

A further effect of increased labor force participation among married women is the increased emphasis placed on the *income-earning* function of the household as opposed to the *consumer-spending* function. The 1970s and 1980s have witnessed a dramatic rise in pressure groups lobbying for jobs, pay, tax preferences, and transfer payments—to the relative neglect of *consumer* interests. Note, for example, the public demand for trade protection, continued subsidies to "save the family farm," deregulation of oil and gas prices, and increased state and local government revenues (tax and otherwise) to protect jobs and raise salaries for teachers. Impact on consumer prices and tax burdens is less-often acknowledged. This fact, by the way, highlights the usefulness of the particular version of the circular flow model employed in this book, namely one that differentiates clearly between the *consumer role* and the *resource-ownership role.* The fact that households increasingly define their economic interests primarily on the *receiving* side of income rather than on *spending* side helps explain an *inflationary bias* in the U.S. economy, i.e., the tendency to *adapt* to rising prices by lobbying for higher money incomes rather than supporting efforts to *restrain* price increases in the first place.

The Citizenship Role

The third function performed by individual members of households is what we have labeled *citizenship.* Referring again to the circular flow model, there is considerable justification for picturing a three-headed individual rather than the Janus figure actually drawn (though it would be troublesome graphically). People make market choices that reflect their interests as *consumers,* decisions oriented to their role as *resource owners,* and still other decisions *beyond* the framework of individual market choice that shape the basic environment for consumer and resource-owner behavior, and also *transcend* those roles. As voters, participants in civic life, or social activists, individuals help modify economic institutions, thereby determining the "rules of the game" and shaping the environment within which we live. (Of course not all individuals fully exercise their citizenship rights. In the 1980 election, only 70% of the voting-age population registered, and only 74% of those registered voted. This means that only 52% of the voting-age population actually voted!)

The *citizenship function* can hardly be ignored in our real-world description of the American economy. As we shall note in Chapter 28, the rising politicization of economic life—as exemplified by political action committees and special-interest lobbies—is a predominant force in the 1980s. As its influence expands, the supra-institution of government steadily displaces the supra-institution of the market as an allocator of resources, distributor of income, determinant of the economy's overall performance. Whether this trend can or should be reversed is an issue of growing controversy.

Selected Readings and References

"Economic Characteristics of Households in the United States: Third Quarter 1983 (Average Monthly Data from the Survey of Income and Program Participation)," *Current Population Reports: Household Economic Studies,* Series P-70, No. 1, U.S. Bureau of the Census, September 1984.

"Money Income and Poverty Status of Families and Persons in the United States: 1983 (Advance Data from the March 1984 Current Population Survey)." *Current Population Reports: Consumer Income,* Series P-60, No. 145, U.S. Bureau of the Census, August 1984.

Economic Indicators. February 1985.

Economic Report of the President 1985.

Statistical Abstract of the United States 1985.

Labor Unions and Collective Bargaining

Although labor unions have existed in the United States since the 1820s and even earlier they did not become a solid fixture in our economy until the 1880s, and membership was small until the 1930s. Unions give workers a stronger voice in dealing with employers regarding wages, hours, working conditions, and job security; and some labor organizations function as sociopolitical pressure groups. Today 23 million men and women, about one-fifth of all American workers, belong to unions (broadly defined). The AFL-CIO is a federation of labor unions that involves itself in national policy issues as well as union affairs.

Man is not only the end, but also the means of production. Out of his dual capacity arises a conflict between his activities as a producer and his interests as a person—a clash between life and work.
—Sumner Slichter

"Organized labor" is an important institution in the American economy. The term refers to the organization of workers into unions, and then linking these unions together through cooperation and affiliation to accomplish certain common goals.

Unions and Collective Bargaining

A *labor union* (or "trade union") is an association of employees. The purpose of unions is to give men and women who work for pay a stronger influence in dealing with employers. Their motto is: "Through union comes strength." Organized labor uses this strength in efforts to gain higher wages, better working conditions, more control over their jobs, and improvements in the social and economic life of working people.

One of labor's principal techniques is *collective bargaining*, which is a process of establishing the terms of employment by means of formal agreements between employers and unions representing employees. Collective bargaining is the essential "bread and butter" function of a union. (In addition to trade unions proper, certain other "employee associations," such as the huge National Education Association, also have collective bargaining rights.)

Collective bargaining agreements typically contain provisions in three areas: (1) *union recognition and security* (e.g., provision for automatic dues "checkoff" and often a "union shop" clause in which the employer promises to require new workers to join the union as a condition for continued employment), along with a statement of *management prerogatives;* (2) *wages and hours,* work loads, seniority arrangements, and other matters related to working conditions and job control; and (3) a *grievance procedure* for dealing with day-to-day disputes during the life of the contract and complaints initiated by individual workers on the job. In the process of collective bargaining, *strikes* (by employees) and *lockouts* (by employers) may legitimately occur—along with the usual strategies of "demands," "final offers," threats, bluffs, attempts to manipulate public opinion, and eventual compromise—but once the contract is signed, such *work stoppages* are forbidden.

Before Unions

We can make use of history (as well as statistics) to analyze the institution of unionism as it developed in the United States and exists today. What was it like to be a worker in America in 1900? Following is a sketch of worklife (compiled from several sources):

- The average worker made about $10 a week for a 60-hour week. Some textile workers put in as many as 84 hours. More than two million children, some 12 years old or younger, worked long hours, frequently at night, for which they were paid no more than 60¢ a day.
- For working 12 hours a day, seven days a week, garment workers were paid three or four dollars a week, out of which they often had to pay fines to their employers for talking, smiling, or breaking needles. The places they worked were "dim, damp, disease-breeding sweat shops." There were no regular hours, no minimum wages, no vacations, and "no human dignity."

And from a handbook for employees of a Chicago department store somewhat earlier:

- Each employee must not pay less than five dollars per year to the church and must attend Sunday school regularly. Men employees are given one evening a week for courting and two if they go to the prayer meeting.
- Any employee who is in the habit of smoking Spanish cigars, being shaved at barbers, going to dances and other places of amusement will surely give his employer reasons to be suspicious of his integrity and honesty.

Because of conditions and practices like these, many workers felt they were being treated more like machines or slaves than free productive men and women with human dignity. To improve their status, more and more employees began to organize unions, or join existing unions. It was not easy. When railroad workers began organizing, George F. Baer, president of the Philadelphia & Reading Railroad, made the following statement (in 1903):

> The rights and interests of the laboring man will be protected and cared for, not by the labor agitators, but by the Christian men to whom God in His infinite wisdom has given control of the property interests of the country. Pray earnestly that the Lord God Omnipotent still reigns and that His reign is one of law and order.

Mr. Baer's pronouncement reflected the thinking of his time. Throughout most of our nation's history, business and all levels of government *opposed* labor unions—sometimes using the police, National Guard, and armies of private detectives to break up strikes and prevent union organizing efforts. Often employees who sympathized with unions were not only fired, but blacklisted. The individualist outlook of the American worker deterred many workers from joining a union, and still does. In general, public sentiment was hostile to organized labor, and government's three branches—legislative, executive, and especially the *judicial*—reflected this attitude. As a result, union membership prior to the 1930s was relatively small.

The Rise of Unionism

Figure 20.1 shows total union membership in the United States from 1900 to 1980. Notice the sharp increase from 3½ million during the early 1930s to 15 million in the 1940s. What factors account for this dramatic rise?

First was the Great Depression, the most severe breakdown our economic system has ever experienced, with by far the highest levels of unemployment. Between 1929 and 1932, millions of workers lost their jobs. During the 4-year period 1932 to 1935, *the nation's unemployment rate never fell below 20%*, and in the worst year, 1933, one worker out of every four was jobless. Millions of families were poverty-stricken. (Unemployment insurance and other income maintenance programs had not yet become available.) The American people lost confidence in the business system and looked for new ways, including unionism, to improve the economy.

The Great Depression triggered a change in government policy. Shortly after his election in 1932, President Franklin Roosevelt publicly stated that "If I were a worker in a factory, the first thing I would do is join a union." In 1935, Congress passed the National Labor Relations Act (Wagner Act), guaranteeing workers the *right to organize unions and bargain collectively* with employers, without interference from management. Employers were now required to bargain in good faith with any union recognized by the National Labor Relations Board as a certified bargaining agent. With the outbreak of World War II and consequent return to full employment, *tight labor markets* also contributed to the growth of unionism.

There have been several changes in the law dealing with unions since the landmark Wagner Act of 1935. Some of the later legislation was designed to *limit the power of unions* (e.g., the 1947 Labor-Management Relations Act, or Taft-Hartley Act) and also to *make unions more responsible* to their members and to the public (e.g., the 1959 Labor-Management Reporting and Disclosure Act, or Landrum-Griffin Act). But today, unions are a solid fixture in our economic world. Indicative of the modern attitude of union acceptance by government and the general public was the 1960 observation by President Dwight Eisenhower (himself a political conservative) that

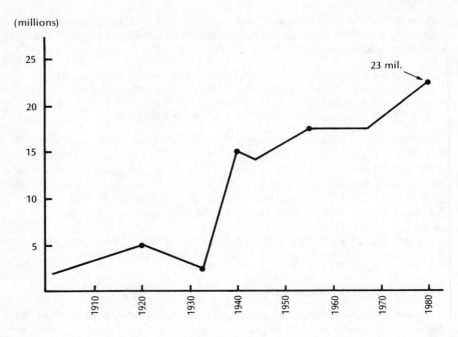

Figure 20.1   *Union Membership in the United States 1900-1980**

*Includes employee associations such as the National Education Association (1.7 million teachers) that have collective bargaining rights but are not always classified as labor unions. They are not affiliated with the AFL-CIO.

Source: *Statistical Abstract of the United States (1981, 1985); Historical Statistics of the United States*

"Only a fool would try to deprive working men and working women of the right to join the union of their choice."

Organized Labor Today

Today, 23 million men and women, about *one-fifth* of all workers in the United States, belong to unions and employee associations (down from one-fourth in the early 1950s). Using only nonsupervisory production employees as a base rather than the total civilian labor force, the union membership ratio rises from 20% to 30%. But totals can be misleading. In certain industries, such as transportation and construction, the *vast majority* of workers are union members. At the other extreme, only about one-sixth of the workers in finance and insurance, service industries, and retail and wholesale trade belong to unions.

A few of the country's 250 national unions are very large. In 1980, the Teamsters union had nearly two million members. The same year, the Auto Workers, Steelworkers, Machinists, Electrical Workers, Food and Commercial Workers, and the State, County, and Municipal Employees (AFSCME) were reported to have over a million members each. By 1983, however, official membership statistics showed sharp reductions for the steelworkers, machinists, and electrical workers. The size and influence of some unions can be compared with the giant corporations with whom they bargain in labor negotiations, such as General Motors, U.S. Steel, General Electric, DuPont, and Procter & Gamble; but recent years have witnessed dramatic setbacks for America's unions. High unemployment rates and concessionary wage agreements became everyday headlines, undermining union membership and morale (not to mention the loss of dues to union treasuries). Between 1975 and 1983, for example, the United Steelworkers alone lost 355,000 members.

What is the *structure of organized labor* in the United States? In general, there are three "layers" of union organization. First there is the *local* union that exists within a particular factory or office building. Above the local is the *national or international* (some U.S. unions include Canadian workers). It is the national union (to which locals belong by charter) that has much of the collective bargaining power, especially in an industry like steel or automobile production. In some unions there are *districts* or *conferences* interposed between the local and national levels, mainly to provide staff support to locals and carry out organizing efforts.

At the top of the structure (though not superior in sovereignty to the nationals) is the AFL-CIO *federation.* The American Federation of Labor and Congress of Industrial Organizations (reunified in 1955 under the leadership of George Meany and Walter Reuther) is not really a union but an association of some 100 unions, including about 14 million members. It serves as the chief spokesman for organized labor on matters of national economic policy and such political issues as election of the President and members of Congress, as well as international issues. Not all labor organizations are affiliated with the AFL-CIO. The Teamsters and the National Education Association—with nearly 4 million members between them—are the largest *independents.*

At the state and local level, there are *labor councils* or "central bodies" (affiliated with the AFL-CIO) that represent organized labor in political affairs, community services, educational activities, and a variety of other areas.

Future of the Labor Movement

The history of organized labor in America is one of struggle and achievement. What is its future? This is a question many people are asking. Some say that unions played their most important role from the mid-1930s to the 1950s and now there is less need for them. With the spread of automation and growing fears of unemployment, however, many workers have turned to unions to help *protect their jobs and incomes* (not only from management, but from other workers!). They feel that labor unions are needed as a "countervailing power" to offset the influence of big business and big government and help achieve economic justice in our mixed economy. Critics of organized labor argue that union work rules often inhibit efficiency, wage rates are sometimes unreasonably high, and strong-arm methods continue to be used against nonunion workers as well as management. What seems generally agreed is that the socioeconomic institution of unionism, "warts and all," is here to stay.

It would hardly be an exaggeration, however, to say that the American labor movement is undergoing an identity crisis in the 1980s. The pages of the weekly *AFL-CIO News* chronicle labor's concerns and frustrations, its unrelenting criticism of business and government, dissenting views on economic policy, appeals for political action, and of course the day-by-day victories and defeats in collective bargaining and litigation (as well as its "good-citizen" activities as a member of

American society and the world community). Yet organized labor clearly remains a vital institution of our mixed economy, as essential today in our basically private-enterprise system as is government regulation of the food and drug industry, the collection of income taxes, and public programs in aid of the poor.

But this is not to say that unions in the future will make their chief contributions as agents bargaining for the highest attainable wages or as sponsors of political action committees (especially in light of the Presidential elections of 1980 and 1984). What labor organizations do best is to ensure that the individual worker on the job has *a voice that will be listened to.* Exploitation, favoritism, corruption, and other abuses of supervisory powers have by no means vanished from the American workplace. Management-controlled procedures for airing grievances ("up in Personnel") are frequently well intentioned and effective; and workers often have further recourse to one or another governmental agency somewhere in the bureaucracy or judicial system.

The *union,* however, is right there at the job site. It exists in the form of fellow workers and the shop stewards they select to stand with them and speak out—as coequals in the work setting—to protect the rights of *individual men and women* as they fulfill their social responsibilities as productive workers. It is one important offset to the "nullity and futility" (see Chapter 31) that people so often suffer in modern life. If labor unions and their leaders have sometimes used ways and means that invite criticism, they nevertheless are part of a movement that has proved beyond question its fundamental and continuing worth in American society.

Selected Readings and References

John R. Commons et al., *History of Labor in the United States.* New York: Macmillan, 1918.

R.L. Darcy and P.E. Powell, *Manpower and Economic Education.* Denver: Love, 1973. (Also see "What All Workers Should Know About Economics," Chapter 11 in *Vocational Education and the Nation's Economy.* Edited by W.G. Meyer; Washington: American Vocational Association, 1977.)

R.L. Heilbroner and A. Singer, *The Economic Transformation of America: 1600 to the Present,* 2d ed. New York: Harcourt Brace Jovanovich, 1984.

M.B. Schnapper, *American Labor* (cited in Chapter 10).

Gerald G. Somers (editor), *Collective Bargaining: Contemporary American Experience.* Madison, Wisconsin: Industrial Relations Research Association, 1980.

Philip Taft, *Organized Labor in American History.* New York: Harper & Row, 1964.

Studs Terkel, *Working.* New York: Random House/Pantheon, 1972.

AFL-CIO News. (Weekly)

Historical Statistics of the United States (cited in Chapter 15).

Information Please Almanac 1985 (cited in Chapter 15).

*Statistical Abstract of the United States/*1981 and 1985 editions (cited in Chapter 15).

Money, Banking, and the Federal Reserve System

Money is anything that is generally accepted in payment for goods or debt. Two-thirds of our *money supply* consists of demand deposits and other checking accounts in *banks and savings institutions*. Money is valuable not because it is "backed by gold" but for what it can buy. A rising price level—inflation—reduces the *value of money*. The federal government carries out its constitutional duty to regulate the value of money primarily through the functioning of the *Federal Reserve System*.

Some men worship rank, some worship heroes, some worship power, some worship God; and over these they dispute. But they all worship money.

— Mark Twain

An economist is a person who knows more about money than people who have it.

— Anonymous

Virtually everyone in the United States knows the importance of money, even if he has never read a book on the subject. But not everyone understands the nature and functions of money, and the structure and functioning of the monetary system of the United States. As we consider these topics in the present chapter, particular emphasis will be placed on the role played by (1) commercial banks and other private-enterprise financial institutions, and (2) the Federal Reserve System, our nation's "independent-within-government" central bank.

Money and the Monetary Stock

Money is defined as anything that is widely accepted in payment for goods or debt. The most familiar forms of money in the United States are *Federal Reserve Notes*— paper currency issued by the 12 regional Federal Reserve Banks; and *coins* issued by the U.S. Treasury. On the other hand, the type of money that is quantitatively most important is the *deposits* that people maintain in commercial banks and "thrift" accounts (e.g., in savings and loan associations) that can be transferred by the simple act of writing a check. More than two-thirds of the narrowly defined money supply, M-1, (which averaged about $550 billion in 1984) consists of *demand deposits* and other *checkable deposits.* The rest of the "monetary stock" consisted of *currency* ($160 billion) and *travelers checks* (about $5 billion). Two significant facts about checkbook money is that (1) most of it is *created by banks* in the process of extending *loans,* and (2) the banks maintain *reserves* that are only a *fraction* of outstanding deposit obligations.

Functions of Money

Money performs several *functions* in the economic process. As we have seen in the circular flow model, money serves as a *medium of exchange.* Consumers trade money for the goods and services they buy in the market; business firms pay money for the resources they employ in production. The circulation of money is the key to our economic communication system; it is what we "vote" with to express preferences in the marketplace. In addition to serving as a medium of exchange, money is a *store of value* (not a very good one during periods of inflation!). The things that function as money in a particular economic system (coins, paper currency, checkable deposits, travelers checks, and—the experts are not quite sure how to regard *this* modern institution—bank credit cards) are all expressed in terms of the nation's *unit of account* (for us, the U.S. dollar).

Value of Money

The *value of money* is determined by what it can purchase in the marketplace. The dollar is valuable not because the U.S. Treasury owns some $11 billion in gold (the value of our current gold stock is only 2% of the total money supply) nor even because the federal government *says* it is worth a dollar. The value of the dollar is determined by the *quantity of goods and services* that can be obtained in exchange for a dollar. And this, of course, depends on the *prices* at which goods and services are sold.

When the general level of prices goes up—as measured, for example, by a rise in the consumer price index *(CPI)*—the purchasing power or value of money declines. Simply put, this is what economists mean by *inflation.* (The colorful expression "too much money chasing too few goods" is not quite accurate as a definition of inflation for two reasons: It confuses cause with effect and implies a particular theory of causation.) As we saw in Chapter 15, the price level nearly tripled between 1967 and 1981, shrinking the value of the dollar to about 36¢ and generating a sense of economic crisis.

We will wait until Part Five to consider the specific *causes* of inflation. But no matter how the problem is explained, it clearly has a lot to do with *money:* how much there is, where it comes from, how it is used, its current purchasing power, and the value people expect it to have in the future.

The Banking System

What determines the quantity of money available in the economic system? As we have seen, it is not simply a matter of how much currency is issued by the U.S Treasury and 12 Federal Reserve Banks. The bulk of the nation's money supply is *created* in the form of checkable deposit obligations by some 40,000 privately owned, profit-seeking business firms whose chief "commodity" happens to be "credit." (There are about 15,000 commercial banks in the United States and 27,000 "thrift" institutions, including savings and loan associations, credit unions, and a small number of mutual savings banks.) When a merchant, for example, needs $100,000 to purchase inventories of goods for his autumn selling season, he goes to his bank, signs over a promissory note, and receives a credit entry increasing the balance in his firm's checking account. The merchant is now free to write $100,000 in checks to pay his suppliers. When the note comes due, the merchant must repay the loan with interest (in practice the interest may be deducted in advance). It is the *interest payment,* of course, that provides the bank's incentive to make the loan; the main source of *bank profits* (apart from financial investments, service charges, etc.) is interest earned on loans. This might not seem to be very lucrative since one assumes that the bank has to *pay* interest to its depositors and therefore gains only the "spread" between the rate paid and the rate charged. But, in fact, our banking system has a special feature— "fractional-reserve banking"—that permits commercial banks to lend money that "didn't exist."

For reasons that are perfectly reasonable and quite legal, banks are required to maintain a cash (or cash-equivalent) *reserve* of only about 10% (rates vary depending on the type and size of deposits) of the *obligations* (promises to pay "on demand") the bank owes to its depositors. After all, it is unlikely that all depositors will show up demanding their money at the same time, so the bank doesn't really need a 100% reserve. As long as the bank has *excess reserves* beyond the legal requirement it can keep extending new loans up to the amount of the excess reserves, thereby creating interest-earning assets for itself and, essentially as a side effect, *increasing the nation's money supply.*

Note that the bank does maintain a 100% "reserve" of *assets*; after all, it holds the merchant's promissory note. But the note is not a "liquid" asset; it doesn't qualify as money because it won't be "widely accepted in payment for goods or debt." In effect, the bank has "monetized" the merchant's promise to pay, which is *not* widely accepted, by substituting its own more acceptable promise to pay "on demand." (We know and trust the bank—which, after all, is regulated by a state or federal agency; we may *not* know the merchant and can't take the time to check into his credit-worthiness).

Role of the "Fed"

Our federal constitution gives Congress the power to "coin money and regulate the value thereof." Although the Department of the Treasury performs a variety of functions in the area of money and banking (e.g., chartering national banks and operating the federal mints and Bureau of Printing and Engraving) it is the *Federal Reserve System*—our nation's "central bank"—that bears the basic *responsibility for monetary policy*. Established in 1913, the FRS consists of a 7-person Board of Governors appointed by the President (for 14-year terms); 12 Federal Reserve Banks situated throughout the country (with 25 branches plus other facilities); the 12-member Federal Open Market Committee, consisting of the Board of Governors and 5 representatives of the Reserve Banks; a 12-member Federal Advisory Council (one from each Federal Reserve district); and some 6,000 member banks. (All national banks must be members, while state-chartered commmercial banks have a member-ship option; the membership provision lost much of its significance when passage of the Depository Institutions Deregulation and Monetary Control Act of 1980—the most sweeping modification of the nation's banking system since the 1930s—provided for *all* commercial banks and thrift institutions to meet FRS reserve requirements on transaction accounts.)

Federal Reserve Banks serve as "banker's banks" and as fiscal agents for the federal government. They clear checks, issue paper currency (examine a dollar bill to see which one of the 12 district Banks issued it), hold the reserves of banks and thrift institutions, supervise and audit member banks, conduct research, and provide a variety of other services. Moreover, they cooperate with the Board of Governors and Federal Open Market Committee in performing the *monetary policy* function that is of critical importance in the context of the macro performance of the American economy.

As we shall see in Chapter 26, the Federal Reserve ("Fed") maintains leverage on banks mainly by influencing the *volume of excess reserves* in the system. If the Fed feels the economy requires a larger supply of money and credit—in order to help achieve the broad goals of economic growth, acceptable levels of unemployment, a reasonably stable price level, and balanced transactions with foreign countries—the Federal Open Market Committee will place *more* reserves in the system. If a "tight-money" policy appears to be needed, opposite actions can be taken to *reduce* the volume of reserves.

A Changing Institution

A quotation at the beginning of this chapter said economists know more about money than people who have it. We stand by that assertion (there are too many economically innocent lottery winners, millionaire relief pitchers, and brothel owners to seriously dispute the claim!). But as was hinted earlier (in the reference to bank credit cards), economists certainly do not know everything they would like to know about money, such as what it really *is* these days. In its monthly *Federal Reserve Bulletin,* for example, the Fed publishes data on five different "concepts of money, liquid assets, and debt"; and the *Statistical Abstract of the United States* (published by the Department of Commerce) lists yet another (narrower) concept of "Money Stock." The Federal Reserve's numbers ranged in late 1984 from $550 billion for M-1 to $2.3 trillion for M-2, $2.9 trillion for M-3, and correspondingly higher for "L" and "Debt." Why the differences?

If money *is* what money *does*, then recall that money is a medium of exchange for transactions *and* a store of value. You can *buy* things with currency, checks, credit cards, etc.; and you can *store* purchasing power for future use in the form of checking deposits, passbook savings accounts, money market accounts (transferable by check), certificates of deposit, Treasury securities, and a variety of other more-or-less liquid assets. Thus, there is no clear-cut category of monetary assets. Small wonder that the Fed has trouble measuring, much less controlling "the money supply"!

The U.S. economy's recent experiences with money and monetary policy illustrate dramatically how economic institutions—such as the Federal Reserve System, and money itself—*change* in response to new technology. For it was clearly the advance in electronic information systems that triggered changes in financial practices´and institutions and led to passage of the Monetary Control Act of 1980.

Selected Readings and References

Federal Reserve Bulletin (cited in Chapter 15).

The Federal Reserve System: Purposes and Functions. Washington: Board of Governors of the Federal Reserve System, 1974. (Additional FRS publications include *The Monetary Control Act of 1980, Federal Reserve Glossary,* and *Federal Reserve Banks;* a listing of titles appears in each issue of the monthly *Federal Reserve Bulletin.*)

Statistical Abstract of the United States (cited in Chapter 15).

Economic Functions of Government

The "public sector" of the American economy refers to the economic activities of all levels of government: *local, state,* and *federal.* Citizens use governmental entities to *make rules* and to engage in activities that influence the *production* of goods and services and the *distribution* of income in our economy. *Government* accounts directly for *one-fifth* of our gross national product.

Government is a contrivance of human wisdom to provide for human wants.
    —*Edmund Burke*

There is no safe depository of the ultimate powers of a society other than the people themselves; and if they are not enlightened enough to exercise control with a wholesome discretion, the remedy is not to take control from them but to inform their discretion by education.
    —*Thomas Jefferson (modified)*

In a democracy, people get the kind of government they deserve.
    —*H.L. Mencken*

The word "government" is used here to include public agencies at all three levels of government. In addition to the federal government, the public sector includes 50 state governments and some 80,000 units of local government (cities, counties, townships, school districts, special districts, etc.). There are 15,000 public school districts in the United States that have *governmental power* to levy taxes (which they used in 1982 to generate *local* revenues of $36 billion, not quite one-third of the $115 billion they *spent*).

Four Economic Functions

What kinds of services do governmental units perform for their citizens? Besides operating schools and providing national defense, they put out fires, build roads, manage hospitals, help the needy, provide police protection, and handle hundreds of other tasks. And, of course, they collect taxes and borrow money to pay for all these activities. From an *economic* viewpoint, we can classify the *functions of government* under four headings:

1. *Rulemaking* (establishing and enforcing civil and criminal laws, public health regulations, antimonopoly statutes, city zoning ordinances, minimum wage rates, etc.).
2. *Producing goods and services* (e.g., streets and bridges, public education, national defense capability).
3. *Transferring income* (taxing, borrowing, and spending, including the payment of social security benefits and welfare assistance).
4. *Stabilizing the economy* (e.g., managing the money supply and raising or lowering taxes and government spending to promote full employment and prevent inflation).

The Growing Role of Government

Government has always played an important part in the economic life of the American people. In the past half-century, however, government's role has grown enormously. In 1929, only 3 million workers (6% of the civilian labor force) were government employees; by 1984 *public employment* had risen to 16 million, or 14% of the labor force. *Tax collections* rose from less than $10 billion to $671 billion (1982)—from $70 to nearly $3,000 on a per capita basis (not adjusted for inflation). *Government expenditures* rose even more, so that *government debt* increased from a little over $30 billion in 1929 to $1,546 billion in 1982. *Government purchases of goods and services* (the narrower measure of government spending used in calculating *GNP*) rose from $8.8 billion to $748 billion (1984). Adjusting for inflation, the real increase was 637%. In relative terms, government's share of *GNP* more than doubled, growing from 8.5% to 20.4%.

In terms of *employment* and *direct absorption of resources,* it is state and local government that dominates the public sector. Four out of every five civilian government workers are on state and local payrolls while 60% of total and 80% of nondefense government purchases of goods and services are accounted for by state and local government. *Taxes* and *transfer payments* are a different matter. Nearly two-thirds of the taxes Americans pay (including social security payroll taxes) go to the *federal government,* and three-fourths of all income-maintenance transfer payments (mainly social security benefits) are paid by federal government.

Rulemaking

Why is government involved in the four kinds of economic activities listed above, and why has this involvement expanded so dramatically since the 1930s? To begin with, *rules and regulations* are obviously necessary to maintain an orderly society for 240 million people spread out 3,000 miles from Atlantic to Pacific and 1,500 miles from Canada to Mexico, plus Hawaii and Alaska! Without clearly formulated and conscientiously enforced *property laws,* for example, the private-enterprise sector of our economy could never function at all. Then, too, wars and other crises have necessitated government action. Moreover, as our socioeconomic life has grown more complex and interdependent the American people have increasingly called upon government for programs of consumer protection, job safety, environmental controls, and a multitude of other regulatory activities.

Government and the Economy's Performance

But why does the government perform the additional functions of *stabilizing* the economy, *producing* goods and services, and *transferring* or redistributing income? One approach to answering this question is to begin by recognizing that we live in a democracy. If government becomes involved in certain activities it is presumably because the people *desire* such involvement. Americans turn to their government *to help solve economic problems* because, rightly or wrongly, they feel that governmental action will generate better outcomes than are forthcoming from the private sector alone. (Recall the quotations at the beginning of the chapter, plus Winston Churchill's observation that "Democracy is the worst possible system of government—except for all the others.")

Bearing in mind the book's structured approach to economic understanding, it should not be surprising to note that the economic problems government is called upon to help solve all derive from the *basic functions that every economic system must perform,* i.e., determining (1) the overall level of production, employment, and income; (2) the specific kinds of goods and services produced; and (3) the distribution of income.

Macroeconomic Stabilization

Prior to the 1930s, standard neoclassical theory held that the market mechanism could be relied upon to generate high overall levels of employment, production, and income. Then came the Great Depression. Real *GNP* fell by 30%, unemployment averaged 19% for an entire decade, and the American people lost confidence in the "self-correcting" powers of the market. Through their representatives in Congress, they decided that the *federal government* should replace the market as the supra-institution ultimately responsible for *stabilizing the economy* (state and local participation in macroeconomic stabilization essentially is limited to administering expenditure programs financed with federal funds). So crucial is the stabilizing function that a separate chapter is devoted to the subject (see Chapter 26). The *theoretical* basis (Keynesian "demand-side" model) for government stabilization policies is summarized in the appendix to the present chapter.

Government as Producer

Just as government stabilization efforts are a response to one of the three basic problems facing the entire economic system, so it is with government's role as a *producer of goods and services.* Most people feel that the private-enterprise market system does a commendable job of producing such items as food, clothing, automobiles, and housing. But market forces alone fail to allocate enough resources to the production of certain other types of goods—such as schooling, health care, and environmental protection. Seldom does the private sector on its own initiative undertake to build roads or dams. And nobody would expect or even permit private enterprise to provide for national defense. Because the members of our society want certain "public" or "social" goods that *must be consumed collectively* (such as national defense), and because we want *greater quantities* of particular kinds of "private" goods than would be supplied by the market (e.g., education, which involves substantial "external benefits" that "spill over" to the community at large), the citizenry instructs local, state, and federal government to engage in the production of goods and services. This involvement may be *direct* as in the case of police protection and the municipal water works, or *indirect* (through contracts with private suppliers of military equipment). The hoped-for result of government production is a *better mix of goods and services* that will enhance the wellbeing of the American people.

Which *levels* of government produce the various public and quasi-public goods that Americans demand, and at what *cost?* A comprehensive answer to this question would require a treatise on the economics of public finance. Here we limit discussion to the data provided in Table 22.1—bearing in mind that inflation and the rising trend of government services make the absolute dollar figures for a given year virtually

Table 22.1
Direct General Expenditures by Function and Level of Government, 1982-83

Function	Local	State	Federal	Total
	Level of Government and Amount Spent (Billions of dollars)			
National defense[1]	—	—	$229	$ 229
Education[2]	$119	$ 45	13	177
Interest on general debt	13	11	109	133
Public welfare	14	44	25	83
Health and hospitals	23	21	12	56
Natural resources[3]	2	6	48	55
Highways	16	21	1	37
Police and fire protection	23	3	2	28
All other functions[4]	71	33	97	202
Totals	$281	$184	$536	$1,000 bil.[5]

[1]Includes "International Relations" of $10 billion.

[2]Intergovernmental expenditures of $89 billion from the federal government to state and local units and $101 billion from state to local governments omitted from federal and state totals, respectively, to avoid double counting.

[3]Includes "farm subsidies" of $31 billion.

[4]Includes governmental administration, housing and urban renewal, veterans services, sewerage and sanitation, parks and recreation, etc.

[5]This compares with *Total Government Expenditures* of $1,351 billion, which includes Insurance Trust Expenditures of $297 billion (e.g., Social Security benefits, unemployment compensation, etc.) as well as enterprise-type expenditures of $53 billion (utility services, state liquor stores).

Source: U.S. Bureau of the Census, *Governmental Finances in 1982-83.*

obsolete by the time they are published! (See statistical references at the end of the chapter.)

The first thing to note about Table 22.1 is that the figures include only *direct general expenditures;* omitted are payments made from insurance trust funds (e.g., social security pensions which mainly affect the distribution rather than the composition of the nation's income), the expenses of such public enterprises as municipal utilities and state liquor stores and intergovernmental transfers (but see the footnotes in the table). Boxes have been drawn around certain dollar amounts to highlight the biggest items of spending by each level of government. For *local* government, the biggest item was $119 billion for education, followed by $23 billion for health and hospitals, with an equal amount for police and fire protection. At the *state* level, education again drew the largest expenditure at $45 billion, followed closely by public welfare. To no one's surprise, national defense was the most costly direct-general-expenditure function of *federal* government ($229 billion for the fiscal year ending in September 1983); but note that *interest on the national debt* ranked second!

For the most part, the functional *pattern* of government spending remains quite stable from year to year, even though the dollar amounts keep rising. It may be interesting to observe that if one subtracts the cost of defense and interest on the debt, the direct general expenditures of the federal government just about equal the total outlays of local governments and run well below state spending.

Sources of Government Funds

Where does the money come from to finance all of these expenditures? Not simply from "the printing press"! Altogether, government collected $666 billion in *general taxes* in fiscal 1983. This included $289 billion in *federal* individual income taxes (down $9 billion from the year before), $84 billion in *state* sales and excise taxes, $86 billion in *local* property taxes, and $37 billion from the federal corporate income tax (a substantial reduction from previous years). A variety of other taxes generated the remaining $170 billion. Miscellaneous revenues of $213 billion and government borrowing (i.e., sale of bonds and other types of securities) provided *funds from nontax sources* to meet expenditure requirements. (Note that all these figures ignore the revenues generated by *insurance trust funds* and *utility and liquor store operations* since we have excluded those items from the present discussion, which focuses on *general* government expenditures.) Total government *debt* rose from $1.6 trillion in 1982 to $1.8 trillion in 1983—the largest percentage rise in public debt since 1945—with the federal government accounting for most of the increase.

Taxes, Spending, and Redistribution

Up to this point we have considered public-sector involvement in *stabilization* and *production* (as well as the more general area of rule-making). Government is also deeply involved with the third basic problem of the economic system, namely *income distribution.* This is unavoidable, for taxing and spending *inevitably* influence the distribution of real income among individuals and groups. *Progressive* taxes (such as the graduated federal personal income tax) take a higher percentage of income from high-income than low-income families. *Regressive* taxes (e.g., flat-rate sales and excise taxes) take a higher percentage of income from low-income than from high-income families. Few if any taxes are effectively *proportional* in the sense that they actually take the same percentage of income from all taxpayers, rich and poor alike. Thus, taxation not only transfers income from the *private* to the *public* sector but almost always, whether intentionally or not, leaves the *after-tax* distribution of income *within* the private sector somewhat different from the *pre-tax* distribution. (A recent study of tax burdens, by Joseph Pechman, indicated that the overall U.S. tax system takes about 20% of the income of the lowest fifth of families, 23% from the middle quintile, and 26% from the highest quintile. It should be noted, however, that even if the overall tax burden is roughly proportional by income class—with regressive state and local taxes offsetting the moderate progressivity of the federal individual income tax—there is still a redistributional effect based on differential patterns of employment, home ownership, and consumer spending *within* the respective income classes.)

Tax = Base x Rate

Before leaving the subject of taxation, a word should be said about popular usage of the word "taxes" and some related terms. Riddle: How can taxes be *reduced* (as happened under the Economic Recovery Tax Act of 1981) and at the same time *increase*? To provide the answer, we need to introduce a simple formula: $T = B \times R$ where T stands for the *amount of tax paid* (and therefore received by government), B is the *tax base* (the object or magnitude used for calculating tax liability), and R is the *tax rate* (the percentage that is applied to the tax base to calculate the amount of tax owed).

The answer to the riddle now becomes clear: People sometimes use the word "tax" to mean the *tax rate (R)* and at other times they use it to mean *amount of tax payment (T)*. As a matter of simple arithmetic, using the $T = B \times R$ formula, one can see that if the tax base *(B)* goes *up* sufficiently it will offset a *decline* in tax rates *(R)*—which is exactly what occurred with the federal individual income tax between 1981 and 1982. Tax *rates* were cut but (despite the economic recession) the nation's Personal Income, and therefore taxable income, went up enough to raise actual tax receipts by some $12 billion.

Recent Trends in Transfers and Taxes

Even apart from differential tax burdens, government *spending* also leaves some people in the position of having gained more income than others. In the case of certain kinds of *transfer payments* (e.g., unemployment compensation and public assistance payments), *redistribution is often the intent* as well as the outcome. This is so not only for humanitarian and political reasons; many economists and others in our society believe that excessive income inequality leads to a serious *misallocation of resources* because it gives some families five times (or 50 or 500 times!) as many "dollar votes" in the marketplace as their less affluent neighbors. In order for the market system to achieve "allocative efficiency" it is necessary, they say, for government to smooth off the roughest edges of poverty and inequality, in part by providing transfer payments to low-income people and by exacting significantly higher tax payments from the well-to-do since they have greater "ability to pay" (see Chapter 27).

In recent years, momentous changes have occurred in the redistributional area. In terms of income maintenance, for example, benefit payments under the Old Age and

Survivors Insurance program alone (it becomes "OASDHI" with the addition of "Disability" and "Health" coverage), rose from $59 billion in 1975 to $149 billion in 1983. *Total* transfer payments in the economy increased from $178 billion to $405 billion during the same period! ("Indexing" of social security benefits to adjust for increases in the cost of living played a major role in lifting older Americans above the poverty line, as noted in Chapter 27.) As a share of Personal Income, transfer payments climbed from less than 10% in 1970 to 14% in 1984.

On the tax side, two developments are especially notable. The contribution rate for the OASDHI program (combined total for employer and employee) increased from 9.6% in 1970 to 13.4% in 1983 while at the same time the tax base (annual maximum taxable earnings) went up from $7,800 to $35,700! The maximum tax payment by an individual worker rose sixfold from $374 in 1970 to $2,392, which means that for a great many lower-income workers the biggest "tax bite" is no longer the progressive federal individual income tax but the regressive Social Security payroll tax (the employer then contributes an additional $2,392 for the worker, resulting in a maximum total payment of $4,784 per year).

A second development is the dramatic reduction in corporate income taxation. Yielding about two-thirds as much in the 1950s as the personal income tax (PIT), the corporation income tax by the 1970s was generating only one-fourth as much revenue as the PIT; and in the early 1980s the figure dropped well below 20%. (Uncertainty about the true incidence of this tax prevents economists from reaching agreement on the effect that the "demise of the corporate income tax" may have on the distribution of income.)

Equally dramatic and much more clear in terms of its distributional impact is the lowering of rates in the personal income tax. Almost without public comment, the top-bracket rate in the federal PIT was cut in 1981 from 70% to 50% (before the rate reductions of the 1950s, marginal rates rose as high as 92%). A further provision that reduces the progressivity of the PIT is indexation to prevent "bracket creep," i.e., moving to income levels subject to higher marginal rates simply because inflation has raised one's nominal money income. Then in 1984 and 1985, proposals were advanced to adopt a flat-rate PIT, or perhaps a two-step or three-step rate structure. The surprising thing about such anti-egalitarian institutional adjustments is that they seem to enjoy widespread support among the very people who object to existing inequalities in the distribution of wealth and income. One of the ironies of economic policy in the 1980s, therefore, is the erosion of support for the one economic institution capable of dealing in a noninflationary way with extreme inequality, namely the graduated personal income tax. Yet the reason for this attitude is not hard to find; there is such widespread dissatisfaction with tax cheating and within-the-law tax avoidance that the American people seem to be giving up in despair. Better to have a *non*progressive tax system that perpetuates extreme inequalities between income classes, they seem to be saying, rather than suffer continued inequity in administering a system so shot through with loopholes and shelters that people who pay anything like their nominal tax bills become targets of ridicule!*

---

*In this author's own judgment, one specific tax reform long overdue is the substitution of tax *credits* (i.e., subtracted form one's bottom-line tax liability) for the present system of personal *exemptions* (subtracted from taxable income). The effect of this change would be to grant everyone the same dollar amount of tax savings instead of the present arrangement which reduces tax liability of high-income people by more *dollars* than the reduction for people in lower tax brackets.

Special-Interest Groups

Is there a linkage between the "momentous changes" that have occurred in the respective areas of income maintenance programs and personal taxation? It seems clear that there is. As Lester Thurow pointed out in the *Zero-Sum Society*, the American people increasingly turn to government to help solve their economic problems. But they are not always realistic in appreciating the *costs* of government programs. Pressure groups and political lobbies have developed great skill in using the mechanisms of democratic government for their own *special* interests. What is lacking in public-sector decisionmaking is an enlightened, disciplined view of the *general* interest, and in particular the ability to make and defend equity decisions involving *the redistribution of income*. (Perhaps our creativity in designing institutional reforms has outstripped our ethical attainments.) Until such ability is developed, the American people may pursue in vain the articulated set of goals they have established for their economy with respect to the overall level, composition, and distribution of income. These issues are faced again in Chapters 27 and 28, and once more in Part Six.

Public-Sector Shortcomings

Despite what was suggested early in the chapter—that the American people call upon government to perform certain economic functions because they want better outcomes than are forthcoming from the private sector alone—we trust that readers are not left with the impression that governmental activities in the areas of rulemaking, producing, transferring, and stabilizing always leave the economy better off than it was before. Indeed, the "theory of public choice" and discussions of "public sector failures" strongly suggest that the supra-institution of government is no more perfect as a mechanism for coordinating economic life than the supra-institution of the market. One is reminded of the late Arthur Okun's dictum that "The Market has a place, and the Market must be kept in its place." It bears repeating for government's place. Not only does "public choice" replace individual, selective, *quid pro quo* market decisionmaking (recall Chapter 17) with collective decisionmaking, indivisibility of benefits, and "nonexclusion" (hence, the "free-rider" problem)—most importantly it substitutes compulsory compliance for voluntary transactions (e.g., you are "buying" nuclear missiles this year whether you want them or not).

Add to those conceptual concerns such mundane public-sector defects as *fiscal illusion* ("Our new Civic Center didn't cost anything; it was paid for with federal money"), the *special-interest effect* ("Yes, Congressman, we want you to cut the defense budget; but don't close our local air base"), election politics, absence of a cost/revenue test, bureaucratic empire-building, a general lack of incentive for efficiency and effort—and one must surely adopt a guarded attitude toward expansion of government's role in economic affairs.

Selected Readings and References

E.K. Browning and W.R. Johnson, *The Distribution of the Tax Burden.* Washington: American Enterprise Institute for Public Policy Research, 1979.

Richard Goode, *The Individual Income Tax,* Rev. ed. Washington: Brookings, 1976.

R.A. Musgrave and P.B. Musgrave, *Public Finance in Theory and Practice,* 3d ed. New York: McGraw-Hill, 1980.

Arthur M. Okun, *Equality and Efficiency: The Big Tradeoff.* Washington: Brookings, 1975.

Joseph A. Pechman, *Who Paid the Taxes: 1966-1985.* Washington: Brookings, 1985.

Lester C. Thurow, *The Zero-Sum Society* (Distribution and the Possibilities for Economic Change). New York: Basic Books, 1980.

Economic Indicators (cited in Chapter 15).

Facts and Figures on Government Finance, 22d biennial ed. 1983. Washington: Tax Foundation, Inc.

Governmental Finances in 1982-83. Government Finances, GF83, No. 5, U.S. Bureau of the Census, October 1984. Washington: U.S. Government Printing Office, 1984.

Statistical Abstract of the United States 1985 (cited in Chapter 11).

Your Federal Income Tax (For Individuals). Publication 17, revised November 1984. Internal Revenue Service, U.S. Department of the Treasury. (Yearly)

APPENDIX: Macroeconomics—The Aggregate-Demand (Keynesian) Theory of National Income, Employment, and Price Level

During the worldwide economic depression of the 1930s, British economist John Maynard Keynes expounded a theory explaining the determination of the overall level of production and employment. Eventually accepted by virtually all mainstream economists, the "Keynesian model" held that in a market economy, *total spending determines the level of national income and employment*. Keynesian macroeconomic theory has provided the *basis for government policies* aimed at reducing unemployment, preventing demand-pull inflation, and promoting full production.

In 1936, during the Great Depression, British economist John Maynard Keynes* published *The General Theory of Employment Interest and Money.* In this book he expounded a theory to explain the process by which the overall levels of production and employment were determined. It was Keynes' idea that the market system, as it existed in the 1930s, did *not* tend automatically to establish an equilibrium level of income *that necessarily ensured full employment.* Since standard neoclassical theory (largely *micro*economics) was a "scarcity" theory based on the assumption of full employment, it could not be applied to a world in which enormous quantities of resources were involuntarily idle. Hence, to make the conventional theory of the market more applicable to the real world it was necessary to explain how unemployment was *caused* and how it could be *eliminated,* i.e., *how full employment could be achieved.* (Keynes has been called "the savior of capitalism," and correspondingly the economist who rescued neoclassical theory from irrelevancy.)

Keynes began by repudiating Say's Law of the Market (see the circular flow model in Chapter 13) which held that *(a)* "supply creates its own demand," and therefore *(b)* the market system always tends toward a full-employment equilibrium. Keynes

---

*His name rhymes with "rains," not "beans"; the theory is "Kainzian," not "Keenzian" or "Keneesian."

pointed out that the process of production does indeed generate the *income* necessary to finance the purchase of the total output, and he agreed that *wants* were unlimited. But he showed that this did not necessarily guarantee that every dollar *received* in a particular income period would automatically be *spent* in that period. In particular, *savings* did not necessarily constitute *effective demand* for capital goods. Aggregate demand (total spending, or *GNP*) might not be sufficient to take off the market all of the goods that were produced. In effect he suggested what might be termed "Keynes' Law of the Market": that *demand* creates its own supply (within the production-possibility limits set by resources and technology).

Keynes persuaded his fellow economists—in Britain, the United States, and elsewhere—that *total spending* (effective aggregate demand) *determines the level of national income and therefore the level of employment.* Spending consists of two parts (ignoring government for the moment): *consumption* (spending on goods to satisfy wants) and *investment* (spending to create new capital equipment). Aggregate income *(Y)* equals consumption *(C)* plus investment *(I): Y = C + I.*

The people who save are not necessarily the same people who make investment decisions: Hence, it is possible for the volume of planned savings to be different from the volume of planned investment. If saving is greater than investment $(S > I)$, more money is being taken out of the income stream than is being put in; income will tend to *fall.* If investment is greater than saving $(I > S)$, more money is being injected into the income stream than is withdrawn ("leaking out") and therefore income *(Y)* will tend to *rise.* When planned saving equals planned investment $(S = I)$, the economy is in a position of equilibrium, though *not necessarily at full employment.*

The rate of investment is determined by the marginal efficiency of capital (MEC)—roughly the discounted expected profitability of investment—in conjunction with the rate of interest *(i).* There are two kinds of investment: autonomous and induced. "Autonomous investment" is *independent* of changes in the level of income, whereas "induced investment" *varies* with changes in the level of income (and consumer spending). We assume in the present discussion, as Keynes himself did, that investment is *autonomous.*

When planned saving equals planned investment† the nation's income is at an equilibrium level: there will be no tendency for it to change until either *S* or *I* changes. Another way of putting this is to say that when aggregate demand $(C + I)$ equals aggregate supply, the nation's income is at an equilibrium level. This is so because the sales revenue of business firms are just large enough to induce them to continue employing a quantity of resources (labor, land, capital) that gives rise to factor payments totaling that level of income which in turn induces the volume of consumption expenditure that—in conjunction with the level of autonomous investment—will maintain the flow of aggregate effective demand unchanged.

The rate of saving (and of consumption) is determined by the community's *propensity to consume,* in conjunction with the level of the nation's *income.*

1. *The average* propensity to consume *(APC)* equals the ratio of consumption to income at any given level of income: $APC = C/Y.$ The *APC* is assumed to be quite stable in the short run.

---

†Or, to generalize the model, when *total leakages* or withdrawals (personal saving + business saving + taxes) equal *total injections* (gross private domestic investment + government purchases of goods and services + net exports), then the nation's income is at an equilibrium level, but not necessarily at full employment.

2. The *average* propensity to *save (APS)* equals the ratio of saving to income at any given level of income: $APS = S/Y$. Since *APC* is stable, *APS* must also be stable.
3. The *marginal* propensity to consume *(MPC)* equals the ratio of a *change* in consumption to a *change* in income: $MPC = \Delta C/\Delta Y$. The *MPC* is assumed to be positive, less than one, and *constant* (indicated by a linear consumption function).
4. The *marginal* propensity to *save (MPS)* equals the ratio of a change in saving to a change in income: $MPS = \Delta S/\Delta Y$. It has the same characteristics as *MPC*.
5. $APC + APS = 1$, and $MPC + MPS = 1$.

The great operational significance of the *MPC* lies in the fact that it determines the numerical value of the investment *multiplier*. The multiplier *(k)* is the ratio of the change in equilibrium income to the change in investment that induces the new level of income: $k = \Delta Y/\Delta I$. It is the number which is multiplied by a change in investment to determine the resulting change in income ($\Delta Y = k \cdot \Delta I$). The multiplier is equal to one over one minus the *MPC*: $k = 1/(1 - MPC)$.‡ This is the same thing as the reciprocal of the *MPS*: i.e., $k = 1/MPS$.

To determine the effect of a change in investment on the equilibrium level of the nation's income, you multiply the change of investment (whether the change is positive or negative) by the multiplier k. Thus, $\Delta Y = \Delta I \cdot k$. For example, if I declines by \$5 billion with $k = 3$, the equilibrium level of Y will decline by \$15 billion. If I increases by \$10 billion with $k = 4$, the equilibrium level of Y will be \$40 billion larger than the previous equilibrium level. (Remember that k is determined by the marginal propensity to consume: $k = 1/(1 - MPC)$.) The new equilibrium income (Y_1) equals the original equilibrium income (Y_0) plus or minus the change in income (ΔY): $Y_1 = Y_0 + \Delta Y$. Note that the multiplier works in *both directions*, up and down. Moreover, it works with injections of government spending *(G)* as well as with changes in private investment (but only *government purchases of goods and services*, not transfer payments).

At this point we add the *government sector* to the model (recall the *policy* orientation of the theory: What can the nation do to achieve full employment?). Our basic income equations become $Y = C + I + G$ on the aggregate-demand side (compare with the U.S. Department of Commerce formula for calculating *GNP*) and either $Y = C + S$ (as before) if government purchases of goods and services (G) is *deficit-financed* (which is more expansionary), or $Y = C + S + T$, if G is financed by taxes (T). As a matter of public policy, if the present equilibrium level of income is *too low* (resulting in *unemployment*), the government can inject new *spending* into the economy. This new spending will increase income by a *multiple* of the increased government spending: $\Delta Y = \Delta G \cdot k$. Alternatively, the government could take action (e.g., with tax changes, transfer payments, debt retirement) designed to alter the level of *consumption* or *investment*.

The basic Keynesian model is graphically illustrated in Figure 22A.1, with explanations provided in the captions.

---

‡Proof:

(1) $k = \Delta Y/\Delta I$

(2) $Y = C + I$

(3) $\Delta Y = \Delta C + \Delta I$

(4) $k = \Delta Y/(\Delta Y - \Delta C)$

(5) $k = \dfrac{\Delta Y/\Delta Y}{(\Delta Y/\Delta Y) - (\Delta C/\Delta Y)} = \dfrac{1}{1 - (\Delta C/\Delta Y)}$

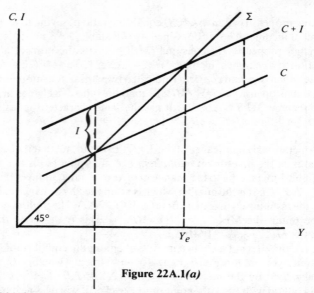

Figure 22A.1(a)

Figure 22A.1(a) shows graphically that the equilibrium level of income (Y_e) is determined by the intersection of the total spending curve (C + I) and the 45-degree line or so-called aggregate supply curve (Σ). Note that the C + I curve is parallel to the C curve (because of autonomous investment).

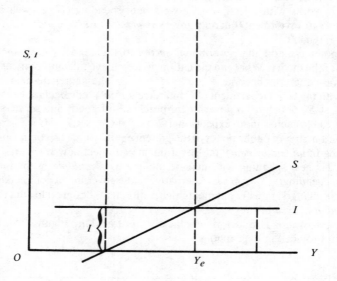

Figure 22A.1(b)

Figure 22A.1(b) shows that the equilibrium level of income (Y_e) is determined by the intersection of the savings and investment curves. Note that the I curve is parallel to the horizontal axis (again, because of autonomous investment).

Observe the relationship between the two diagrams. At equilibrium Y_e (above), the vertical distance between the C curve and $C + I$ curve is exactly equal to the distance between the S curve and the horizontal axis (below).

In Figure 22A.1, the equilibrium level of income Y_e is *not necessarily the full-employment level.* There may exist a "deflationary gap" or "unemployment gap" where the aggregate demand curve intersects the 45-degree line at an income *too low* to provide full employment. Or, an "inflationary gap" may exist, with aggregate demand intersecting the 45-degree line at an income *too high* to provide full-employment-without-inflation. See Figure 22A.2. The basic policy implication of Keynesian theory is that the national government has the power, through appropriate

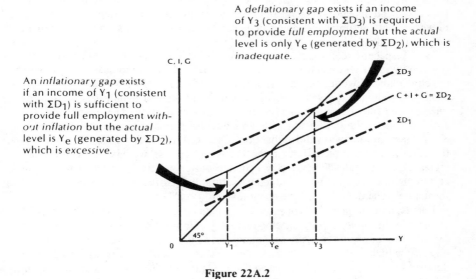

A *deflationary gap* exists if an income of Y_3 (consistent with ΣD_3) is required to provide *full employment* but the *actual* level is only Y_e (generated by ΣD_2), which is *inadequate.*

An *inflationary gap* exists if an income of Y_1 (consistent with ΣD_1) is sufficient to provide full employment *without inflation* but the *actual* level is Y_e (generated by ΣD_2), which is *excessive.*

Figure 22A.2

Note that the *equilibrium* level of income may not necessarily be the level that provides full employment without inflation.

monetary and fiscal policies, to help eliminate deflationary or inflationary gaps. In the United States, the federal government also has the *legal responsibility* to do so, i.e., "to promote maximum employment, production, and purchasing power" (under provisions of the Employment Act of 1946), as well as prevent inflation (Full Employment and Balanced Growth Act of 1978).

In the diagram, the *size of the deflationary gap* is measured on the *vertical* axis; it is equal to the difference in equilibrium *income,* measured on the *horizontal* axis, divided by the multiplier. This yields the vertical distance between the two aggregate demand curves (i.e., Deflationary Gap = $(Y_3 - Y_e)/k$). One way to eliminate the gap is to increase government purchases (G) by an amount that will shift aggregate demand upward from ΣD_2 to ΣD_3.

The concept of the *inflationary* gap is more slippery. One can calculate its size as $(Y_e - Y_1)/k$ but, in the real world, if aggregate demand were excessive at ΣD_2 it is doubtful that income could truly be in equilibrium (at Y_2) since the existence of inflation disturbs all economic calculations, including investment and the propensity to consume (as the stagflation-prone market economies of Europe and America were to learn after the mid-1960s). Policy actions that could eliminate the inflationary gap include *spending cuts by government* and *higher taxes* that would induce reductions in consumption and investment.

The above sketch of national income theory is based on the simple Keynesian model, expounded half a century ago. The essence of the theory is still accepted by most economists. In the past four decades, however, the theory has been tested, criticized, and refined at many points. For example, it was originally assumed that the propensity to consume was quite stable and therefore fluctuations in income were largely attributable to shifts in autonomous investment. Experience has shown, however, that consumer spending can be very *un*stable; it is not a simple function of current income alone.

With respect to inflation, Keynes assumed that the price level would not rise until full employment was reached, or at least approached, i.e., an increase in aggregate effective demand would expand employment and real output, not just increase the monetary value of a given level of output. With 18% of a nation's labor force unemployed (the actual average rate of unemployment in the U.S. throughout the entire decade of the 1930s) and with large quantities of land and capital goods idle, Keynes' assumption was valid at that time. On the other hand, with only 5% or 6% of the labor force unemployed (as in the 1960s and 1970s), we have learned that an increase in aggregate demand may generate only a relatively small expansion in employment and output while inducing a substantial *rise in the price level* because of "structural" characteristics of the economy.

Finally, until the late 1960s or early 1970s, many (Keynesian) economists regarded changes in the *money supply* as being relatively unimportant as a determinant of the overall level of economic activity. Today, just as in a sense "we are all Keynesians now," it is likewise true that "we are all monetarists now" (at least in considerable degree). Growing numbers have joined Nobel laureate Milton Friedman in viewing the money supply as a highly important variable that directly influences macroeconomic performance.

In sum, the Keynesian model, as economists view it today, is considered a useful but rather "blunt" instrument for guiding stabilization policy—still a *necessary* tool for preventing the classic problems of "cyclical" unemployment and demand-pull inflation, but *insufficient* to cope with structural realities in today's economy. In other words, it fulfills its promise as a theory of aggregate demand but offers no solution to the modern problems of structural unemployment, cost-push inflation, and that legacy of the Viet Nam era, "stagflation."

Foreign Trade and the International Sector of the Economy

When nations follow the *Law of Comparative Advantage*, specializing in what they can produce most efficiently and trading with other countries, world output increases. Differences in the monetary units of sovereign nations make *international trade* more complex than domestic trade because of variations in *foreign exchange rates*. A country's *international balance of payments* is a structured summary of all transactions between that nation and the rest of the world. Because of its commitment to economic growth and status as the world's largest economy, the United States plays a dominant role in international trade and finance.

Specialization is limited by the extent of the market.
— *Adam Smith*

The general public remains insufficiently aware of the growing links among nations over the past few decades, and of the extent today of international economic interdependence.
— *The World Bank*

If specialization and the division of labor contribute to greater productive efficiency *within* a nation (recall Chapter 12), it seems logical that the same would be true *between* and among nations. Indeed, this observation provides the foundation for a theory of international trade.

Law of Comparative Advantage

As expressed in the Law of Comparative Advantage, if nations having different cost-of-production patterns for two or more commodities will specialize in producing the goods for which their costs are relatively lowest, then total output will increase and international trade can result in increased real income for all countries. It is not *absolute* cost advantages (measured in hours of labor, or monetary outlays) that matter, but only comparative, or *relative* differentials. In terms of production possibilities and opportunity costs (see Chapters 11 and 12, including Appendix), all that is required to make specialization and trade worthwhile between two countries is that their respective cost structures, or "transformation ratios," for producing two or more commodities have significant differences. Thus (using hypothetical data), if Brazil can produce 1,000 tons of coffee with a given quantity of resources, but only 100 motorboats, whereas the United States can produce 100 motorboats with the same "package" of resources, but only 200 tons of coffee, then a significant difference exists in opportunity costs. By choosing one pattern of resource allocation over another, Brazil "transforms" 100 motorboats into 1,000 units of coffee ($C/B = 10:1$); compared with the USA's 100 motorboats into only 200 units of coffee ($C/B = 2:1$). With such dramatic differences in productive efficiency, is it any wonder that Brazil specializes in coffee production, leaving the motorboat industry to the USA? The particular circumstances that give rise to cost differentials may vary from differences in climate, land resources, labor and management skills, etc., to such circumstances as tradition, "impetus of an early start," and deliberate incubation and nurturing of an industry by government through planning, subsidies, and protective trade policies.

In the real world of the early 1980s, the United States enjoyed a comparative advantage in producing a variety of agricultural commodities, certain types of machinery and motor vehicles, coal, chemicals, aircraft, scientific instruments, and numerous other commodities leading to total U.S. merchandise exports of over $200 billion per year. On the other hand, our comparative *dis*advantage in the production of such items as petroleum, smaller automobiles, clothing, iron and steel, alcoholic beverages, coffee, fish, certain electronic products, and other goods resulted in merchandise *imports* averaging *$230* billion. Because this "trade deficit" has been both substantial and rising, it is one of the concerns we shall return to in Chapter 29 when we consider some of our nation's international economic problems.

Foreign Exchange

The *economic basis* for international trade is thus essentially the same as for interpersonal or interregional trade, namely *specialization according to comparative efficiency*. But two interrelated facts make international trade significantly *different* from domestic trade. First is the *political sovereignty* of the respective nations, meaning that they are free to establish their own "rules of the game." A second fact is implied by the first, namely that each nation has the power to establish and regulate the value of its own *currency*. International trade therefore involves different monetary units.

When American farmers export soybeans to England, the Americans want to be paid in U.S. dollars. English importers must take their own currency, British pounds, and convert in into *foreign exchange*—the general term for currency of other nations—in order to obtain the dollars required to make payment. Thus, *two* sets of transactions are involved when goods flow across national boundaries, one for the *commodity* and another for the *currency* needed to pay for the commodity. Consequently, two *prices* are involved, the dollar price of soybeans and the pound price of dollars. The latter price is called the *foreign exchange rate,* defined as the price of (one unit of) a foreign currency expressed in terms of the domestic currency. From the viewpoint of the U.S. dollar, the foreign exchange rate on the British pound in 1985, for example, fluctuated around $1.20.

Under a system of "flexible" or "floating" exchange rates (which has prevailed in the world economy since "fixed" or "pegged" rates were abandoned in the early 1970s), prices of foreign currencies are determined by the forces of supply and demand. Greater demand for dollars, e.g., to buy high-yield U.S. securities, tends to raise the price (= value) of the dollar—making it "stronger" in world markets—and vice versa (which is perfectly consistent with the general supply-and-demand theory of price determination explained in the appendix to Chapter 17.) "Strength" of the dollar increases its buying power, making foreign goods cheaper for people who hold dollars, including American consumers—thereby stimulating imports. The other side of the coin is that a "strong" dollar makes it more expensive for foreigners to buy the dollars they need to finance purchases of American goods, hence U.S. *exports* are discouraged. Somewhat ironically, therefore, a "strong" dollar means a "weaker" export sector, as exemplified by the plight of American farmers whose foreign markets have in recent years eroded (not only by the "strong" dollar, of course, but also by such governmental "rule changes" as temporarily embargoing the shipment of American grain to the Soviet Union.)

International Balance of Payments

Table 23.1 presents a summary of all transactions between individuals, business firms, and governmental agencies of the United States and their counterparts in the rest of the world for 1980. This type of annual accounting statement is called a nation's *international balance of payments.* While the format for such a statement is not completely standardized, it typically displays (among other elements) a *Current Account* summarizing the value of all merchandise exports and imports during the year, payments made and received for "services" (including investment income received by Americans for having made "capital" available to foreigners), and a variety of other entries. It is within this account that one finds such highly publicized figures as the nation's "merchandise trade deficit" (or surplus), as well as the more comprehensive "Balance on Goods and Services" and "Balance on Current Account."

Next is the *Capital Account* showing the flow of investment funds into and out of the country (which eventually give rise to investment income and payments as recorded under "Services" in the Current Account). Closely related (surprising as this may seem) is the entry labeled *Statistical Discrepancy.* The connection stems from the fact that many of the "Errors and Omissions" are actually unrecorded private capital flows. These are perfectly legal transactions, such as the purchase by foreigners of U.S. Treasury securities in order to obtain high-interest yields on risk-free financial investments, but the system of reporting does not routinely record them.

Finally, the international balance of payments records changes in *Official Reserve Assets* owned by the nation's government (the U.S. Treasury in our example), reserve assets owned by foreign governments, and transactions involving operations of the

International Monetary Fund. By definition the balance-of-payments statement must balance (as does a balance sheet in ordinary business accounting); but sometimes a "memorandum" entry is provided to indicate the magnitude of *"balancing"*

Table 23.1

International Balance of Payments, United States, 1980
(Billions of Dollars)

I. Current Account
   A. Merchandise trade (excl. military)

Exports		+224.0
Imports		-249.3
Merchandise Trade Balance		[-25.3]

   B. Services   +36.1

Investment income, net	+29.9	
Other services, net	+ 6.2	
Balance on Goods and Services[1]		[+10.8]

   C. Private remittances vs. govt. pensions, etc.   -2.4

   Balance on goods, services, and remittances   [+8.4]

   D. Government grants (excl. military g & s, net)   -4.7

   E. Memo: U.S. military grants of goods and services [net -.6]

   Balance on Current Account   [+3.7]

II. Capital Account
   A. Private   -36.7

Increase in U.S. assets abroad	-71.5	
Increase in foreign assets in U.S.	+34.8	

   B. Government
      Increase in assets other than official reserves   -5.2

III. Statistical Discrepancy (or errors and omissions including   +29.6
     large unrecorded private capital flows—net foreign
     funds invested in the U.S.)

   Balance on Capital Account and Statistical Discrepancy   [-12.3]

IV. Official Reserve Assets and Balancing Transactions
   A. Increase in official U.S. reserve assets   -8.2

   B. Increase in foreign official reserve assets in U.S., net   +15.5

   C. Allocation of Special Drawing Rights (SDRs)   +1.2

   Memo: "Balance of Payments Deficit"   [-8.6]

---

[1]Total exports of goods and services equalled $344.7 billion and total imports $333.9 billion.

Source: *Survey of Current Business,* March 1982

transactions that were required to accommodate the more autonomous flows recorded above (e.g., the $8.6 billion entry in Table 23.1).

Detailed balance-of-payments information is collected, analyzed, and published by agencies of the respective countries. These statements are of great interest to the International Monetary Fund, a multilateral organization established in the 1940s to help stabilize economic relations among nations of the world. In the United States, the U.S. Department of Commerce publishes current balance-of-payments data in its monthly *Survey of Current Business.*

Internationalization and Interdependence

If Japan's rise to trillionaire status since the 1960s (joining the USA and USSR in that exclusive club) is one "miracle" of today's world economy, a phenomenon of even greater global significance is the unprecedented internationalization of production, investment, labor supply, and ownership. Traditional theory held that international trade was a necessary consequence of the *immobility of resources* across national borders. Since land, labor, capital, and enterprise were not free to move from one country to another, resources could not be efficiently allocated. International specialization in *production,* however, and *trade* helped compensate for this inefficiency by "embodying" resources in commodities and shipping *them* abroad.

The dramatic rise of the multinational (or "transnational") corporation in recent years runs counter to the traditional pattern, entailing enormous flows of capital, labor, and entrepreneurship across national borders. In addition, "guest-worker" programs and permissive immigration policies (e.g., in the European Common Market, the Middle East, and the United States) have created huge expatriate or immigrant populations. Presumably this reflects not only the high valuation of economic considerations but also powerful centrifugal *cultural* forces at work in today's world.

Partly because of these "countertrends," it is difficult to provide a simple numerical indicator of the importance of international trade and investment in the world economy. In calculations of *GNP*, the international sector is represented by the very modest statistic known as "net exports" (for the U.S. economy, typically no more than 2% of *GNP* whether positive, or as in recent years *negative*). Looking at gross data, however, exports of goods and services in 1984 equalled 10% of *GNP,* and the value of exports-plus-imports totaled 22% of *GNP!* In the early 1980s, one of every seven manufacturing jobs and one-third of our farm acres were producing for export.

In fact, the United States leads the world in both exports and imports; after all, 22% of a multitrillion dollar *GNP* makes for huge waves in the world economy! But West Germany, Japan, Britain, France, the Soviet Union, Italy, Canada, and even tiny Belgium-Luxembourg, The Netherlands, and Saudi Arabia are also major world traders. On the basis of exports as a percentage of *GNP,* a good indicator of *dependence on the international sector,* all of these nations rank much higher than the United States. And that is only from the viewpoint of production, jobs, and markets. Nations also become highly dependent on international trade in terms of what they *import*—especially food, fuel, strategic minerals, etc. A dramatic example once again is The Netherlands, whose imports of goods and services equal 40% of that nation's *GNP* and for whom the ratio of exports-plus-imports to *GNP* exceeds 80%!

With regard to the international movement of *resources,* in a number of smaller nations, more than one-fifth of the resident labor force consists of foreign workers.

(Accurate statistics are not available for the United States on the total number of foreign workers in our labor force, but we know that some eight million immigrant and nonimmigrant aliens officially enter the country each year—including students and short-term visitors—and also that perhaps as many as two million or more "undocumented aliens" cross over into the United States annually.)

International movements of capital and enterprise are symbolized by the *multinational corporation,* which on the one hand brings modern technology and new jobs to the host country while at the same time inciting fears that its economy (and perhaps even its culture and politics) will be "taken over by foreign capital." Using the United States as an example, the U.S. Department of Commerce reports that in 1980 Americans owned $214 billion of direct investment assets abroad, while foreigners had $66 billion of direct investments (i.e., excluding bank deposits, government securities, etc.) in this country. Also of interest is the fact that, as of 1983, foreigners held $150 billion in U.S. Treasury securities, accounting for one-eighth of our nation's public debt. American trade missions and even state governors increasingly strive to lure foreign investments to this country, notably from Japan.

Statistics such as these remind us of a lesson learned in Chapter 12, namely that *interdependence* is the other side of the coin in a specialized, efficiency-oriented economic system. To the extent that resources become allocated worldwide on the basis of comparative advantage, in effect an interdependent "world economy" is created. But we continue to live in a system of politically *independent* nations whose sovereignty enables them to establish their own "rules of the game." Among the rules of international trade (broadly construed to encompass foreign investment, labor mobility, and foreign exchange policy) are the arrangements under which goods, resources, and money will move across national boundaries. In simplest terms, this is the issue of "free trade" and "open borders" versus "interventionism," "controls," and "protectionism." (Note that the free-trade argument, based on increased world production, logically extends to resource mobility as well as the flow of goods and services; this implies an "open border" policy for labor, capital, and entrepreneurship— with land, for the most part, being intrinsically immobile.)

The "Free Trade" Issue

Since the time of Adam Smith, *free trade* has been one of the basic "articles of faith" for mainstream economists, sometimes even cited as the litmus test of economic understanding. Those who favor free trade are "sophisticated," and those who lean toward protectionism are "uninformed and short-sighted." But the case for free trade, as we have seen, is essentially based on a single criterion, namely *increased production* (with correspondingly lower prices and greater consumption). (As we shall consider in Chapter 30, single-criterion thinking often is not at all sophisticated.) Increased production and lower world prices, however, are not the only effects of international specialization and trade. As Third World commodity producers and American auto workers have learned, it may not be an easy matter to find new jobs for half a million workers displaced by foreign competition. (The same theoretical model that demonstrates aggregate gains and lower *world* prices also discloses, but with less fanfare, that domestic consumers will actually pay *higher* prices for export goods than they paid *before* specialization and trade.) Nor is there any assurance that the "terms of trade"—the *structure* of world prices—and the respective *gains* from trade will be "fair." It is because of these and other "side effects"—both short-run and long-run—

plus a wide range of political and cultural considerations, that many nations of the world remain unconvinced about the virtues of free trade (and American workers increasingly are of like mind).

The policy antithesis of free trade and open borders is interventionism. This entails *controls, regulations, taxes,* and *subsidies.* Perhaps the best-known technique is the *protective tariff,* actually a high selective sales tax imposed on imports. The effect of import duties in general is to increase costs to the businesses which import goods from abroad, and these costs are passed along to consumers in the form of higher prices. If the tax is "moderate," the foreign-made goods will continue entering the country and the main effects will be higher prices and tax revenues collected by the government. Of course, prices will still be lower than domestic prices or the goods wouldn't be imported at all.

On the other hand, if tariff rates are quite high, the effect might be to raise the price of the imported commodity to levels that could not compete with domestic goods. The home industry (markets, profits, and jobs) would thus be "protected from foreign competition," but at the expense of consumers who are denied access to lower-priced foreign goods. (Quality differences are ignored in this brief discussion.)

Tariffs are by no means the only techniques used to prevent foreign goods from entering a country's markets. The full arsenal of trade barriers includes import quotas (maximum quantities of a good allowed to enter the country), foreign exchange controls, arbitrary technical standards, import licensing, disruptive regulations (e.g., administrative red tape in customs), and so-called voluntary restraint agreements (such as the negotiated arrangement by which Japan "voluntarily" limited auto exports to the United States).

On the supply side of the market, governments can manipulate the rules of the game by subsidizing exports, granting special tax treatment, and exempting exporters from certain trade practices that might be illegal within the country.

U.S. Trade Policy

The ups and downs of free trade versus protectionism throughout history make a fascinating story, including linkages between the American political revolution of 1776 and the free-trade doctrines of Adam Smith's book *The Wealth of Nations* published the same year. Within our own 20th century, we note that U.S. policy at first was basically high-tariff, except for a brief period around World War I; but beginning in the mid-1930s, tariff rates have declined to such *low* levels that we presently qualify as the world's leading advocate of free trade (with perhaps no greater champion than President Reagan). In part this goal has been pursued within the framework of a multilateral organization called GATT (General Agreement on Tariffs and Trade, established in 1947) that continues to strive for the reduction of trade restrictions. This is not to say that everyone in the United States favors free trade, nor does government policy always advance the cause of free trade. Pleas for protection of American business and labor from foreign competition are increasingly heard, especially during periods of economic recession and high unemployment, as for example, during the downturns of 1980-1982. The omnibus Trade and Tariff Act of 1984, while generally promoting freer trade, nevertheless contained a number of protectionist provisions. The so-called voluntary restraint agreements (VRAs) mentioned earlier in the context of Japanese cars, are also finding expanded application, notably to limit steel imports.

From the broader perspective of the world economy, the trend in recent (recession-plagued) years has been *away* from comprehensive free trade rather than toward it, with tariffs remaining high in some sectors and nontariff barriers finding increasing expression.

Selected Readings and References

R.E. Caves and R.W. Jones, *World Trade and Payments,* 3d ed. Boston: Little Brown, 1981.

Economic Indicators (cited in Chapter 15).

Economic Report of the President (cited in Chapter 15).

Federal Reserve Bulletin (cited in Chapter 15).

International Monetary Fund, *International Financial Statistics* (monthly and Yearbook). Also *IMF Survey, Balance of Payments Statistics* (monthly and Yearbook), *Direction of Trade Statistics* (monthly and Yearbook), *Government Finance Statistics Yearbook,* and annual *World Economic Outlook.*

Statistical Abstract of the United States (cited in Chapter 15).

Survey of Current Business (cited in Chapter 15).

World Bank, *World Development Report 1984.* New York: Oxford University Press (for the World Bank), 1984. (Annual)

Economic Growth:
Processes and Consequences

Economic growth is defined as an increase in the production of goods and services over a significant period of time. One common measure of growth is the *annual rise in total GNP;* another is the year-to-year *increase in per capita GNP* (both expressed in *real* terms). With an annual growth rate of 2%, per capita *GNP* doubles in 35 years, as it did in the United States between 1950 and 1985. The *causes* and *processes* of growth were topics of particular interest to Adam Smith and the early classical economists. Since the 1950s, increasing attention has been given to the *side effects* and limits of growth. For today's American economy, growth is a *goal* and at the same time a *problem.*

In the past 100 years, U.S. economic growth has created 90 million jobs, increased the average consumer's real income fourfold, cut the work week from 63 to 35 hours, and produced the world's first multitrillion-dollar economy.

At current rates of industrial growth, exhaustion of natural resources and pollution of the environment within the next century will threaten the existence of life on this planet.

A capitalist economy must grow or die.

—(paraphrased from various sources)

No topic in economics is more inclusive, complex, and intriguing than growth— the "life process of mankind" so far as material wellbeing is concerned. Growth in this broad sense examines not just the structure and functioning of the economic system at a point in time but its "laws of motion" and trajectory over a period of years. It is concerned, therefore, with both the present and future of the economic process and, most significantly, with the "life process" by which the seeds of the present yield their fruit in the future. Since growth occurs over a span of time, there are few if any constants in the economic process; "static" analysis, with its fixed data and ceteris paribus assumption, gives way to *dynamic analysis* in which virtually everything changes and interacts with everything else.

"Growth" Defined in Quantitative Terms

Such breadth of scope can be intimidating from the viewpoint of meaningful analysis, and it will therefore be necessary to draw some boundaries. For the present discussion, economic growth is defined in a purely *quantitative* sense as the increase in production of goods and services over a significant period of time. Growth can be measured as the annual *increase* in (1) *total GNP* or (2) *per capita GNP*—both expressed in *real* terms, i.e., adjusted for changes in the price level. (Two further definitions of growth also make good sense: an increase in *potential* as opposed to *actual GNP,* and an increase in *productivity*; but both entail measurement problems as well as suffering conceptual limitations.) Largely excluded from consideration in the present chapter are the topics of "development" and "progress," which carry more *qualitative* connotations (addressed in Part Six).

Because no definitive statistics are available for *GNP* prior to 1929, earlier data on U.S. output are to some extent "guesstimates." Even if our present system of national income accounting did go back to the 19th century, however, comparisons would be highly suspect because of the fundamental *transformation* that has occurred in product quality, the composition of *GNP,* and consumer lifestyles (contrast life before and after telephones, electric lights and power, automobiles, television, and computers!). Economically speaking, we live in such a different world from that of our great-grandparents that any quantitative comparison requires great caution.

Some widely used estimates based on cumulative growth rates (calculated by Nobel laureate Simon Kuznets, "father" of our national income accounting system) suggest that real *GNP* per person was more than four times as great in 1980 as one hundred years earlier. By 1982 (see Table 29.1), per capita *GNP* stood at $13,200 after rising at an annual rate of about 2% since 1950 (2.2% since 1960). At a 2% growth rate, income doubles every 35 years, as it did in the United States between 1950 and 1985; at 2.2% the 1982 figure will double (in just under 32 years) to $26,400 per person in *real* terms by the year 2014.

Sources of Growth

What causes an economy to grow? Adam Smith stressed the importance of *specialization* and division of labor, *capital formation,* and *free trade.* Of central importance in his "classical theory of growth" was the process by which business *profits* were converted into personal *savings,* which in turn were *invested* in the accumulation of real capital equipment, i.e., savers directly or indirectly used their surplus funds for the purchase of newly produced plant and equipment, thereby channeling resources away from consumer goods to the production of capital goods. More equipment per worker meant *higher productivity* (output per unit of input), and *therefore* (assuming no reduction in hours of work) more output, i.e., *a higher GNP.*

(Note the socially productive role assigned by this theory to profits, income inequality, and personal saving—the rationale for a "trickle-down" growth strategy. "You can have millionaires, high investment, and growth *or* income equality, low investment, and stagnation.")

Later economists, notably Karl Marx in Europe and Thorstein Veblen in America, adopted a more "qualitative" approach to explaining growth, attributing increased output not just to larger accumulations of physical capital and a bigger labor force but most importantly to *changing technology.* As perceptive social scientists could readily observe after a century of ongoing "industrial revolutions" (recall Chapters 7 and 10), modern economies not only had *more* capital and labor, the resources were qualitatively *better.* Recognition of the dynamic influence of technological progress was the beginning of modern growth theory, and indeed the key to a deeper understanding of the economic process.

Empirical studies during the past 25 years acknowledge the contributions to growth made by technological advance and qualitative improvements in labor (from increased schooling, etc.) as well as capital formation, increased labor supply, economies of large-scale production, and such sources as the reallocation of labor from low-productivity agriculture to higher-productivity industry. The upshot is that economists today explain the process of growth in essentially the same terms we have been using in this book to explain the larger economic process: *Growth is caused by quantitative increases and qualitative improvements in resources, technology, and institutions.*

In a famous study of the sources of U.S. growth for the period 1929-1957, Edward Denison attributed 34% of the increase in output to the quantitative increase in hours of labor; 23% to improvements in the quality of labor resulting from "investments" in education; 20% to advances in technology; 15% to the increased stock of capital; and 9% to economies of scale. In a subsequent study for 1948-1969 he found that increased labor contributed 24%, increased capital 21%, increased education 12%, improvements in resource allocation 9%, and improved technology 34%. (Updated to 1981, the latter study found labor's quantitative contribution to be 19% and capital's 15% with education contributing 19% while technology and other factors accounted for 47% of the increase in production.)

Looking beyond specific numbers, it is clear that growth results chiefly from *more labor and capital,* from the *embodiment of knowledge* in both capital and labor, and from a variety of *institutional changes* that improve the allocation of resources. It should be noted that when the stock of capital is increased, the new plant and equipment typically embody the latest technology; hence capital formation and technological improvements are conjoined. *Capital investment is the operational mechanism for introducing advanced technology into the system.*

For a particular country at a given stage of economic development, an appropriate growth strategy may focus on capital formation and resource reallocation; for another economy, the current need may be qualitative improvements in the labor force. A more mature economy may require major breakthroughs in new technology. There is no simple formula that will ensure optimal growth for all countries at all times. In the 1980s, a low-income economy like China's, for example, appears to be benefiting most from increased reliance on market-type institutions plus the accumulation of relatively unsophisticated capital. For the United States, the emphasis on modernization of physical capital (as opposed, for example, to heavier outlays on education) seems to be proving effective, though not without opportunity costs and side effects. After eight years of stagnation in productivity growth, averaging well below 1% per year, output per hour in 1983 and 1984—for a number of reasons, to be sure—rose 3% per year in the American economy.

Consequences of Growth

The *effects* of growth are manifold. Higher *GNP* means a larger income pie—more goods and services to consume, more capacity for capital formation, and more resources available for allocation through the public sector (to strengthen national security, for example, and to provide social goods such as education as well as creating a more favorable political climate for antipoverty programs). To quote a popular showtune, "What you get depends on what you want"; the *effects* of growth depend to a great extent on value decisions that people make about its preferred *uses.*

Historically, Americans have opted to use their growing output for all of the purposes indicated above—consumption, investment, and public goods—as well as for more *leisure* (the average work week declined from 63 hours in 1880 to 35 in 1982), improvements in the conditions of worklife (e.g., higher standards for occupational health and safety), protection of the environment, and aid to less fortunate peoples at home and abroad (through public and private economic assistance). Such choices are a reflection of the nation's overall value system, including the traditional American propensity for more-always-more consumer goods and services (particularly services, the desire for which may truly be insatiable!).

Growth has given Americans indoor plumbing, central heating, electricity, telephone service (in 97% of households), and home appliances (142 million TV sets in 1980); abundant (and relatively safe) food and drugs; and 130 million automobiles, along with four million miles of highways. It has raised the average person's schooling from less than a grammar school education before 1900 to a level beyond high school graduation today, with one of every four adults holding a 4-year college degree. Growth also enables us (and makes it necessary?) to spend some $400 billion per year on medical care and almost as much for "protective services"—national security, police protection, etc.—such "defensive" goods and services accounting for about one-fifth of our *GNP.*

Not all effects of growth are determined by such discretionary actions as the choices people make in consumer markets or through the institutions of democratic government. (In speaking of "effects" of growth, one tends to think in scientific terms of cause-and-effect, the demonstration of which is sometimes dubious to say the least. The present discussion focuses on concomitants, correlates, or consequences of growth as experienced historically in the United States and other industrial economies.) Much has been proclaimed, for example, about water and air pollution (recall the musical satire: "Don't drink the water and don't breathe the air"); land pollution (radiation, herbicides, pesticides, erosion, pit-mine despoliation); urban blight (slums, crime, congestion, noise, personal isolation); thermal pollution (the greenhouse effect of heat generated by industrial processes on the earth's surface); and increased population both worldwide (up from 1 billion in 1850 to 2 billion by 1930 and 4.7 billion in 1983) and in the United States (from 140 million in 1946 to 240 million today). Perhaps the most harmful of growth's side effects is the "encapsula-tion" of individuals by collective thinking and materialistic values—the ultimate "dark-side" expression of Thorstein Veblen's "cultural incidence of the machine process."

Growth and Economic Wellbeing

It should be clear from the foregoing discussion that economic growth is not necessarily synonymous with increased wellbeing. *GNP* is a measure of production and quite properly is regarded as one important indicator of a system's performance. But "other things" are not always equal in the economic world. The processes and outputs of production historically have generated detriments as well as benefits, "bads" along with goods. (Ironically, when economic actions are taken simply to offset the "bads" this may show up as an *increase* in *GNP*. Example: When "defensive expenditures" of $5 billion are made to produce antipollution equipment needed to prevent further damage to human health, the nation's *GNP* rises by $5 billion! When increased outlays are required for police protection and private security systems, does the resulting *GNP* increase really indicate improvements in wellbeing?)

The phenomenon of growth is, therefore, at one and the same time not only a *goal* but a *problem*. Insufficient growth ("stagnation") results in unemployment, business failures, lagging output, rising poverty, declining per-capita incomes, loss of international markets, and a host of other symptoms not excluding diminished national prestige in the world community. It has been argued that a capitalistic market system "must grow or die." Without year-by-year increases in aggregate demand the economy cannot provide full employment—nor meet other requisites for survival—and will therefore stagnate. Sociopolitical pressures arising from "zero economic growth" could trigger such widespread adjustments in economic institutions (notably an expansion of government planning) that capitalism would erode away. (Failure to make the institutional adjustments might lead to utter collapse of the economic system, perhaps along lines of the Marxist scenario.)

Too Much Success?

On the other hand, if the goal of continuing growth is *achieved,* energy and other natural resources are depleted, the environment is polluted, income inequality and world poverty increase (see Chapter 29), and in such affluent industrial nations as the United States *individuals* "drown in a sea of goods, statistics, and uncontrollable technological change." Doomsday studies such as the highly publicized statement in the 1970s by the Club of Rome (an international organization of business leaders, scientists, and academicians) predict that the limits of world economic growth may be reached before the year 2100. (Such long-range forecasts are always notoriously unreliable, even though the studies are valuable for creating awareness of real problems.)

Somewhat cynically perhaps, others acknowledge that economic growth can continue indefinitely as consumers increasingly "take in each others' washing," i.e., as the composition of *GNP* turns from goods to such labor-intensive *services* as child care, fast-food/restaurant dining, commercial entertainment, mass lifelong education, information processing and sales activities, litigation, and government services—all of which swell the *GNP* statistics. Whether such growth is real or illusory, clearly it *differs* in a substantial way from the industrial growth experience of the first two-thirds of the 20th century.

Beyond Quantitative Growth

If economic *growth* were somehow an adequate goal for the U.S. economy in years past, it hardly seems so today. (Note, however, that what may be true for us is not necessarily true for other countries; economic growth remains a useful rule-of-thumb objective for many low-income nations of the world.) What the American economy needs in the 1980s and 1990s, as more and more observers avow, is not merely quantitative growth but *qualitative development* and genuine *progress*. The meaning of these terms, and some key considerations in pursuing the goals, will be considered in Part Six.

Selected Readings and References

Edward F. Denison, *The Sources of Economic Growth in the United States and the Alternatives Before Us.* Supplementary Paper No. 13. New York: Committee for Economic Development, January 1962. (Denison is also the author of *Why Growth Rates Differ,* Brookings Institution, 1967; *Accounting for U.S. Economic Growth 1929-1969,* Brookings, 1974; and *Accounting for Slower Economic Growth: The United States in the 1970s,* Brookings, 1979.)

Simon Kuznets, "The Pattern of U.S. Economic Growth," in *The Goal of Economic Growth,* Rev. ed. Edited by Edmund S. Phelps. New York: W.W. Norton, 1969.

W. Arthur Lewis, *The Theory of Economic Growth.* Homewood, IL: Irwin, 1955.

R.G. Lipsey and P.O. Steiner, "Are There Limits to Growth?" pp. 815-818 in the sixth edition of their book *Economics* (cited in Chapter 1).

P.A. Samuelson and W.D. Nordhaus, *Economics,* 12th ed. (cited in Chapter 6).

E.F. Schumacher, *Small is Beautiful: Economics as if People Mattered* (cited in Appendix to Chapter 14).

Adam Smith, *The Wealth of Nations* (cited in Chapter 12).

Paul M. Sweezy, *The Theory of Capitalist Development.* New York: Oxford University Press, 1942.

Economic Report of the President (cited in Chapter 15).

Statistical Abstract of the United States (cited in Chapter 15).

Survey of Current Business (cited in Chapter 15).

Productivity Policy: Key to the Nation's Economic Future. A Statement on National Policy. New York: Committee for Economic Development, April 1983.

PART FIVE
PROBLEMS, POLICIES, AND THE CHALLENGE OF INSTITUTIONAL ADJUSTMENT

Not only are the next five chapters longer than most of the earlier ones, the topics are also among the most challenging. Three persistent problems of the American economy—*instability, inequality,* and *power*—are analyzed, along with the multifaceted problems of *international economic relations.* Policies for coping with these problems must reflect not only theory and ideology but the volatile facts and values that are asserting their force in the nation and around the world. In response to *dynamic technology,* societies must unceasingly adjust their *institutional arrangements* in the interest of more effective and equitable economic performance. (Note: Chapter 8 should be reviewed, especially the concluding section on the principles of institutional adjustment.) Chapters 25 and 26 deal with the historic bugaboo of market economies, macroeconomic instability resulting in *unemployment* and *inflation.* Chapter 27 applies the five-step method of policy analysis to capitalism's endemic problem of inequality and *poverty.* Chapter 28 extends the analysis of inequality to the sociopolitical sphere with an examination of the *concentration of power.* And Chapter 29 looks at *international problems* concerning trade, the continuing struggle between capitalism and socialism, and the plight of the poor nations. Because policy discussions inevitably reflect the perceptions and values of particular individuals, readers should take any conclusions and recommendations with a grain of salt; there are no universally correct answers in the field of economic policy.

The Business Cycle, Unemployment, and Inflation

Throughout the 250-year era of industrial capitalism, periodic "recessions" and "recoveries" have characterized the market economies. Since 1854, a total of 30 *business cycles* have been experienced in the United States, an average of one every 4½ years. No simple theory of causation has evolved. Effects of short-run instability include lost output, insecurity, and human burdens distributed unequally among workers, consumers, business firms, and governmental units. A major problem of recession is higher *unemployment*, while periods of economic expansion have stimulated *inflation*. Since the late 1960s, high unemployment and inflation have often occurred simultaneously, giving rise to the problem of *"stagflation."*

What goes up must come down.

Instability, like inequality, is a congenital disease of capitalism.
  —(conventional aphorisms)

If a standard supply-and-demand diagram symbolizes *microeconomic equilibrium*, then Figure 25.1, showing ups and downs of the nation's overall economic activity, may perhaps be regarded as the classic symbol of *macroeconomic instability*. Indeed, the supply-and-demand model shows how employed resources are (more of less) efficiently allocated among alternative uses, whereas Figure 25.1 reminds us that large quantities of available resources periodically are *not employed at all* (while at other times, spending outstrips resource supply and triggers inflation.)

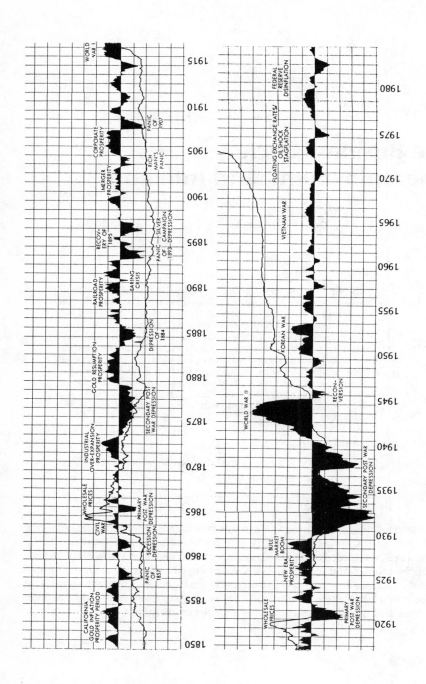

Figure 25.1   Business Cycles in the United States, 1850 to 1983

Source: The Ameritrust Company, Cleveland, Ohio

History of Business Cycles

Charts such as these (sometimes measuring more than a yard across) depict 30 business cycles occurring since 1854. On the down side, the biggest blob of black ink (which should be red!) is the decade-long Great Depression of the 1930s. Since World War II ended in 1945, the National Bureau of Economic Research (a nongovernmental organization that serves as our nation's unofficial "cycle watcher") has recorded nine cycles; and as this book goes to press in late 1985 economists are predicting number 10. It has been said that death and taxes are the two things that cannot be avoided in this world. In market economies it hardly seems an exaggeration to add the business cycle as a third inevitability. (Whether and to what extent similar economic cycles occur in planned socialist economies is subject to some debate.)

Phases of the Cycle

Figure 25.2 illustrates the four phases of the business cycle: *expansion, peak, recession,* and *trough.* (The rich vocabulary of cycle literature also includes such terms as recovery, upper turning point, contraction, and lower turning point; prosperity and depression; upswing and downswing; boom and bust; growth recessions; and even "rolling readjustments.") The frequency and duration of cycles varies considerably but averages one about every 4½ years (or one every 8-10 years for "major cycles"). Recessions typically last a year to 18 months, while expansions average about three years (the two compressed cycles of 1980-1982 were highly unusual). The most recent trough, as of this writing, was November 1982, followed by a strong recovery in 1983 and 1984 (recording the highest year-to-year economic growth in over 30 years) and continuing in 1985. If the economy turns downward in 1986 it should not surprise students of economic history. On the other hand, there is certainly nothing automatic or inevitable about a four- or five-year cycle. There is not

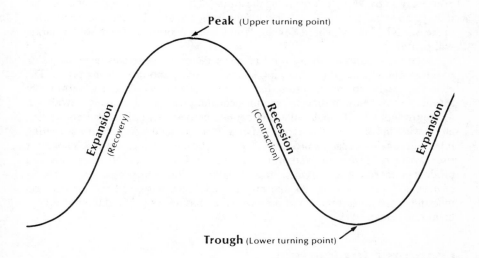

Figure 25.2   *The Four Phases of the Business Cycle*

even a "formula" definition of recession and the other phases of the cycle. (The National Bureau rejects the rule-of-thumb view that two consecutive quarters of decline in real *GNP* constitutes a recession; their own definition of recession as "a recurring period of decline in total output, income, employment, and trade, usually lasting six months to a year..." relies upon the professional judgment of their Business Cycle Dating Committee to designate peaks and troughs.)

The Cycle in Economic Theory

The phenomenon of periodic "general gluts" (as T. R. Malthus termed the recession problem in the early 1800s) or cycles of "prosperity and depression" (the title of a classic book published by the League of Nations in 1937) has lurked in the background of mainstream economics for two centuries. The endemic instability of capitalism, with its recurring "industrial crises," was a major theme of Karl Marx. American economic history is replete with accounts of periodic financial "panics" (e.g., the Panic of 1837, of 1857, 1873, 1893, 1907, etc.). Every schoolchild has heard of the Great Stock Market Crash (of October 1929), leading to the Great Depression ("cured" after 11 painful years not by rational economic policy but, as certain economists take impish pleasure in pointing out, by Adolf Hitler and Japanese imperialism).

Although numerous explanations have been proposed (including financial specula-tion, investment surges prompted by technological innovations, errors of public policy, random events, sunspots, etc.), no definitive theory of business cycles has been forthcoming. This is not really surprising. Given the intricacy and dynamism of the economic process *seasonal, short-run,* and *long-run* fluctuations in economic activity are inevitable; why, then, expect a simple theory for such a complex phenomenon? Thanks to modern statistical programs and econometric techniques however—such as the system of "leading economic indicators"—a great deal is known about the *behavior* of economic cycles. And history does suggest that "what comes down will eventually go back up." (Forecasting the timing of the ups and downs remains an art rather than an exact science—a talent that offers rich financial rewards for those who, in the words of John Maynard Keynes, "know better than the market how the market will perform.")

Economic *expansion* (the upward phase of the cycle) generates increased sales, profits, employment, production, investment, income, and often rising prices. The economy begins to import more, interest rates edge upward, and governmental revenues grow. New businesses are formed; the poverty rate moves downward. Money wages rise, through collective bargaining between unions and employers, along with "normal" market forces. After a period of recovery, industry utilization rates press against capacity, productivity growth begins to slow, and unit labor costs rise. During *recession* sales and profits decline, workers are laid off, wage rates and product prices stabilize, consumers react to falling incomes by postponing purchases of durable goods (such as cars and major appliances), business firms cut back on investment spending, production declines, some businesses fail, and the unemploy-ment rate rises.

Economic Insecurity

While the above sketch approximates reality, in practice the scenario varies from cycle to cycle. What is clear is that many people—but by no means all!—are *hurt* by economic downturns; and *burdens are unevenly distributed* among various business firms, workers, consumers, and the providers and beneficiaries of government services. Periodic recessions cost the American economy $100 billion per year or more in lost output—vast quantities of housing, food, mass transit, capital equipment, environmental improvements, and other valuable goods and services that might have been made available to the American people (not to mention poverty-stricken peoples of the Third World).

In terms of individual human beings, there is loss of income and self-esteem accompanying unemployment, financial and personal tragedies associated with business failure; there is a rise in social dependency and such pathologies as alcoholism, drug abuse, violence, marital breakdown, crime, suicide, and both physical and mental illness (all of which are documented correlates of joblessness). Moreover, the past record of economic instability breeds the expectation that the whole pattern will repeat itself again and again, and the fear that sooner or later the worker's own number will come up. (Among other effects this sense of insecurity can undermine the spririt of workers and induce social and political behavior aimed at preserving one's own job "at all costs," regardless of implications for productivity, equity, or human dignity.)

As many economists have pointed out (see the quote from Keynes in Chapter 27), *instability* and *inequality* seem to be inherent in a market society. And it is precisely in the *downward phase of the business cycle* that these two problems manifest themselves so dramatically, in *unemployment* and *loss of earnings*. Information about employment and unemployment has already been presented in a variety of contexts in this book (e.g., in Chapters 6, 15, 19, 20, and 22). What remains to be done with the subject in this chapter and the next is to sketch a framework for viewing the overall problem of unemployment—types, causes, effects—and consider the various approaches required for dealing with the problem.

Unemployment

We learned in Chapter 15 that "unemployment" is not quite the same thing as not having a job. For purposes of economic analysis, only *involuntary* unemployment is taken into account; a worker is involuntarily unemployed only if he or she doesn't have a job but is able to work and is actively seeking employment. The Bureau of Labor Statistics calculates unemployment rates for the overall labor force as well as particular categories of workers. In 1982, for example, the total unemployment rate *(TUR)* averaged 9.5% (the highest level since 1941). In seeking to explain *why* unemployment was that high a manpower economist might begin by pointing out that the 9.5% rate reflected *three types of unemployment:* (1) *cyclical,* caused by insufficient market demand (see Chapter 22, including Appendix); (2) *structural;* and (3) *frictional.* While one-third to one-half of the 9.5% rate could be accounted for in cyclical terms, perhaps as much as two-thirds of total unemployment arose from "structural" and "frictional" causes. In other words, a substantial amount was "core unemployment" in the sense that it would not melt away by cyclical expansion, as indeed the experience of 1983 and 1984 demonstrated.

The cause of "cyclical unemployment" is insufficient spending in product markets to enable business firms to sell all the goods and services that can be produced by the nation's available resources. This insufficiency of aggregate demand (i.e., *GNP* spending by consumers, business investors, government, and foreigners buying our exports) typically occurs during the recession phase of the business cycle, hence the name. But this spending shortfall could also exist in other situations such as during the expansion phase of a low-level cycle that never carries actual production to the economy's full potential. Since the "age of Keynes," this type of unemployment has been considered more controllable by short-run public policy than the other kinds. In fact, according to Keynesian theory, appropriate monetary and fiscal policies (discussed in Chapter 26) would completely eliminate cyclical unemployment, thereby achieving "full employment," defined as an unemployment rate of somewhere around 3% to 4%.

What remained would be *structural* unemployment—caused by technological changes, geographic shifts of industry, foreign competition, obsolete worker skills, and generally a mismatch of employment opportunities and available human resources—and *frictional* unemployment—caused by imperfections or "frictions" in the system such as delays in job placement, geographic relocation of workers, seasonal variations in production and sales, and the like. This persistent core of unemployment could be pushed lower only through institutional adjustments that improved the structure of the economy and made labor markets more effective. (Thus, "full employment" really means jobs for about 96% of the labor force, not 100%.) Note that workers who are unemployed for structural and frictional reasons are nevertheless *involuntarily* unemployed, and in fact may be worse off than cyclically unemployed "job losers" because they may not be qualified for unemployment compensation and certain other labor-market benefits. This group of nonjob-losers includes new entrants to the labor force (e.g., recent graduates) and re-entrants (e.g., "displaced homemakers") as well as job-changers.

By mid-1985, after 32 months of cyclical expansion, the *TUR* was down to 7.3% and holding steady. No one could say for sure how much of this unemployment could still be attributed to insufficient aggregate demand, but many economists were beginning to think that the new level of "full employment," at least for the next few years, will leave "core unemployment" around 7%. Structural adjustments and supply-side policies such as deregulation of industry, modernization of capital, expanded research and development, better educational programs, stronger incentives for work and investment, improvements in labor-market information (perhaps through revitalization of the Public Employment Service), and time itself would be required to reduce this core rate.

Demand-Pull Inflation

In the expansion phase of the cycle, the economy may "overheat" and trigger the particular type of inflation called *"demand-pull" inflation* (recall from Chapter 22 of the definition of inflation as a rise in the general level of prices). This is the counterpart in Keynesian macroeconomic theory (see appendix to Chapter 22) of insufficient-demand unemployment. Thus, not enough market demand (*GNP* expenditures) causes *unemployment,* too much market demand causes *inflation,* and precisely the right amount of demand generates *full-employment-without-inflation.*

Demand-pull inflation results from "too much spending chasing too few goods." Recalling the four groups of spenders in the *GNP* equation *($GNP = C + I + G + X_n$),* one cannot say off-hand that demand-pull inflation is caused by "too much government spending," for example, any more than one can place the blame specifically on consumers or business investors or exporters. It is *total* spending that is excessive in relation to the economy's ability to produce sufficient quantities of output to meet market demand at existing prices. Essentially this inability arises when additional spending (typically financed by the expansion of credit and growth of the monetary stock) can no longer call forth additional resources for production because the pool of previously unemployed resources has been exhausted. In other words, demand-pull inflation occurs when spending continues to rise after full employment is achieved. The cure for the problem, therefore, is to reduce aggregate demand or find a quick way to increase output (which is no easy task). Public policies for coping with this and other types of inflation, as well as unemployment and lagging growth, are discussed in the next chapter.

Cost-Push Inflation and Other Types

Demand-pull (or "classic") inflation is not the only type of inflation that plagues the U.S. economy; there is also *cost-push inflation.* (Two further types that warrant identification are "structural" and "random-shock" inflation. *Structural inflation* results from changes in the composition of demand such that prices rise, predictably, in expanding industries where demand temporarily outstrips supply; but in shrinking industries, where supply exceeds demand, market power prevents price reductions. *Random-shock inflation*—a variant of the cost-push hypothesis—is caused by such events as wars, crop failures, and OPEC's 1973-1974 embargo and 1979-1980 oil price increases.) With cost-push inflation it is not simply increased demand that forces the price level up but increases in wages, interest rates, the cost of materials, and even taxes and required profit margins. (In technical terms, higher costs of production shift supply curves to the left where they intersect demand curves at higher prices.) As applied to labor costs, this is the familiar "wage-price spiral." For example, unions and management negotiate a 6% increase in money wages and the corporation announces higher prices for its products—even before aggregate demand rises. But the same thing can also happen with other factor costs, notably interest. If a merchant must pay 15% to borrow funds to purchase his inventory, other things being equal in our less-than-perfectly competitive economy, he will pass along the interest costs by charging his customers higher prices. The overwhelming effect of high mortgage rates on construction and home purchases is well known.

It should be noted that the cost-push explanation is not purely a one-sided theory of inflation; it still requires assumptions about demand, just as the demand-pull theory assumes certain conditions regarding supply. The chief merit of the cost-push hypothesis lies in its focus on such real-world circumstances as market power (of corporations and unions), expectations ("rational" and otherwise), and governmental responsibilities (e.g., legislative mandates to promote full unemployment)—thereby inducing a much-needed reexamination of the simplified Keynesian model.

The Problem of "Stagflation"

Until the 1970s it was customary for economists to consider the problems of unemployment and inflation in terms of either-or. "Today we are suffering unemployment, but at least the price level is under control; next year we hope for full employment but probably will be battling inflation." Textbooks displayed a "Phillips curve" showing the tradeoff between given rates of unemployment and inflation; designated fiscal and monetary policies could supposedly be implemented to put the economy anywhere on the curve that we might choose. No more. For a decade the U.S. economy experienced *"stagflation"*—the simultaneous occurrence of high unemployment (and lagging growth) *plus* high inflation (i.e., stagnation + inflation). In 1974, for example, with unemployment at 5.6% (considerably above the 3% to 4% "full employment" level) the Consumer Price Index rose 12.2%; in 1977 the *TUR* averaged 7.1% while the *CPI* rose 6.8%. And on the eve of President Reagan's election in 1980, unemployment stood at 7.1% in tandem with double-digit inflation (13.3% in 1979, 12.4% in 1980). The dean of American economists, Professor Paul Samuelson of M.I.T. (himself a Nobel laureate) observed that a Nobel Prize awaited the person who could show the guided market economies of the West how to cope with "this new scourge."

So far no economist has claimed the prize. There have been no theoretical breakthroughs within the neoclassical tradition to explain the phenomenon of stagflation, although two important changes in macroeconomic thinking have occurred. First, a great deal more attention is now paid to the *monetary stock* and the influence it has on aggregate demand and the general level of prices. And second, there has been a resurgence of interest in the *supply side* of the economic process, including the effect of "autonomous" cost increases on prices, production, and employment. Both factors influence current thinking about *public policies* aimed at promoting stability and growth, the subject of the next chapter.

The problem of stagflation has also brought home to mainstream economists some insights from the legacy of evolutionary-institutional economics. Prominent among these lessons are the impact of technological change on the institutional fabric of society, the powerful influence of social and political forces on economic life, and the centrality of value issues (see Chapter 30) in developing policies for economic progress. It is no accident that Adam Smith's term "Political Economy" is staging a comeback as a label for the economics discipline, nor that economists of the left and right have reached so much agreement on the need for institutional adjustments of one kind or another to reinvigorate the American economy.

Selected Readings and References

R.L. Heilbroner and A. Singer, *The Economic Transformation of America* (cited in Chapter 20).

C.H. Hession and H. Sardy, *Ascent to Affluence: A History of American Economic Development* (cited in Chapter 10).

Wesley Clair Mitchell, *Business Cycles and their Causes.* Berkeley: University of California Press, 1941. (Originally published as Part III of *Business Cycles,* 1913.)

Geoffrey H. Moore, *Business Cycles, Inflation, and Forecasting,* 2d ed. Cambridge, MA: Ballinger, 1980 (for National Bureau of Economic Research).

R.D. Peterson, "Business Cycles: Recessions and Depressions," *Colorado Economic Issues,* Vol. 5, No. 5 (January 1981), Colorado State University, Fort Collins, Colorado. (Distinguishes six phases of a business cycle: Peak, Contraction, Recession, Trough, Recovery, Expansion; and depicts the economy's growth trend in relation to recurring cycles.)

Paul Studenski and H.E. Krooss, *Financial History of the United States,* 2d ed. (Fiscal, Monetary, Banking, and Tariff). New York: McGraw-Hill, 1963.

Business Conditions Digest. Bureau of Economic Analysis, U.S. Department of Commerce. (Monthly)

Economic Report of the President (cited in Chapter 15).
Statistical Abstract of the United States (cited in Chapter 15).
Historical Statistics of the United States, Colonial Times to 1970 (cited in Chapter 15).
Survey of Current Business (cited in Chapter 15).

Public Policies for Stability and Growth

Since the 1940s it has been the declared responsibility of the federal government to promote *macroeconomic stability*. Although a wide range of policy instruments can be used to pursue the goals of stability and growth, major reliance traditionally was placed on "demand-side" *fiscal* and *monetary* policies. With stagflation reaching crisis proportions in the late 1970s, however, increased attention turned to "supply-side" policies designed to correct structural problems and promote *growth* in the American economy. By 1982, the *inflation* rate had dropped sharply and remained moderate throughout the vigorous economic expansion of 1983-1984. Meanwhile, after rising to distressingly high levels in 1982-1983, *unemployment* declined in 1984 but continued well above rates traditionally associated with full employment.

"The Congress hereby declares that it is the continuing policy and responsibility of the Federal Government to use all practical means...to promote maximum employment, production, and purchasing power."
   —Employment Act of 1946

"[It is the] policy and responsibility of the Federal Government...to promote full employment and production, increased real income, balanced growth, a balanced Federal budget...and reasonable price stability ...[and] to rely principally on the private sector for expansion of economic activity and creation of new jobs for a growing labor force."
   —Full Employment and Balanced Growth Act of 1978

The back-to-back occurrence of the Great Depression (1930-1941) and World War II (1942-1945) seem from the economist's point of view almost like a "controlled experiment" decreed by fate. The two events set the stage for enactment of what has been called the most significant piece of economic legislation in American history, the Employment Act of 1946.

The Depression appeared to demonstrate that a mature market economy, left to its own tendencies, might remain far below the full-employment level not just for two or three years but indefinitely. Unemployment, which had climbed from 3.2% in 1929 to a depression peak of 24.9% in 1933 (see Statistical Reference Table in Chapter 15), still measured 14.6% in 1940 and 9.9% in 1941. World War II showed that a massive infusion of government spending (in this case, for wartime mobilization) could restore the nation to full employment and full production. The total unemployment rate for all civilian workers dropped to 4.7% in 1942 and below 2% for the remaining three years of the war. Real *GNP* rose by 15% in 1942 and by 1944 was 42% above the 1941 level. (True, the drain of people into the armed forces removed large numbers of potentially unemployed workers; but new entrants into the labor force fully offset the drain, and *civilian employment* rose by several millions.)

Government's "War Against Unemployment"

When the war ended, Congress was determined not to permit the country to slide back into a major economic depression. With bipartisan support, the Employment Act of 1946 was passed (see the "Declaration of Policy" quoted above). Although deliberately vague when it came to quantitative goals and particular instruments of policy, the Act laid the groundwork for carrying out its general mandate by creating an information system and institutionalizing responsibility for policy leadership, planning, and review. The law established (to assist the President), a three-person Council of Economic Advisers and required publication of an annual *Economic Report of the President,* to be carefully reviewed by a Joint Economic Committee of the Congress (which also exercises initiative in policy studies and deliberation). Through a 1949 resolution, Congress provided for publication of the monthly *Economic Indicators* which, along with the annual Economic Report, serves as an authoritative source of current statistics for monitoring the performance of our economy.

The vagueness in defining policy objectives was overcome some 30 years later with passage of the Full Employment and Balanced Growth Act of 1978 (popularly called the Humphrey-Hawkins Act). In a classic illustration of "enantiodromia" (a tendency to swing toward the opposite), the 1978 legislation (see quote at beginning of chapter) spells out in great detail a laundry list of ancillary goals, constraints, and guidelines along with quantitative specifications that even at that time were generally regarded as unattainable—4% unemployment by 1983 and 0% inflation by 1988. Perhaps the greatest significance of the Act was its explicit commitment to controlling *inflation* and recognition that long-term growth considerations must be kept in mind when formulating policies for short-run economic stabilization. (The language of the Act shows how "the medium can be the message" insofar as its provisions suggest quite dramatically the complexity, multidimensionality, and limited efficacy of modern economic policy, all in all an attitude that contrasts markedly with the "fine-tuning" optimism of the mid-1960s.)

Approaches to Policy

In the previous chapter and brief section above, we have in effect addressed Steps 1 and 2 in the Five-Step Method of Economic Reasoning. The *problems* of unemployment and inflation were defined, and the *goals* of "full employment" and "reasonable price-level stability" along with "balanced growth," were identified. Step 3 calls for consideration of *alternative methods* that might be implemented to pursue the stated goals. (Except for some pertinent observations offered in Chapter 31, we shall leave Step 4—analyzing the probable benefits, costs, and other effects—to the Council of Economic Advisers, Congressional Budget Office, Federal Reserve research staff, and such nongovernmental "think tanks" as Data Resources Inc.; and Step 5—choosing the best solution—to the President, Congress, and Federal Reserve.) In the present context, we want to know *what policy strategies are potentially available for use in seeking to achieve macroeconomic stability and growth.*

Six broad approaches may be identified:

1. General demand-side policies (fiscal policy, monetary policy).
2. Moral suasion (including "guideposts").
3. Structural and supply-side policies.
4. Selective market transactions.
5. Incomes policies.
6. Direct mandatory controls.

Each will be discussed in turn, beginning with general policies that operate on the demand side of the market.

Fiscal Policy

Fiscal policy is the deliberate use of government spending, taxing, and borrowing to influence the overall level of economic activity. In the present context "government" means strictly the federal government, and the intended influence is focused on reducing unemployment and/or inflation. The agents of fiscal policy are the President and Congress, with the Treasury Department providing supportive services (and in some instances the Council of Economic Advisers recommending particular strategies). "Discretionary" policy as opposed to "automatic built-in stabilization" is emphasized, and unless otherwise stated Keynesian aggregate-demand theory serves as the basic guide to policy action.

If the economy is threatened with *insufficient demand* (recall Chapter 25), compensatory fiscal policy calls for tax cuts, increased government purchases of goods and services, increased government transfers payments, and deficit-financing (i.e., Treasury borrowing to make up the difference between expenditures and tax revenues). *Tax cuts*—such as lower rates or higher exemptions in the personal income tax, which can take effect quickly through reduced withholding—will leave households with more disposable income and therefore encourage increased personal consumption expenditures. Other things being equal, this raises *GNP* (effective aggregate demand) thereby stimulating sales, production, and employment. Reductions in excise taxes, social security contributions, and business taxes also tend to counter cyclical unemployment. On the other hand, structural and frictional unemployment are unresponsive to general tax reductions per se.

On the *spending* side, government can pump income into the economy by launching public works projects (e.g., building or repairing highways, bridges, dams, etc.), undertaking environmental improvements, or speeding up procurements in defense or other areas. This type of spending ("government purchases of goods and services") directly increases aggregate demand. (Note that the "general" nature of fiscal policy is already dubious in that expenditures do not rise across the board but involve particular projects.) With one in every three Americans participating in government benefit programs (see References, Chapter 19), it becomes administratively easier to pump purchasing power into the economy by means of transfer payments. While this form of government spending is not as direct as purchases of goods and services, it has the advantage of reaching people who are extremely likely to spend their newly-found income without delay.

When spending exceeds tax revenues, the federal budget incurs a *deficit* (the opposite of a budget surplus). Money could be directly created to cover the deficit (under the Constitution, Congress has power to "coin money"), but tradition calls for the Treasury to *borrow* from banks, households, business, or foreigners, thereby increasing the *national debt*. It is true that public borrowing may reduce private purchasing power, but until recent concern with the "crowding-out" effect on private investment, Keynesians did not regard this as a serious difficulty.

Fiscal Policy to Fight Inflation

If expansionary fiscal policy can help prevent or cure cyclical unemployment, what can fiscal policy do about *inflation?* The answer is the reverse of what was said above: Anti-inflationary fiscal policy may prevent or cure *demand-pull* inflation, but can do very little about cost-push or other types of inflation. If the threat is excessive demand, government can raise taxes and/or cut its own spending. ("Can" is not the same as "will"; political considerations, such as affinities for campaign contributions and votes at election time, often get in the way of rational economic policy.) Again, it is virtually impossible to raise taxes or cut spending "in general." There are always burdens to distribute, which fall on particular groups and individuals. The upshot is that *expansionary* fiscal policy has always been more popular than *anti-inflationary* ("restrictive") fiscal policy. Given the cyclical nature of macroeconomic instability, an *inflationary bias* is introduced into the policy system, and this tends to diminish professional support for *discretionary* fiscal policy (based on ad hoc decisionmaking) as opposed to *built-in stability.*

Monetary Policy and the Federal Reserve

Monetary policy refers to actions taken by the Federal Reserve System to influence the cost and availability of money and credit for the purpose of promoting economic stability and growth. Our nation's *monetary authority* (or "central bank") is the Federal Reserve System (see Chapter 21), operating under powers delegated by Congress. The direct agents of monetary policy, therefore, are not the President and Congress but principally the Board of Governors of the Federal Reserve System, its Chairman, and the Federal Open Market Committee (with the Treasury Department of course performing various functions that affect money, credit, and interest rates).

To understand the role of the "Fed," it is essential to bear in mind that its basic purpose is to ensure that the U.S. economy has a sound financial structure "in all seasons," so to speak. This means promoting efficient day-to-day banking, providing sufficient money and credit growth in the long run, and adapting its policies in the short run to help combat inflationary pressures, unemployment, or imbalances in transactions with foreign countries. It is not just a mechanism for implementing Keynesian monetary policy.

The tools of monetary policy include open-market operations, discount policy, and changing reserve requirements. (Selective credit controls are mentioned below under the heading of direct controls.) With the economy facing a situation of insufficient aggregate demand, the Fed is likely to initiate an "easy money" policy (to work in tandem with expansionary fiscal policy). Actions would include lowering the discount rate (the interest rate Federal Reserve Banks charge on loans to their commercial-bank clients) and—far more important—*buying* government securities on the open market (i.e., from business firms, banks, and households, NOT new issues from Treasury). The effect would be to increase the excess reserves of banks, thereby enabling them to create *new money* via the lending process (recall Chapter 21).

The Fed could also reduce reserve requirements (the percentage of current deposit obligations that banks must hold in the form of vault cash or balances at Federal Reserve Banks); but this technique is seldom utilized. *Open market operations*—the purchase and sales of government securities—constitute the *principal tool of monetary policy.* (The buying and selling decisions are made by the Federal Open Market Committee and implemented by the Federal Reserve Bank of New York.) An increase in the monetary stock (resulting from an open-market purchase) tends to reduce interest rates, which in turn encourages investment (as well as consumption expenditure) and thereby raises aggregate demand.

This money-interest-investment chain of reasoning represents the Keynesian view. During the past decade or so, increasing numbers of economists have become "believers" in a more *direct* mechanism. Following the lead of Nobel laureate Milton Friedman, "monetarists" hold that an increase in the money supply raises aggregate demand directly without having to rely on a tenuous linkage with interest rates and investment.

The Equation of Exchange: MV = PQ

These economists make use of an old truistic formula, the equation of exchange: $MV = PQ$, according to which (by definition) total spending for newly produced goods and services equals the value of production. Thus, the money stock, M, times its velocity of circulation, V, (the number of times each unit of money turns over during the year), equals the average price, P, of newly produced goods and services, Q, i.e., equals P times Q. When certain empirical assumptions are made about the behavior of M, V, P, and Q, the equation of exchange moves beyond truism to become an empirical *theory*. Specifically, when V is assumed to be constant, or to change in a stable, predictable way, one can then predict that a 10% rise in M, for example, would (after a certain time lag) trigger a 10% rise in aggregate demand. Unless production (Q) could somehow rise by 10%, it would inevitably follow that the price level (P) would rise, i.e., *inflation* would result. Why? Because the rise in total spending necessarily triggers a corresponding 10% rise in the money value of the nation's output (they are two sides of the same coin!); and if the quantity of that output cannot rise sufficiently and quickly (because of full employment or rigidities in the employment and production system), the only variable that can change is *P,* the price level. Thus, excessive monetary growth directly triggers inflation.

Monetary Policy to Counter Inflation

When the economy is threatened with demand-pull inflation, the prescription calls for a "tight money" policy. The Fed raises the discount rate (partly to signal the direction that policy is taking) and engages in open-market *sales.* The result is to reduce bank reserves and prevent any further expansion in the supply of money and credit (perhaps even induce reductions). The Fed could also raise reserve requirements (but prefers to avoid this "meat-axe" approach). Interest rates tend to rise, thus discouraging business firms from borrowing to finance real investment; aggregate demand is restrained.

In the monetarist scheme, limiting the growth rate of the monetary stock checks spending directly and prevents further increases in the monetary value of the nation's output. Monetarists basically do not like discretionary monetary policy (making "judgment calls" on when to turn the monetary spigot on or off), preferring the "monetary rule" of a steady increase in the money supply corresponding to the economy's long-run growth pattern.

Inadequacy of Monetary and Fiscal Policy

General fiscal and monetary policy enjoyed high credibility among economists in the 1950s and 1960s on grounds that they were adequate instruments for achieving stabilization while avoiding selective intervention in particular sectors of the economy. Our experience with stagflation proved otherwise. Policy commitments to full employment tended to generate and sustain inflation; after all, high aggregate demand is not only the textbook *cure* for cyclical unemployment but also the *cause* of demand-pull inflation. Nor does "equal treatment" (the premise of general as opposed to selective policy strategies) necessarily distribute burdens evenly among people in *different circumstances.* Squeezing inflation out of the economy through restrictive monetary policy, with its predictable high interest rates, wreaks havoc on the construction industry and home buyers. Expansionary policies that rekindle inflation can wipe out the purchasing power of pensions and savings that are vitally needed by retired persons. Curing inflation with fiscal and monetary restraint can leave millions of workers unemployed and deprived of adequate income, not because that was the *intent* of the policy but nevertheless was a predictable "side effect."

These burdens are illustrated in the experience of the early 1980s, as recounted in Chapter 25. Chiefly as the result of restrictive monetary policy, the rate of inflation was cut from 13.3% in 1979 and 12.4% in 1980 to 3.9% in 1982, 3.8% in 1983, and 4.0% in 1984. Meanwhile the unemployment rate climbed from 7.0% in 1980 to a plateau of 9.5% in 1982 and 1983 before falling back to 7.4% in 1984 (still high by historical standards). What made the situation easier to bear, and lent credibility to the overall mix of economic policies during this period (at least for the people who were not unemployed!) was the dramatic growth the nation experienced in output, capital formation, productivity, and real per-capita income (see Table 15.2).

"Jaw-Boning"

The six broad policy approaches listed above constitute a sort of spectrum from most-*general* to most-*specific* instruments of economic intervention by government. (General as opposed to selective/mandatory policies are regarded as being more *neutral* in terms of the impact they have on market decisions and resource allocation.) Number 2 on the list is *moral suasion,* or exhortation (sometimes called "jaw-boning"). Prominent leaders in effect exhort participants in the economic process to "be reasonable, consider the public interest, and exercise self-restraint." President Kennedy, for example, appealed to the steel industry in 1962 to hold the line on prices; many Presidents have asked labor unions to moderate their wage demands. Federal Reserve officials on occasion pass the word to financial institutions that it is especially important at this time to weigh carefully all loan requests. A key feature of moral suasion (which is always being applied to some extent by wielders of economic power) is voluntary compliance. Of course there is social pressure, sometimes magnified by an accommodating press, but there are seldom outright threats. Wage-and-price guideposts of the 1960s provide an example of moral suasion in *quantified* form ("Do something for your country—don't ask for wage increases that exceed last year's average national increase in productivity"). The trouble is, exhortation doesn't always work—as President Carter learned when he tried it as an anti-stagflation strategy in the late 1970s.

Structural and Supply-Side Approaches

Structural and supply-side policies—Number 3 on the list of approaches—are not really new. Antitrust laws to preserve business competition, labor legislation, and public funding of education and research are familiar examples. But increased attention to the supply side came in the late 1970s in the wake of our long-continuing stagflation. In 1978 the Congressional Joint Economic Committee concluded a 3-year study on prospects for economic growth which stressed that the American economy was entering "a new era in its economic development." In its 1980 bipartisan annual report (issued nine months before President Reagan's election and reiterating themes from its 1979 report), the Committee's Democratic chairman observed that "The past [was] dominated by economists who focused almost exclusively on the *demand* side of the economy and who, as a result, were trapped into believing that there is an inevitable tradeoff between unemployment and inflation." What was needed for the 1980s, by contrast, was adoption of "a comprehensive set of policies designed to enhance the...*supply* side of the economy" (emphasis added).

With the election of Ronald Reagan, the "new era of economic thinking" called for by the JEC (and numerous nonpartisan observers outside government) found expression in "supply-side economics" and "Reaganomics." Putting aside media distortion and extremist versions, President Reagan's supply-side economics was essentially a reaffirmation of classical growth theory (a la Adam Smith, updated to reflect today's high technology) and a marked downgrading of the demand-side theories associated with John Maynard Keynes.

With structural and supply-side policies, emphasis turns from short-run "quick fixes" to the longer run; from compensatory fiscal policy to such structural changes as tax cuts (to raise incentives for work and investment), deregulation, and free trade. In essence, President Reagan's version of supply-side economics placed greater reliance on markets and individual performance, less on regulation and government policies. As of the mid-1980s, the early results include the "mixed bag" of increased output, a remarkably stable price level, higher unemployment, and increased inequality in the distribution of wealth and income. (One structural improvement not yet addressed in the 1980s, despite the Reagan Administration's "efficiency" orientation, is the creation of an effective system of labor-market intermediaries—whether public, private, or cooperative—to help reduce frictional and structural unemployment. Institutional adjustment is sorely needed in this area on grounds of human dignity, to serve workers' needs, as well as efficiency.)

Selective Market Transactions

A fourth policy approach, *selective market transactions,* is by definition more limited than general demand-side policies, moral suasion, or structural and supply-side strategies. Examples include commodity sales from government stockpiles (to augment market supply during periods of temporary shortage, thereby preventing inflationary price increases), intervention in foreign-exchange markets, and *direct job creation* (i.e., if labor demand in normal markets is insufficient to provide jobs for everybody, government enters the market on the demand side as "employer of last resort").

Incomes Policies

Continuing along the spectrum of policy approaches to Number 5, the instrument known as *incomes policies* has attracted professional and political attention for a quarter of a century (in part because a number of European countries have experimented with variants of the strategy). The basic logic of incomes policies is quite simple: If wages, interests, rent, and profits can be prevented from rising excessively, inflation can be prevented. (Income constraints would also be applied to transfer payments and dividends.) As a practical matter, attention has focused on constraining increases in *money wages,* by far the biggest source of personal income and largest component of production costs (hence, a key leverage point for preventing either cost-push *or* demand-pull inflation). Organized labor objects to singling out wages, insisting that all income shares should be subject to the same constraints. This seems quite reasonable but overlooks important problems of an administrative nature as well as complications arising out of the nature of "property" income. In the narrow sense in which "incomes policies" is used in the present discussion—differentiated from *(a)* voluntary compliance, with guideposts established under a strategy of moral suasion, and *(b)* direct mandatory controls over prices, wages, and perhaps other income shares—the United States has never actually tried this approach. Perhaps the most mature proposal was the tax-based incomes policy (TIP) described in Jimmy Carter's last *Economic Report of the President* (January 1981). Employees of firms whose rate of wage increase complied with explicit standards would be awarded a tax *credit;* those employed by firms whose wage increases exceeded the standard would be assessed a tax *penalty.* Application of the TIP to *prices* (which, of course, help determine the incomes of business firms) would pose such overwhelming difficulties that, at most, the program would probably have to be limited to very large firms. (It should be noted that some economists use "incomes policy" to encompass the full range of schemes for constraining wage and price increases, whether compliance is voluntary, mandatory, or subject to rewards or penalties.)

Direct Controls

The sixth and last policy approach for achieving stability and growth reaches the upper limit of the spectrum, *direct mandatory controls*. The classic example is a wartime economy in which prices, wages, profits, and other forms of income are frozen; materials and labor are allocated according to government priorities; and consumer goods are rationed to preserve some measure of equity in the face of scarcities. In other words, the market mechanism is temporarily shelved in the interests of effective mobilization for the war effort. (Another example is the *comprehensive planning* practiced by socialist/communist economies as a *peacetime* norm.) During World War II, the U.S. economy was indeed subjected to comprehensive wage and price controls. During the Korean War, controls were more limited. On several occasions *selective credit controls* have been imposed (e.g., on home buying, purchases of automobiles, and frequently on borrowing to purchase shares of stock, i.e., "margin requirements"). In 1971, in an effort to cope with "the new scourge" of stagflation, President Nixon issued an Executive Order freezing prices, wages, and rents. This provided the U.S. economy its most recent experience with wage-price controls.

One never knows the full effects of direct mandatory controls—on production, employment, resource allocation, incentives, saving, investment, productivity, or even on actual prices paid and received in the market. Inequity, circumvention of controls, and profiteering are virtually inevitable. Trading on "the black market" undermines the tax system, social morality, and the accuracy of economic statistics (which are used, among other purposes, to evaluate the effectiveness of the price-control program). Illicit transactions are also known to promote violent crime.

To the extent that one respects the market as a mechanism for allocating resources and motivating production, controls are more or less anathema. What the record shows for the period of the Nixon price-wage freeze is that the rate of inflation (measured by the Consumer Price Index) declined from 5.5% in 1970 to a plateau of 3.4% in 1971 and 1972, then rose to 8.8% in 1973. By 1974, when the freeze was phased out (also the year of the first OPEC oil-price shock), the inflation rate soared to double digits (12.2%) for the first time since 1946 (when price controls were removed at the end of World War II).

For reasons enumerated above, economists generally do not like direct mandatory controls. Because they are temporary, they may do little more than postpone a rise in prices ("repressed inflation"), meanwhile engendering allocative inefficiencies, disincentives, and inequities. In wartime, when military victory is the goal and patriotism combined with force is the mechanism, price and wage controls are imperative and reasonably effective; in peacetime, American society does not seem ready to accommodate that particular form of institutional adjustment.

The "Uneasy Triangle"

Figure 26.1 illustrates the "Triangle of Policy Goals." Before the Great Depression, mainstream economists held that all three goals were simultaneously attainable

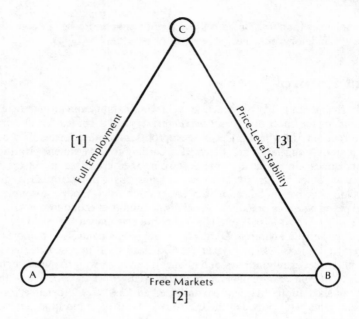

Figure 26.1   *The Uneasy Triangle of Policy Goals*

through the normal functioning of the market. In his 1936 book, Keynes argued that institutional characteristics being what they were in the modern economy (notably money, market power, and attitudes about wage rates), the only way all three goals could be achieved is through government control of aggregate demand, using compensatory fiscal and monetary policies. By the 1960s (under the influence of the Phillips-curve hypothesis alluded to in Chapter 25), many Keynesians in effect had added the letters A, B, C to the diagram. These represented "policy packages" that were capable of delivering any *two* of the goals, but at the cost of sacrificing the third. Option "A" entailed the selection of free markets and full employment as priority goals, while relegating a stable price level to secondary status. Option "B" emphasized free markets and avoidance of inflation at the cost of high unemployment. Option "C" placed top priority on full employment and price-level stability even if it required some form of wage-price controls. (Liberal Democrats tended to favor A while conservative Republicans leaned toward B. Advocates of Option C offered cogent arguments but seldom mustered broad political support.)

The stagflation of the 1970s forced a total reexamination of the "uneasy-triangle" framework, based as it was on Keynesian demand-side theory. Today there is a growing consensus that none of the designated options is truly viable. This is the message of the Joint Economic Committee report cited earlier and in effect represents the "new era of economic thinking" that focuses on structural and supply-side policies. By no means will this approach be limited to President Reagan's "neo-laissez-faire" policy, however. Future administrations predictably will swing back to greater reliance on programs entailing government expenditures to promote growth and stability. But almost certainly the emphasis will be on the *structure* of the economy rather than predominantly demand-side as was the case for some 40 years.

Historians will likely view the early 1980s as a watershed in American economic policy. This is true not only because of the role that monetary policy played in "the miracle of disinflation" but more importantly for the basic reorientation from short-run to longer-run considerations, and from demand-side to supply-side and structural strategies.

Selected Readings and References

Joint Economic Committee, "A New Economic Era," from *Report on the January 1980 Economic Report of the President.* U.S. Congress, February 1980.

Economic Indicators (cited in Chapter 15).

Economic Report of the President (cited in Chapter 15; Data and information drawn from 1972, 1973, 1974, 1975, 1981, and 1985 Reports).

The Federal Reserve System: Purposes and Functions (cited in Chapter 21), along with other FRS publications.

Productivity Policy: Key to the Nation's Economic Future (cited in Chapter 24).

Poverty, Insecurity, and Inequality: Issues in the Distribution of Income and Wealth

Despite the U.S. economy's $4 trillion annual production and income, 35 million Americans remain poor—with money incomes below the official poverty thresholds (in 1983, $10,200 a year for a four-person family and $6,500 for a couple). Although median family income in 1983 was $24,580, nearly one-fourth of all families lived on an income of below $12,500. The richest 20% of American families get 43% of the nation's income, while the poorest 20% get only 5%.

The outstanding faults of the economic society in which we live are its failure to provide for full employment and its arbitrary and inequitable distribution of wealth and incomes.
        —John Maynard Keynes

It is the policy of the United States to eliminate the paradox of poverty in the midst of plenty in this Nation.
        —Economic Opportunity Act of 1964

If we cannot learn to make, impose, and defend equity decisions, we are not going to solve any of our economic problems.
        Lester C. Thurow, The Zero-Sum Society

The above quotation from John Maynard Keynes is especially interesting in view of the fact that the famous English economist—who ranks with Adam Smith and Karl Marx among the world's most influential economists—was himself a millionaire described as an "upper-crust snob." In the concluding chapter of his 1936 classic, *The General Theory of Employment, Interest, and Money,* he wrote: "There is social and psychological justification for significant inequalities of incomes and wealth, but not for such large disparities as exist today."

How Much Inequality?

What *are* the magnitudes of disparity that exist in market capitalism, and does Keynes' statement apply as much today as it did 50 years ago?

Table 27.1 shows the distribution of money income among families before federal income taxes from 1929 to 1983 (adding historical perspective to Table 19.2). Between 1936 and 1947, a significant reduction in inequality occurred, with the bottom 40% of families increasing their share of the nation's income from 13.3% to 16.8% and the top quintile (20%) of families experiencing a reduction from 51.7% of total income down to 43.0%. The highest 5% of families took a sharp cut from 26.5% to 17.2% of total income. During the past four decades *little change has taken place in the pre-tax distribution of money income* in terms of quintiles. (To express the relative shares of Table 27.1 in approximate *dollar* terms, note that aggregate personal income in 1983 was $2.7 trillion.)

Table 27.1

Percent of Family Income Received by Each Quintile and Top Five Percent in Selected Years

	1983	1965	1947	1941	1935-36	1929
Families ranked by income						
Total, 100%	100.0%	100.0%	100.0%	100.0%	100.0%	100.0%
Lowest 20%	4.7	5.2	5.0	4	4.1	13
Second 20%	11.1	12.2	11.8	10	9.2	13
Middle 20%	17.1	17.8	17.0	15	14.1	14
Fourth 20%	24.4	23.9	23.1	22	20.9	19
Highest 20%	42.7	40.9	43.0	49	51.7	54
(Top 5%)	(15.8)	(15.5)	(17.2)	(24)	(26.5)	(30)

Source: *Statistical Abstract of the United States 1985,* and *Historical Statistics of the United States.*

Substantial inequality exists in the distribution of income whether we look at income before or after taxes. According to Joseph Pechman's study of 1980 income (his book *Who Paid the Taxes, 1966-85* utilizes concepts and procedures that differ somewhat from the census data reported in Table 27.1), the lowest one-fifth of families received 4.1% of adjusted family income before taxes and 4.3% after all taxes (not just the federal income tax but all federal, state, and local taxes combined). The second quintile got 9.7% of the nation's total income before and 10.1% after taxes. For the middle quintile the figures were 15.4% and 15.6%; for the fourth quintile, 21.9% and 22.0%; and for the highest one-fifth of families, the share of total income was 48.9% before and 48.0% after taxes. With respect to the persistent pattern of income inequality both before and after taxes during the past 20 years, Pechman points out that rising transfer payments received by the lowest income groups during this period have been offset by growing inequality of *factor income* (derived from market activity).

Of all the various types of taxes used in the United States (e.g., property, corporation income, payroll, sales) the personal income tax is the most progressive— ranging from a burden of about 3% for the lowest quintile to 8% for the middle and 13% for the highest quintile—and therefore has the greatest potential for moderating extreme inequality in the distribution of income. Because of limitations on graduated rates, however, and heavy reliance on other types of taxes to generate the bulk of tax receipts, the distributional impact of the federal income tax is actually quite small. (Richard Goode points out in *The Individual Income Tax* that if the *entire burden* of the federal individual income tax in 1966 had been assessed against the richest 5% of family units, that group would still have had 13% of total after-tax income!)

Neither the census data cited in Table 27.1 nor Pechman's estimates is entirely acceptable to all economists. Disagreements exist on (1) the appropriate definition of income and (2) assumptions concerning the incidence of tax burdens (e.g., are property taxes paid by the owners of capital, or shifted to consumers in the form of higher prices?). Edgar Browning in particular has argued that if income were defined to include non-cash items such as food stamps, medical services, and subsidized housing, and if different assumptions were made about tax incidence, the actual pattern of income distribution in the United States would appear to be much more equal. (To generate better data on the real income of households, the Census Bureau in 1983 initiated a new "Survey of Income and Program Participation/SIPP," which includes data on government programs providing non-cash benefits to families. This sample survey should eventually help resolve disagreements about the amounts and types of real income accruing to various households, information which previously had often been based on personal, not unbiased, estimates made by the researcher.)

Inequality and Poverty

What is the connection between *inequality* and *poverty?* According to the Census Bureau, the cutoff line dividing the lowest quintile from the second 20% of families in 1983 was about $11,600. The nation's *8 million poor families* plus most of the 6 million near-poor (below 125% of the poverty level) were in this lowest quintile, and all together they received about 5% of the nation's money income. At the opposite end of the income scale, the *richest 12 million families had more than eight times as much income in the aggregate as the 12 million families at the low end.* (As reported in Chapter 19, there were 62 million families in 1983, approximately 12 million families in each income quintile.) Median income in 1983 was $24,580 for all families (but only $11,790 for families headed by a female, no husband present). More will be said later about linkages between inequality and poverty.

Distribution of Wealth

Statistics on the distribution of *accumulated wealth* disclose even greater inequality than is the case with annual incomes. One reason for this is a simple matter of arithmetic: Higher incomes (or inherited wealth) make it possible to *save* more, and (as explained in Chapter 15) the "miracle" of compound interest spawns additional dollars like mushrooms in the forest. An absolutely risk-free financial investment of

$1 million *doubles* in value to $2 million in *seven* years at an interest rate of 10%; and when the rate climbs to 14%, the $2 million becomes *$4 million* in just *five* years! (a graphic illustration of David Harum's adage that "Them that has, gets.").

Of the economy's $5.6 trillion of personal assets in 1976, the top one-half of 1% of persons held 14% of total assets. This same group held 38% of the personally held corporate stock (institutions such as insurance companies and retirement funds are the biggest stockholders). The historical trend has been *away* from extreme inequality, however, with the share of personal wealth held by the top 1% declining from 36% in 1929 to 26% in 1956 and 21% in 1972.

The concentration of economic wealth and power has held a strong fascination for the American people (see Chapter 28 on our nation's real-world dynasties as opposed to the immensely popular TV programs). Since 1982, *Forbes* magazine has published the "Forbes 400," an annual listing of the 400 richest people in America. Topping the list in 1984 were a dozen individuals reportedly "worth" $1 billion or more (including such familiar names as Getty, Hunt, Rockefeller, and also such newer rich-and-famous names as Wang, Perot, and Walton). The *least* affluent member of the 400 had assets valued at a minimum of $150 million. Total net worth of the group was estimated at $125 *billion!* (In terms of corporate-held wealth, the "Fortune 500"—another well known annual magazine feature, cited in Chapter 18—listed assets of $63 billion for Exxon, $52 billion for General Motors, and $43 billion for IBM, the latter generating after-tax *profits* in the excess of $6 billion on 1984 business. More on this in the next chapter.)

Is There a Problem?

Whether the above data indicate that a *problem* exists in the United States with respect to the distribution of wealth and income depends on society's values and perceptions. Many political leaders, writers, and other Americans have expressed deep concern in recent years over the paradox of poverty amid economic abundance in the United States. Michael Harrington's 1962 book, *The Other America,* poignantly described the deprivation and misery of millions of low-income Americans, existing as if in an invisible world, side-by-side with the affluent majority. In 1964, the Congress passed the Economic Opportunity Act, declaring a war against poverty, the objective of which was "to eliminate the paradox of poverty in the midst of plenty in this Nation." Economic growth along with government programs adopted in the 1960s and 1970s helped lower the poverty rate significantly. Yet many people are frustrated over our persistent failure to structure the institutions and opportunities of the U.S. economy in such a way that American affluence is more widely shared among our own citizens. In 1984, per capita personal income was $12,730—enough income to provide a three-person family $38,190 and a four-person family $50,920. But as we have seen, the *actual* distribution leaves millions of families with only a fraction of those incomes. (Readers should bear in mind the need to update dollar figures reported in this chapter year by year, predictably at an approximate 5% annual rate.)

The Five-Step Method of Analysis

In Chapter 16, we described a five-step method of economic reasoning that we shall now use in analyzing the issue of *poverty in America.* It involves (1) defining the problem, (2) identifying goals, (3) considering the possible courses of action available to us as a nation, (4) analyzing the probable consequences of the alternative courses of action, and (5) choosing the policy that seems most promising for achieving the stated goals. Since the following section cannot realistically be an entire book within a book, the analysis must necessarily be illustrative rather than exhaustive. Conscientious use will be made of history, statistics, and economic theory.

Step 1—Define the Problem

Despite our $4 trillion economy, some 35 million Americans—seven million unrelated individuals plus the members of nearly 8 million poor families—have incomes that fall below the official poverty thresholds specified by the federal government. (In 1983, the poverty-income standard was $5,061 for a 1-person household, $6,483 for two persons, $7,938 for three persons, $10,178 for four persons, $12,049 for a 5-person household, and correspondingly higher for larger families.) Meanwhile, median family income in 1983 was $24,580; and 30% of American families had money incomes above $35,000 a year. In effect, the 8 million families with incomes below the official poverty standard had combined earnings from employment and property income *plus* transfer payment (public assistance, social insurance, or other cash income) amounting to far below *half* the nation's *average* family income and equal to about *one-tenth* of the income received by the nation's 8 million *richest* families (with incomes ranging $35,000 per year to several millions).

Of the 35 million persons who were poor in 1983 (15% of the total U.S. population), *24 million were white* (12% of all white persons) and *10 million were black* (36% of that population group). For persons of Spanish origin (of any race) the poverty rate was 28%. Some *14 million children* under 18 years of age were growing up in poor families. The poverty rate for one-parent families headed by a woman was 36%; and note that families headed by women (no husband present) accounted for 47% of all poor families! Note also that all of the estimates of poverty reported here, based on census survey data, reflect only *cash* income (see references listed at the end of the chapter).

Historically, the poor have always been with us, but not in the same numbers. Between 1960 and 1973, the incidence of poverty (poor persons divided by total population) declined from 22% to 11%, and the number of persons falling below the poverty-income line dropped from 40 million to 23 million (while the nation's total population was growing by 30 million!). In the late 1970s, however, the poverty rate began an upward trend that has continued without interruption through the 1983 survey. In its report for that year, the Census Bureau indicated an income deficit per family member of $1,100, with a figure of $2,230 for unrelated individuals. This translates into an aggregate *poverty-income gap of $46 billion,* the amount—somewhat more than 1% of *GNP*—required to raise all of the nation's poor persons to incomes above the poverty level.

Theory and Income Distribution

So much for a *statistical* definition of the problem. What light does *theory* shed on the nature, causes, and consequences of poverty? In neoclassical economics, the *marginal productivity theory* of wages teaches that a person will be employed as a worker only if he or she is productive enough (when used in combination with land, capital, and other human resources) to add to the revenues of the business firm an amount equal to or greater than the wage that the employer must pay him (as determined by competition, union contracts, or minimum wage legislation). Unemployment, low wages, and poverty can thus be caused by *low productivity* (or zero productivity in the case of small children and other persons not in the labor force). At a higher level of generalization, conventional economics holds a *market-value theory of income distribution:* To the extent that a person possesses valuable land, capital, or labor resources, he will enjoy commensurate income. (A human being is "worth" what the market says he is worth!) But note that relatively few of America's 240 million people own significant property resources. And the assumption that human beings are so homogeneous and socially adapted that in a nation of 240 million individuals each and every one will have marketable labor services—energy, skills, personality attributes—*and* employment opportunities sufficient to earn a living wage year-in and year-out would seem to require the most devout faith in market processes.

In deference to the pecuniary orientation of standard economics, the "definition of the problem" so far has been expressed in terms of *income poverty*: not enough money to provide goods and services needed for a decent level of living—whether by *absolute* or *relative* standards—in the context of present-day America. But to many social scientists, a more holistic theory of poverty is required as a basis for effective programs of remediation. In this view, the problem of poverty lies not solely in a deficiency of income but in the feelings of hopelessness, helplessness, and isolation that certain (but not all) low-income people suffer, plus the *social behavior* that such feelings precipitate. An insufficiency of income, whether temporary or permanent, is only one aspect of "powerlessness"; but in a society in which money buys not only the material means of life but also largely determines social status and even one's own self-esteem, economic deprivation can be catastrophic.

The concept of a "culture of poverty" has been described by anthropologist Oscar Lewis, and a vast literature has been produced on the social and psychological dimensions of poverty. Research has established links between low incomes on the one hand and crime, suicide, mental illness, poor health (including irreversible brain damage to babies), and other pathologies. Poverty is therefore seen as a *social* problem that not only imposes heavy burdens on individuals and families but also takes its toll on the community as a whole.

Links Between Inequality and Poverty

Returning to the relationship between poverty and inequality, it should be pointed out that there is a *definitional* issue and a *causal* connection as well. Some people say that "poverty" just means "having less than your neighbor," i.e., poverty has no meaning beyond inequality. This is a *relativistic* definition; and, in fact, there is considerable intellectual support for defining poverty in terms of family incomes that fall below 50% of the nation's median family income. At present, however, the *official* definition of poverty used in the United States is an *absolute* standard in the sense that it is based on estimates of income required to provide food, housing, and other goods and services that are judged necessary for a decent level of living in the present-day setting of American life. According to this approach, it is possible to *retain* substantial inequality while *eliminating* poverty by raising all families to a specified absolute minimum (adjusted annually for inflation).

With respect to the *causal* (or associative) connection between inequality and poverty, it is instructive to focus on the *upper* end of the income scale. If Gloria Vanderbilt and Michael Jackson have personal incomes of, say, $10 million a year (sports celebrities such as Dan Marino and Mary Lou Retton demand and get "only" $1 or $2 million per year) does this affect the incomes of people at the lower end of the scale? In monetary terms it is high product and ticket prices that generate incomes in excess of competitive levels (i.e., monopoly prices charged for highly differentiated commodities: "all the traffic will bear"). This enormous purchasing power in turn enables the Vanderbilts and Jacksons to "raid the circular flow" of real income, commanding resources and appropriating goods and services that otherwise might be available to lower-income consumers.

The Tax System as Part of the Problem

Given the idiosyncracies of market valuations and the monopoly power of the super-rich (much of whose income is "economic rent" in the sense that it greatly exceeds the opportunity cost of the individual's labor services, in real terms), gross inequalities may seem inevitable in a market society. There is no law prohibiting consumers from voluntarily paying monopoly prices. But when a nation levies taxes, opportunities exist to alter the *after-tax distribution of income* (as is done in many European nations). To the extent that extreme inequality persists *after* taxes it seems clear that low-income taxpayers (reference here is not solely to personal income taxes) are "subsidizing" the rich in the sense that lower-income people must pay whatever tax dollars are not paid by those with higher incomes. (According to the study by Pechman cited in Chapter 22, the two lowest quintiles paid 21% of their incomes in taxes—mostly sales, excise, and payroll taxes—while the top two quintiles paid 25%. Note that if tax payments *in total* are deficient the result will be demand-pull inflation, with the poor predictably suffering a loss of real income.)

Thus, the unwillingness of the super-rich to pay high taxes has the effect of shifting tax burdens to the poor, and to middle-income families (there *is* a law against not paying your taxes, unless you are cunning enough to "shelter" the income). Earlier it was observed that American ingenuity and energy applied to legal tax avoidance have undermined the one institutional structure capable of dealing in a noninflationary way with extreme inequality, namely the progressive individual income tax. (In defense of tax-dodging by the super-rich, one can imagine Finley Peter Dunne's *Mr. Dooley* saying, tongue-in-cheek: "Sure, it's a crime for government to tax away big incomes that free men stole fair and square.")

One of the most puzzling economic attitudes held by the American people is the notion that the rich and super-rich (including entertainers, sports figures, and their lawyer-agents) somehow amass their fortunes in ways that do not entail diverting incomes from other people, such as "the fans" (credit the self-serving remarks of some high-salaried players at the time of the 1985 baseball strike with helping American consumers begin to learn the score!). Similar is the notion that million-dollar winners in state lotteries are getting their money from a computer rather than from the pockets of ticket-buying "taxpayers" who can ill afford the outlays—which, to be sure, are voluntary but paid simply because the ticket buyers know very well that this is the only investment they can make that offers even a one-in-a-million chance of attaining "the American dream." (The reader will recognize that much of this discussion applies as much to the near-poor and middle-income population as to the 15% of Americans officially counted as poor.)

Step 2—Identify Goals

Although this step is both subtle and crucial, we shall deal with it succinctly here and invite reconsideration later in the context of the value analysis presented in Part Six. Americans have long advocated equality of opportunity, freedom of choice, the dignity and supreme importance of the individual, distributive justice, and economic security. These values serve as *criteria of choice* (see Chapter 30) in the selection of social goals, such as the elimination of poverty (recall the policy declaration in the Economic Opportunity Act of 1964).

The American people have expressed their commitment to eliminate poverty amid affluence in the United States. But the question is, *how to do it?* "Do not show the goal without the way," social philosopher Ferdinand LaSalle warned, "for way and goal on earth are so entwined that each upon the other's change depends, and different paths lead into different ends." When it comes to selecting the *means* of poverty elimination—actual programs and procedures—other values, such as the work ethic and the market principle of quid pro quo, stand in the way of social consensus. The *values, perceptions, attitudes,* and *lifestyles* of the poor, not simply their *income-earning capacity,* may differ from the nonpoor. *Who* or *what* will change? When a specific approach or combination of ways to eliminate poverty is adopted, conflicts emerge and action is stalled. Indeed, it may be true that until we find a satisfactory way to cope with value differences there will be no solution to the poverty problem or, as Lester Thurow suggests, any of our other economic problems for that matter. For present purposes, we shall take the language of the Economic Opportunity Act literally and identify our goal as the *elimination of poverty;* but we shall be mindful that a broad range of values will influence the choice of *means* employed in the pursuit of this goal.

Step 3—Consider Alternatives

A truly comprehensive, open-ended approach to policy analysis dealing with the problem of poverty would adopt the attitude: "Anything goes." All of the possible courses of action would be considered, from *(a)* government confiscation of private incomes and subsequent allocation of equal shares per capita (which hardly anyone would favor) to *(b)* a piecemeal high-employment-plus-tax-and-transfer system (basically our current policy) to *(c)* a consolidated basic independent income/ negative income tax plan along lines that have been proposed by conservative and liberal economists alike.

In this brief treatment, we shall describe only a narrow range of "reasonable" alternatives classified according to whether they represent a *market approach* (involving payments either for work performed or for the contribution of nonhuman resources to production); or a *nonmarket approach*. The latter includes channeling more income to the poor in the form of cash transfers, goods and services in kind, and/or vouchers while also reducing the burden of sales, excise, property, payroll, and income taxes that the poor pay to federal, state, and local government.

Market Approaches

As reported in Chapter 19, the nation's personal income in 1984 totaled $3.0 trillion, of which one-fourth came from "property" income: dividends, interest, rent, and profits of unincorporated enterprises. (Three-fifths was accounted for by "wage" payments to human resources, while one-seventh was derived from transfer payments.) One possible way to wipe out poverty would be to ensure that everyone in the country, including the poor, received *property income;* then they could live off their dividends, rent, interest, and profits without having to rely on wages. This system of "people's capitalism" has been advocated by some businessmen and writers (though it does not, at present, appear to rank very high in feasibility).

The other market approach to providing the poor with more income centers on *jobs and earnings.* Those who have counseled their fellow citizens to: "Join the war against poverty—get a job!" have a point. But several complications arise:

1. Should children under age 18 be working to support themselves?
2. Should men and women 65 and over be participating in the labor force?
3. Should mothers of young children seek employment while somebody else assumes the child-care function? (Apparently so, judging from the public subsidies pouring into this growth industry!)
4. Is it reasonable to demand that all of this nation's physically, mentally, and emotionally handicapped men and women find and hold good jobs?

Indeed, is it realistic to expect everyone to work his way out of poverty when the number of jobs in the economy often falls short of the number of workers by eight or 10 million? Or when wages may be so low that even full-time, year-round employment leaves the worker's family with a poverty-level income? Example: Working 40 hours a week, 52 weeks a year at the $3.35 per-hour legal minimum wage will generate total earnings of less than $7,000 per year, some $3,000 below the poverty threshold for a 4-person family. (Was Karl Marx right when he predicted that the growing immiserization of workers under a capitalist system would eventually force women and children into the labor force?)

The traditional employment-and-earnings strategy nevertheless merits further priority attention. Possible actions include: (1) strengthening the *demand* for labor, (2) providing government subsidies for manpower training to improve the *supply* of labor, and (3) improving the efficiency of the *manpower market* itself (e.g., through better matching of jobs and workers).

On the *demand* side, appropriate fiscal and monetary policies can help bring the unemployment rate for the nation down to something like 5% to 6%. In addition, special job-creation programs (e.g., public works projects, subsidized private-sector jobs, and public service employment) could provide some of the poor with employment and earnings opportunities. On the *supply* side, manpower development and training programs, easier access to schooling, health and nutrition programs, counseling, helping workers relocate to where the jobs are, supportive services, and a host of other "investments in human capital," can help increase the employability, employment, productivity, job tenure, and earnings of low-income men and women who enter the labor force. With respect to the interactive *market mechanism* itself, programs can be implemented to reduce discrimination against minorities (and women, youth, and older workers), increase the flow of job information (e.g., through a rejuvenated Public Employment Service), improve public transportation and child-care systems, and the like. Such actions create a more favorable socioeconomic environment for bringing potential manpower demand and supply into balance at high enough levels to help squeeze out a portion of the nation's job-related poverty. None of this is new, but there is always room for improvement.

Nonmarket Approaches

Public policy can thus strive to make better use of market strategies for raising the incomes of the poor. As suggested above, however, not all Americans own resources (including sufficiently productive labor power) that can be exchanged in the market for a nonpoverty level of income, nor does it seem reasonable to expect that all Americans will acquire such resources. Supplementary *nonmarket strategies* will therefore be necessary to help eliminate poverty. These nonmarket strategies may be classified under three major headings:

1. Cash transfers
   (a) Social insurance (e.g., OASDHI and Unemployment Insurance).
   (b) Public assistance (e.g., AFDC and Old Age Assistance).
   (c) Basic independent income (discussed below).
2. In-kind goods and services (e.g., medical care, food stamps, housing, counseling, remedial education, and supportive services).
3. Tax reductions (e.g., sales and property tax exemption, credits, or refunds for persons designated as poor).

Basic Independent Income

All of the above have been utilized (though not necessarily at optimal levels) with one exception: basic independent income (BII). The rationale of this program is to provide every citizen in the nation a *basic* level of income that is *independent* of his employment status, ownership of nonhuman resources, demonstrated need (i.e., meeting the "means" test), qualification for a social insurance program, or any other traditional criterion. The plan (proposed in the 1950s by C. E. Ayres), is not designed to cure poverty but to *prevent* it. All families and individuals would nominally receive the BII (paid on a weekly, biweekly, or monthly basis), and the payments would be included in taxable income. People with high incomes derived from work or investments would, of course, have "positive" tax liability sufficient to offset their BII payments; so only low-income households would actually receive such payments.

The case for a basic independent income is simple: In a $4-trillion-dollar "economy of abundance," why deprive millions of fellow Americans, especially children, of the goods and services they need to maintain a decent life (whether they "deserve" it or not)? Since the taproot of our economic affluence is the *social* accumulation of technological knowledge, why should that affluence be distributed among society's members in such outrageously unequal shares? Why let families fall below the poverty line and then implement costly and demeaning programs to raise them up again, when poverty can be prevented by setting a floor under the household's income in the first place? (In the heyday of Keynesian theory, it was also argued that increasing the incomes of the poor would raise the propensity to consume, and thereby promote macroeconomic stability.) Variations on the BII plan have been widely discussed in recent years, notably the *negative income tax* (NIT), which is really a way of administering a guaranteed minimum income program, and President

Nixon's proposed Family Assistance Plan (which was limited to families with *children* and conceived as a welfare reform program limited to the poor).

As indicated in the discussion of Step 4 that follows, adoption of a basic independent income plan would eliminate the need for many, though not all, of the other cash-transfer and in-kind programs that presently exist.

Step 4—Analyze the Consequences

It is one thing to conceive a plan for eliminating poverty and quite another to assess carefully the probable *benefits, costs,* and *other effects* associated with its implementation. In general, we know for example that the benefits of a BII/NIT plan would include the virtual elimination of income poverty (there will always be a certain "frictional level" of poverty, largely associated with emotional disorders which lead individuals to behave as if they are "their own worst enemies") and corresponding improvements in health, education, social attitudes, socioeconomic environment, etc., as well as a reduction in crime, dependency, and other forms of social pathology. Numerous government programs that grant categorical financial assistance and in-kind or voucher-type benefits would no longer be required (vital human-service programs would need to continue).

Costs and Side Effects

The anticipated benefits sound impressive; what about the *costs?* Rough estimates (based on assumptions about labor-force behavior and other variables) indicate that the total cost of a BII/NIT plan would be in the range of $120-$160 billion, about 3% to 4% of *GNP*. Ironically, less than half of this amount would go to the poor (completely closing the poverty-income gap), with the remainder "spilling over" to the near-poor and other lower-income households. Such spillover benefits result from a fractional "benefit-loss rate" (say, 50%) designed to preserve *work incentives* and *equity* by allowing persons who are employed to retain a significant portion of their income advantage over non-earners.

How a Negative Income Tax Would Work

Up to a specified "break-even level," earners would receive BII payments equal to one-half the difference between their earned income and the break-even level of income. For example, assuming a guaranteed minimum income of $10,000 and benefit-loss rate of 50%, the break-even level of income would be $20,000. Every household in the nation with an income below $20,000 would receive some amount of net payment; households above the break-even level would receive nothing (and like everybody else would be liable for *positive* tax payments to government on income above $20,000). If a particular household has $6,000 of earnings—or, for that matter $6,000 of income from *any* source—the BII payment would be calculated at 50% of the difference between $20,000 and $6,000, or $7,000. This household will wind up with a final income of $13,000, leaving the family $3,000 better off financially than the no-earner household, whose income will be the guaranteed minimum of $10,000.

Talking about costs in aggregative terms (especially when the figures run in billions) is very impersonal. A key question is: How will the costs be divided among particular groups in society? Referring again to Table 19.2, it is clear that asking the two lowest quintiles to bear the burden would defeat the purpose of the program. That leaves the middle and top two quintiles, consisting of families that are popularly (if inaccurately) known as "the middle class." Depending on the interplay of society's values and perceptions (including priorities assigned to compassion, the quality of our socioeconomic environment, and economic growth), the financial costs of a BII/NIT program would presumably wind up falling mainly on households enjoying incomes of $35-$40,000 and over. However, these are precisely the people who possess the greatest sociopolitical power. And it will do no good to have one group of $40-$50,000-a-year families (such as two-earner households deriving their incomes from the public sector) lobbying aggressively to shift the burden, directly or indirectly, to a different group of $40-$50,000-a-year families (say, in the business sector). In other words, the costs of eliminating income poverty in all likelihood will have to be paid in the form of higher *personal* income taxes by middle and upper-income families; and only when these groups *willingly accept* higher taxes for themselves will the poverty problem be resolved.

Analyzing the likely consequences of alternative solutions (only one such alternative is pursued here, for illustrative purposes) must include not only prediction of benefits and costs, but also of *other effects.* As we shall note in Chapter 30, ignoring "side effects" is a major pitfall in decisionmaking. Whether intended or unintended, outcomes of public programs will unavoidably affect the lives of people, for better and for worse, often in totally unpredictable ways (today's "side effect" can very well become tomorrow's obsession, as the issues of environmental quality and sex equity testify.) With respect to a basic independent income program, critics and supporters alike have recognized that some beneficiaries might elect to "live on the dole," which would reduce the nation's active labor force and perhaps even contribute to an erosion of personal character. (One controversial suggestion is to add a "workfare" provision.) Income maintenance programs, such as unemployment compensation, are already blamed for raising the core rate of unemployment and exacerbating the problem of stagflation (by reduced the job-seeking pressure on unemployed workers, some of whom prefer to subsist on transfer payments rather than accept a low-wage, disagreeable job). Some harmful effects of such socioeconomic programs are virtually inevitable; indeed, few institutional arrangements are entirely free of shortcomings.

Economists do not know all the facts about the costs, benefits, and side effects of eliminating poverty, though research in the past 25 years has helped illuminate some of these consequences. Clearly, there would be tradeoffs involved in an all-out national effort to abolish poverty. Yet most scholars are convinced that the goal is *economically* feasible and the adoption of an effective program awaits only a social consensus on the *equity* decisions required to carry it out (plus favorable timing with respect to, for example, federal budget deficits and the business cycle).

Step 5—Choose Best Course of Action

There is no one "right" solution to the poverty problem, and there is insufficient knowledge of benefits and costs to point unequivocally toward a "best" course of action. But careful analysis reveals certain facts about the problem of poverty-amid-affluence, suggests feasible alternatives, and generates useful approximations concerning the effects of various alternatives. Whatever choices the American people make, they almost certainly will have to stand ready to adjust their proposed strategies in light of actual experience. Thus, the rational-empirical-comprehensive method of policy analysis (as Figure 16.1 illustrated) is a *continuing process of implementation, learning from experience, and revision.* Meanwhile, some form of "war against poverty" and social effort to correct what Keynes called the "arbitrary and inequitable distribution of wealth and incomes" will go on in our democratic society, waning at times when such issues as environmental protection, stagflation, national defense, and budget deficits capture the public's mind, and then regaining priority when the sensitivity of the majority *nonpoor* once more is rekindled into compassionate social action to alleviate the plight of the nation's poor.

Poverty Not the Only Problem

This chapter addresses both poverty *and* inequality in the distribution of income and wealth. (The terrible problem of economic *insecurity* was passed over entirely.) Because of space limitations, the five-step method of policy analysis was only applied explicitly to the poverty issue. This should not be interpreted as implying that America's only distributional problem is poverty; indeed it can be cogently argued that extreme inequality is a cancer infecting people in the upper range of incomes as well as those at the bottom (though few in the top decile will acknowledge that too much money, like too much ice cream, can make you sick). Moreover, as will be discussed in the next chapter, huge disparities in personal income and wealth create dangerous power problems in an otherwise free, democratic society.

It has already been suggested that inequality itself is not necessarily a problem, only *too much* inequality; how much is too much? Discussions of an optimal level of after-tax inequality suggest that the highest quintile might appropriately have three or four times as much income as the lowest quintile, in contrast to the 8:1 or 9:1 ratio that now prevails. The top 5% of families might then content itself with, say, no more than 10 or 15 times as much as the lowest 5% rather than the present ratio of 20:1, which of course still entails ratios of 100:1 and 1000:1 toward the extremes of the income range. Doubtless, this sort of distribution will be achieved only if and when high-income individuals themselves decide to forego the magnitudes of wealth that, throughout the 20th century, have been the object of public adulation and envy, even in civilized and democratic nations such as the United States of America.

Selected Readings and References

E.K. Browning and W.R. Johnson, *The Distribution of the Tax Burden* (cited in Chapter 22); also see E.K. Browning and J.M. Browning, *Public Finance and the Price System,* 2nd ed. New York: Macmillan, 1983.

C.E. Ayres, *The Industrial Economy* (cited in Chapter 5).

Louis A. Ferman et al., *Poverty in America*, Rev. ed. Ann Arbor: University of Michigan Press, 1968. (Contains numerous references to "the culture of poverty.")

Richard Goode, *The Individual Income Tax* (cited in Chapter 22).

John Maynard Keynes, "Concluding Notes on the Social Philosophy Towards Which the General Theory Might Lead" (cited in Chapter 14).

Ferdinand Lundberg, *The Rich and the Super-Rich: A Study in the Power of Money Today.* New York: Lyle Stuart, 1968.

R.A. Musgrave and P.B. Musgrave, *Public Finance in Theory and Practice,* 3rd ed. (cited in Chapter 22).

Joseph A. Pechman, *Who Paid the Taxes, 1966-85?* (cited in Chapter 22).

George Bernard Shaw, *The Intelligent Woman's Guide to Socialism, Capitalism, Sovietism, and Fascism.* New York: Penguin, 1937. (1st ed. published in 1928).

P.M. Stern and G. deVincent, *The Shame of A Nation.* New York: Ivan Obelensky, 1965.

"Economic Characteristics of Households in the United States/SIPP" (cited in Chapter 19).

"The Forbes 400: The 400 Richest People in America," *Forbes,* Special Issue, October 1, 1984.

"The Fortune 500: The Largest U.S. Industrial Corporations" (cited in Chapter 18).

"Money Income and Poverty Status of Families and Persons in the United States: 1983," (cited in Chapter 19).

Statistical Abstract of the United States 1985 (cited in Chapter 11).

Concentrations of Economic Power, and the New Political Economy

Along with instability and inequality, the concentration of *economic power* has been a persistent problem of the American economy. The three problems are interrelated in that a highly unequal division of wealth and income in a market society necessarily implies great disparities of economic, social, and political power, which in turn serve to perpetuate the inequality. Economic instability is both a cause and an effect of concentrated power. Until the 1930s, economic power was largely in the hands of *business;* but the past half-century has witnessed the rise of *other power blocs*—including labor unions, the government establishment, farm groups, and, especially since the 1960s, an assortment of single-issue, special-interest lobbies—which effectively politicize the economic system. The power and influence of organized crime have been pervasive since the 1920s.

The monopolists, by keeping the market under-stocked...sell their commodities much above the natural price and raise their emoluments, whether they consist in wages or profit, greatly above their natural rate.
    —Adam Smith

With the widespread disappearance of competition in its classical form, new restraints on private economic power [appeared] not with competitors but [on the opposite side of the market] with customers and suppliers...[The creation and] support of countervailing power has become in modern times perhaps the major domestic peacetime function of the federal government.
    —John Kenneth Galbraith

Social philosophers have long been concerned with problems of wealth and power, as indicated by the sampling of quotations listed above and in the box below. Since antiquity (and probably in prehistory as well) power and wealth have not only gone hand in hand but have been concentrated in small elitist groups, whether warriors, kings, priests, or business entrepreneurs and government officials. Indeed many people are convinced that extreme inequality of economic and sociopolitical power is a basic, immutable fact of human society. And yet—particularly in a democratic age inspired by the 18th-century revolutionary ideals of liberty, justice, and equality— there remains a certain uneasiness about the disparities that are so evident in contemporary American life, and perhaps a lingering hope that the ideals of democracy can somehow find happier expression in the future.

The Issue of Economic Power

Beyond some initial remarks, the present discussion is limited to economic power held in the *private* sector. When such power is concentrated in the hands of *government,* society must pray that public officials are generously endowed with the traditional virtues of Prudence, Justice, Courage, and Temperance (see Chapter 30); or, alternatively, that a fundamental restructuring of society is imminent. Even with competent and well-intentioned, (i.e., virtuous) leadership, control of the economy by government may yield socioeconomic outcomes inferior to those generated by a market system—assuredly so in the view of adherents to the ideology of capitalism. For economists like Nobel laureates Friedrich von Hayek and Milton Friedman, no society can be free without private ownership and decentralized control of productive resources.

The modern discipline of economics (originally well-named Political Economy) grew out of policy conflicts involving government and business (18th-century mercantilism versus laissez-faire capitalism) and a power struggle between land-owners and industrial capitalists over the distribution of income. Followers of Adam Smith argued that economic power should be widely dispersed in a system of private enterprise and "atomistic competition" rather than concentrated in the hands of government, whose mercantilistic regulations and controls had been undermining the economy's efficiency. Not only in Britain and on the European continent did Smith's ideas enjoy popularity but in America as well. We earlier noted the significant coincidence in 1776 of the American Revolution that freed the Colonies from politico-economic subjugation by the British Crown, and publication of *The Wealth of Nations* heralding a new economic regime in the mother country itself.

America's "Royal Families"

During the first century of our nation's existence, economic power seemed reasonably decentralized. Then came industrialization and the era of the "robber barons," "captains of industry," and the "money lords" (see Selected Readings at the end of this chapter). Starting in the boom years after the Civil War, swashbuckling individuals and the companies they headed amassed enormous wealth and power; names like Carnegie, J. P. Morgan, Rockefeller, Mellon, Jay Gould, Harriman, Vanderbilt, Edison, Ford, and DuPont became established in the lore of American history (not unlike the "noble class" and royal families of Europe!). The great

The phenomenon of economic power has attracted comment not only from modern economists but from philosophers and writers since earliest times. Following is a sample of their observations on the themes of wealth and power.

Wealth maketh many friends.

Holy Bible, Proverbs 19:4

Alle thynges obeyen to moneye.

Chaucer

Wealth is intrinsically honorable and so confers honor on its possessor [irrespective of the source].

Thorstein Veblen

Wealth is power usurped by the few to compel the many to labor for their benefit.
Percy Bysshe Shelley

As wealth is power, so all power will infallibly draw wealth to itself by some means or other.

Edmund Burke

Politics is the conduct of public affairs for private advantage.

Ambrose Bierce

The opposite of love is not hate, but power.

C.G. Jung

An honest man can feel no pleasure in the exercise of power over his fellow citizens.
Thomas Jefferson

Power tends to corrupt; absolute power corrupts absolutely.

Lord Acton

industrial giants such as Standard Oil, U.S. Steel, and General Motors not only survived the economy's recurring business cycles (gaining market shares from the collapse of smaller firms) but contributed insidiously to the pattern of growing concentration of power, wealth, and income which led to the Great Depression of the 1930s. (Accounts of financial chicanery and political corruption, with swindles and bribes exposed at all levels of government, contribute fascinating chapters to American history books and the biographies of some of our nation's celebrated entrepreneurs.)

Because wealth indeed "maketh friends" and economic power tends to attract political power, the great fortunes of America's first families of business and finance have wielded immense influence in virtually every facet of American life from fashion and morals to education and government. Today's numerous grant-dispensing foundations serve effectively to perpetuate the names of their benefactors. Dynasties of wealth and power, perhaps less well known, have continued to be established in finance and industry (e.g., those of banker A. P. Giannini, utilities magnate Samuel Insull, the VanSweringens, Alfred Sloan, Joseph Kennedy, Howard Hughes, and oil billionaires H. L. Hunt and J. Paul Getty). Then, following World War II, a new power bloc established itself as a dominant institution in the U.S. economy: the "military-industrial complex" so labeled by President Eisenhower in a famous 1961 address to the nation. (He described it as "a disastrous rise of misplaced power [that] exists and will persist.") Subsequently redesignated the military-industrial-*academic* complex, this coalition of interest groups has an enormous financial stake in research, development, and production in the fields of defense and space. By the 1980s, the federal budget for defense plus space research exceeded a quarter of a *trillion* dollars and accounted, directly and indirectly, for one of every six jobs in the American economy. In 1984 alone, half a dozen "private-enterprise" corporations in this field had military sales in excess of $4 billion each.

The 1960s and 1970s witnessed another "aristocratic" development that promises to be of more than passing interest: the emergence of the Age of Entertainers. Personalities in TV, cinema, rock music, and sports—aided and abetted by retinues of attorney-agents, publicists, and accountants—began exploiting the strong demand for their unique (sometimes strange) services to command multi-million dollar incomes, acquire worshipful followers, and turn their fame and fortune toward political power. Whether providing support for causes and candidates or seeking elective office directly, the "superstar" entertainers find that a combination of personal popularity, media skill, and wealth creates immense power not only on stage, screen, and playing fields but in sociopolitical life as well.

Corporate Power

Although power ultimately is held by individuals, it is wielded largely through institutional structures like corporations, labor unions, and the three branches of government. In Chapter 18, data were reported showing the dominance of large corporations in the business sector of the economy. This is by no means a purely recent phenomenon, as the chronicles of the "robber barons" indicated. In their 1932 classic, *The Modern Corporation and Private Property,* Adolf Berle and Gardiner Means estimated that the 200 largest nonfinancial corporations (i.e., less than 1% of all business firms) as of 1929 held 49% of all corporate wealth, 39% of all business wealth, and 22% of the entire wealth of the nation. Subsequent studies indicate that, between 1929 and 1980, the share of *manufacturing* assets held by the 200 largest corporations rose from 46% to 60%.

Concentration ratios in manufacturing—showing the percentage of industry output accounted for by the four largest firms (using data from the U.S. Census of Manufacturing)—for the years 1947 and 1977 exceeded 40 in the production of motor vehicles, steel, telephone and telegraph, photographic equipment and supplies, aircraft, and several other industries. In some industries the top four firms accounted for more than 90% of the U.S. output in their specific product line. (It should be noted that foreign competition serves to reduce the market power of domestic producers, in effect giving American consumers more freedom of choice in their buying decisions.)

Protective Strategies

How can society protect its members from concentrations of economic power in the hands of private parties? One approach to the "social control of business" (and labor, agriculture, and other power blocs) has been through *regulation*. Readers are familiar with state public utility commissions that set rates and prescribe service standards for such "natural monopolies" as the purveyors of electricity and natural gas. The list of federal regulatory agencies, boards, commissions, and administrations fills 200 pages in the U.S. *Government Manual!* (Many of their names, abbreviations, and acronyms have everyday familiarity: Commission on Civil Rights, Federal Energy Regulatory Commission (formerly the FPC), Consumer Product Safety Commission, SEC, ICC, FDA, EPA, FCC, FTC, NLRB, OSHA, ERDA, EEOC, et al.)

During the past two decades regulatory agencies have shown increased concern not just for pricing and service but for the *conditions* surrounding the production and use of goods and services, including *worker and consumer safety* and *environmental impact.* The effectiveness and cost burdens of government regulation vary by program and agency, but—reflecting widespread public dissatisfaction—it is notable that the general swing in recent years has been sharply in the direction of "regulatory relief" and *de*regulation.

Antitrust Policy

A second approach to private economic power is *structural* in the sense of preventing the existence or exercise of excessive *market* power. This strategy finds expression in *antitrust* legislation and enforcement. (The term reflects the fact that many of the monopolistic businesses in the late 19th century were corporations that used the legal device of the "trust agreement" to achieve control.)

In 1890, the famous Sherman Antitrust Act was passed, not for the purpose of outlawing "bigness" but to make it illegal for firms to combine or conspire "in restraint of trade among the several States." Reflecting the nation's outrage at the behavior of the robber-baron corporations, the act declared violations to be criminal misdemeanors subject to fines and imprisonment (prompting historians to observe, somewhat prematurely perhaps, that the century-long honeymoon between businessmen and the American public was just about over). In 1911, the Standard Oil Company of New Jersey, controlling 90% of all the oil refined in the United States, was prosecuted under the Sherman Act in a highly celebrated case and ordered *dissolved.*

Despite off-and-on enforcement campaigns and additional legislation—including the Clayton Act of 1914 (which contained a provision to exempt labor unions from antitrust prosecution), the Federal Trade Commission Act of 1914, and the rather modest Antitrust Improvement Act of 1976—the record is decidedly mixed on the extent to which market power has been deconcentrated and competition effectively promoted in the U.S. economy. (With respect to organized labor, legislation such as the Wagner Act made clear the government's intent to *support* the market power of unions rather than seek a competitive structure in labor markets.) The Antitrust Division of the Department of Justice makes occasional headlines with cases such as that which led to the 1982 breakup of AT&T, and of course the existence of the laws and enforcement machinery may help deter monopolistic exploitation. There is no doubt, however, that awesome concentrations of private economic power persist in the American economy. Recall from Chapter 18 Exxon Corporation's assets of $63 billion and 1984 sales approaching $100 billion! (Before changing its name in 1968, Exxon was the Standard Oil Company of New Jersey; one wonders how big it would be today in the absence of the 1911 dissolution!)

Countervailing Powers

If economic power cannot be effectively dispersed in the mode of atomistic competition, for example through enforcement of the antitrust laws, there remains the possibility of providing "equilibrium" by means of a balance of power. In his 1952 book *American Capitalism,* John Kenneth Galbraith suggested that "countervailing powers" tend to develop as offsets to corporations (or other economic entities) which have acquired considerable market power. These self-generating countervailing powers arise not on the same side of the market, but on the opposite side. Thus, big processors and manufacturers on the selling side are confronted with giant retail firms and chain stores on the buying side of the market. Strong labor unions are organized to bargain with management in the oligopolistic auto and steel industries.

Not all private-sector countervailing powers are self-generated. In the case of agriculture, government has deliberately created market power previously unavailable to competitive farmers. Through direct and indirect subsidies, administered prices, trade policies, etc., the federal government has strengthened the economic power of farmers (frequently at the expense of consumers and taxpayers). Since the 1930s, as Galbraith points out, the support of countervailing power has become a prominent function of government.

Of course this development is hardly something entirely new; "neomercantilism" is one label attached to the phenomenon. More than a century ago, the politicization of economic life by special-interest groups was the target of Frederic Bastiat's devastatingly witty *Economic Sophisms;* today the same theme, more soberly treated, dominates such books as Mancur Olson's *The Rise and Decline of Nations,* Milton and Rose Friedman's *Tyranny of the Status Quo,* and Lester Thurow's *The Zero-Sum Society.*

It would seem that self-generating mechanisms (classical competition and countervailing power), antitrust programs, and government regulation have not solved the persistent problem of the concentration of economic power. (Nor has the system of personal income and wealth taxation!) Given the complexities of modern technology and economies of large-scale operations (especially in marketing), it is virtually unthinkable that competitive markets in their classical form could or should be established. As for self-generating countervailing powers, they *proliferate* rather than eliminate concentrations of economic power; moreover, innocent third parties are often injured in the cross fire. *Regulation* may be more or less effective in certain areas, such as health, safety, and public utilities, but elsewhere it has lost credibility— among professional economists, politicians and the general public.

That leaves the *economic interest groups* that operate through government. But before commenting further on the mass politicization of economic life, something should be said about a topic often neglected in economic discussions, namely the role of *organized crime* in the American economy.

Organized Crime

*Un*organized crime is certainly a serious economic problem in the United States, the costs of which are increasingly being studied by economists (as well as sociologists). But it is not a problem of economic *power* in the sense of the present chapter. *Organized crime,* however, is a genuine manifestation of socioeconomic power, one that is often ignored because it is beyond the domain of conventional theory and polite politics. Richly chronicled in books and films about such cities as Chicago and New York (often as tales of excitement and adventure), the story of "crime and wealth" is described from an economic and national perspective in a fascinating chapter in Ferdinand Lundberg's 1960 tome, *The Rich and the Super-Rich.* Lundberg describes a remarkable interplay between the underworld and the "upperworld" in their mutual quests for wealth and economic power. Moreover, apart from standard gangster practices of murdering the competition (after first breaking their legs as a warning), the methods by which executives of the respective worlds operate are often quite similar, especially in the skillful use of political power ("clout") and bribes.

One of the legacies of the 1920s (the era of Prohibition, bootleggers, and organization of the crime syndicates) is the takeover of legitimate businesses by gangsters who have used their wealth to purchase not only legal immunity but respectability and political power. (Recall Veblen's observation that wealth is *intrinsically* honorable, hence bestows honor on whoever possesses it.) Especially insidious is the widespread public acceptance of pervasive crime, graft, and political corruption—not just in two or three "notorious" big cities but throughout the nation (at local, state, and federal levels) and in all branches of government. A further irony is that, labor organizations aside, two of the three industries in which organized crime got its start have now become legitimate enterprises of government, namely *liquor sales* and *gambling* (i.e., the old numbers racket repackaged in the form of the state lotteries).

PACs and Other Special Interests

Returning to the topic of countervailing powers operating through government—the 1980s version of the New Political Economy—the politicization of economic life has become an issue of spirited controversy. The rise of PACs (political action committees) prompted a 1983 headline: "The Best Congress Money Can Buy." In the name of pluralism and participatory democracy, more and more Americans are joining the traditional business and labor pressure groups to promote their own causes in the councils of government at all levels. Whether the goal is increased spending for education, conservation, trade protection, tax relief for the wealthy, or saving the family farm, the single-issue groups—so often the direct beneficiaries of the spending hikes or tax cuts they lobby for—represent their aims as reasonable, legitimate, and somehow in the best interests of society. It is only "the other guy" who seeks "favored treatment," "subsidies," and "tax loopholes."

For these groups, quite often the ends justify the means, and the whole range of power techniques comes into play, from "war chests" to slanted information, sophisticated techniques of persuasion, orchestrated letter and telephone campaigns, boycotts, and "demonstrations" (not always peaceful). When special-interest groups acknowledge their selfish motives, they seek to justify the self-serving behavior on grounds that "everybody else is doing it, why not us?—it's the American way." And, of course, the stakes are high.

A Washington lawyer-turned-editor, commenting on the growing power of such organizations, describes America as no longer a nation concerned with the public interest but "a committee of lobbies." Indeed, of all the contemporary manifestations of power, the army of PACs and self-interest lobbies with their pressure tactics for politicizing economic life may prove to be the most destructive (particularly in the context of stagflation). The phenomenon illustrates that, while self-serving behavior may be a more-or-less reasonable guide for the economy when decisionmakers possess only limited power (as in the case of individual households and small business firms) it is an entirely different matter—to paraphrase Thomas Nixon Carver—when the creatures grow from housecat to Bengal tiger or attain the strength of marauding wolf packs. Supporters of "participatory democracy" who advocate power tactics to achieve social reform seem sometimes to forget that the same resources and techniques are available to groups seeking less-desirable objectives, and often the victory goes not to the right but to the mighty. The use of raw power (again, on grounds that "the ends justify the means") to achieve social goals seems more akin to the law of the jungle than the ways of enlightened democracy. (In *People of the Lie,* psychologist M. S. Peck equates the use of political power—"the imposition of one's will upon others by overt or covert coercion"—with "evil" because such tactics harm both society and one's self.)

Some Limited Strategies

The problem of economic and political power essentially must be dealt with in such contexts as value theory and depth psychology, topics to be addressed in Part Six. In a more limited sense, however, there are some strategies beyond antitrust enforcement, prosecution of organized crime and institutionalized political corruption, and special-interest lobbying that offer promise in coping with concentrations of economic power.

One technique is what C. E. Ayres termed "better streetlighting," by which he meant increased public disclosure of information relevant to the existence and exercise of economic power. (The incidence of violent crime is higher on dark streets, just as white-collar crime flourishes in the seclusion of the smoke-filled room.) Information made available to the public must be accurate and published on a systematic basis, not selectively for headlines, intimidation, or punishment. Streetlighting could also be served through public representation on boards of directors and governing councils of corporations, labor and farm organizations, and government agencies.

A step beyond streetlighting is bona fide public-interest analysis and education, along the lines of Common Cause and (despite their subtle biases) such organizations as the Committee for Economic Development and Public Citizen (the Ralph Nader organization). While these are advocacy groups they often provide accurate information and a balanced analysis of issues. Professional journalists, particularly in the fields of television news and commentary, are uniquely positioned to illuminate issues that are related to economic power but too often lack the necessary understanding, commitment, or freedom to do the job.

While it seems clear that no designated *social structure* can ensure a satisfactory management of economic and political power (compare the situation in the Soviet

Union with circumstances that seem troubling to us in the United States!), there is one further institutional adjustment that perhaps could help, namely a more frequent "changing of the guard." Not only does power tend to corrupt, but power held over long periods of time breeds even more insidious *forms* and *degrees* of corruption. Sooner or later the incumbent leader identifies the organization—whether a business corporation, Congressional committee, academic program, or labor union—with his own ego and suffers "psychological inflation" (reminiscent of Louis XIV of France: "L'etat, c'est moi"), with correspondingly irresponsible behavior. Periodically "rotating the rascals out" would help prevent some of the worst abuses of power, whether in the public or private sector. In Chapter 31, a more personal approach is suggested for coping with the problem of power.

Selected Readings and References

Matthew Josephson, *The Robber Barons*. (The Great American Capitalists, 1861-1901). New York: Harcourt Brace, 1934.

Matthew Josephson, *The Money Lords*. (The Great Finance Capitalists, 1925-1950). New York: Weybright & Talley, 1972.

Ferdinand Lundberg, *The Rich and the Super-Rich: A Study in the Power of Money Today* (cited in Chapter 27).

George Murray, *The Legacy of Al Capone*. New York: Putnam's, 1975.

John T. Noonan, *Bribes*. New York: Macmillan, 1985.

M. Scott Peck, *People of the Lie: The Hope for Healing Human Evil*. New York: Simon & Schuster, 1983.

Robert B. Reich, *The Next American Frontier* (cited in Chapter 18).

Gus Tyler (editor), *Organized Crime in America*. Ann Arbor: University of Michigan Press, 1962.

"The Forbes 400: The 400 Richest People in America" (cited in Chapter 27).

"The Fortune 500: The Largest U.S. Industrial Corporations" (cited in Chapter 27).

Statistical Abstract of the United States 1985 (cited in Chapter 11).

International Economic Relations: Trade, Ideological Conflict, and the Plight of the Less-Developed Countries

To achieve "international balance," the American economy must deal effectively with problems in three areas of international economic relations: (1) *foreign trade,* (2) competition between capitalist and *communist nations,* and (3) issues arising from the poverty and aspirations of the world's *less-developed countries.* America's policy judgments are guided not only by the economic principles of efficiency and growth, but also such considerations as national security, ideology, humanitarianism, and expedience. Decisions made in one sphere inevitably produce consequences in the other areas.

Our goal is a system of free and fair trade in goods, services and capital.
—Ronald Reagan, Economic Report of the President 1985

We will bury you!
—Nikita Kruschyev

For how long will the rich nations, with one-sixth of the world's population, continue to consume two-thirds of the world's income and resources?... There is need to establish a New International Economic Order that will correct inequalities, redress existing injustices, and eliminate the widening gap between the developed and the developing countries.
—United Nations Conference on Trade and Development (UNCTAD)

Earlier we identified "international balance" as one of the six major goals of the American economy (Chapter 5). This is a deliberately broad label intended to suggest the complexity and multidimensionality of international economic relations. In this domain there is no sharp line between economics and politics, no simple criterion of satisfactory performance. It is a bargaining game of give and take, short run versus long run, tangibles versus intangibles.

Problems, policies, and issues concerning institutional adjustment in international economic relations arise from the three interrelated areas of: (1) foreign trade, including investment and finance; (2) competition between market and nonmarket economies, i.e., capitalism and communism; and (3) the poverty and aspirations of the world's less-developed countries. Depending on the situation and mood of the moment, concerns in one or another of these areas may hold sway—import restrictions to offset trade deficits, grain embargoes to punish the Soviet Union for invading Afghanistan, credit bailouts to keep developing countries from catastrophic retrenchment or default on international debt—but there are also unavoidable and lasting side effects in the other spheres.

Global Perspective

It is helpful to begin with a global perspective. In 1985 the world's output of goods and services totaled some $15 trillion, an average income of $3,000 for each of the world's five billion people. Yet half of Earth's inhabitants must live on less than $500 per year, and three out of every five have annual incomes below $1,500. Meanwhile the most affluent of the industrial market economies, including the United States, enjoy per capita incomes well above $10,000 per year (and a trio of small Middle East oil-exporting nations are at or above the $20,000 figure). A World Bank study indicated that, in 1980, 79% of total world output was produced in the *developed* countries, where 25% of the world's people live, while the remaining 21% was shared by the other 75% of the population. The "low-income economies" such as China, India, Bangladesh, certain Latin America countries, and those of tropical Africa, with 47% of the world's population, had to share a meager 5% of world income. Moreover, the income gap between rich and poor nations has been widening. The $6,860 gap between the United States and India in 1955, for example, had nearly doubled to $11,300 by 1980 (constant 1980 dollars). World Bank statistics on population and income for six categories of economies and for selected countries appear in Table 29.1.

America and the LDCs

What do these worldwide statistics have to do with problems and policies of the American economy, one might ask; after all, low incomes in Asia, Africa, and Latin America are *their* problem, not ours. As we noted in Chapter 27, however, poverty and inequality create problems not only for the poor themselves but for the entire community, whether national or global, in which the "disease" of poverty exists. For a host of reasons—ranging from humanitarianism and desire for mutually profitable trade, to the ongoing world conflict between capitalism and communism and the growing dissatisfaction expressed by less-developed countries (LDCs)—"their" problem becomes "our" problem. (To a great extent this dissatisfaction is a side effect of technological advances in communication and transportation, which serve to highlight the extremes of poverty and affluence in the world community.)

Providing a focal point for LDC protest is the 1974 declaration introduced into the United Nations for establishment of a New International Economic Order (NIEO).

Table 29.1

Population and *GNP* per Capita by Categories of Economies and for Selected Countries, 1982

		Population (millions)	GNP per capita
I.	Industrial market economies (*N* = 19)*	733	$11,070
	Switzerland	6	17,010
	Norway	4	14,280
	Sweden	8	14,040
	United States	232	13,160
	West Germany	62	12,460
	France	54	11,680
	Canada	25	11,320
	Japan	118	10,080
	United Kingdom	56	9,660
	Italy	56	6,840
	Ireland	4	5,150
II.	East European nonmarket economies (*N* =8)*	383	$(4,900)†
	East Germany	17	(8,000)†
	Czechoslovakia	15	(6,000)†
	USSR	270	(5,000)†
	Poland	36	(4,000)†
III.	Low-income economies (*N* = 34)*	2,266	$ 280
	Pakistan	87	380
	China	1,008	310
	India	717	260
	Ethiopia	33	140
	Bangladesh	93	140
IV.	Lower middle-income economies (*N* = 38)*	670	$ 840
	Turkey	46	1,370
	Nigeria	91	860
	Egypt	44	690
	Indonesia	150	580
V.	Upper middle-income economies (*N* = 22)*	489	$ 2,490
	Hong Kong	5	5,340
	Israel	4	5,090
	Yugoslavia	23	2,800
	Mexico	73	2,270
	Brazil	127	2,240
	South Korea	39	1,910
VI.	High-income oil exporters (*N* = 5)*	17	$14,820
	United Arab Emirates	1	23,770
	Kuwait	2	19,870
	Saudi Arabia	10	16,000
	Libya	3	8,510

*Data reported only for countries with population more than one million (*N* = 126). For each of the six categories, per capita *GNP* is a weighted average of *all* countries comprising the group.

† Because of unresolved methodological issues in estimating *GNP* for centrally planned (nonmarket) economies, the World Bank after 1980 discontinued reporting income data for these countries. Figures in parentheses are crude approximations obtained by the author from other sources.

Sources: Adapted from World Bank, *World Development Report 1984,* pp. 218f., and other sources.

The declaration calls for changes in (1) the world pricing system, (2) the international monetary system and procedures for management of debt, and (3) a host of other arrangements including tariffs and trade restrictions, control of multinational corporations and technology transfer, plus increased development assistance, support of labor-intensive industries in the LDCs, and expanded utilization of cartels by the LDCs. As the world's largest economy, U.S. policies inevitably have significant impact on "agenda items" in all the broad fields of trade, finance, investment, and aid.

Regarding *economic aid,* the United States has opportunities to provide developmental assistance *multilaterally* through such organizations as the World Bank, International Monetary Fund, and United Nations as well as *bilaterally* through its own Agency for International Development and other programs. LDCs have asked the developed countries to contribute seven-tenths of one percent of their respective *GNPs* for direct assistance, but while several countries approximate or even exceed this figure (notably Saudi Arabia), U.S. *economic aid* has averaged about one-fourth of 1% of *GNP.* Nor has American aid gone to the neediest countries. Proposals for increased assistance generate controversy for a variety of reasons, including allegations of waste or inefficiency in using the funds, a preference for remediating poverty at home before sending money overseas, and the need for federal budget austerity in times of high deficits and inflation. Unconvinced by such arguments, some observers warn that, if the developed countries do not *willingly* increase their level of aid, tactics of desperation if not aggression are likely to be adopted eventually by the LDCs that will *compel* a more positive response.

Capitalism versus Communism

A second facet of international economic relations involves our ongoing struggle with the Soviet Union. Viewed as an *ideological conflict* between "world communism" and "democratic capitalism"—or "totalitarianism versus freedom"—the continuing tension between the United States and the USSR clearly has dominated international relations since the end of World War II. (Note the categories of Table 29.1, with the industrial market economies as the "first world," the nonmarket economies as the "second world," and many of the 72 countries of Categories III and IV as the Third World. To some extent, of course, classification is a matter of judgment—Rich/Poor, Developed/Developing, North/South, Advanced/Less-Developed, etc.—with China always presenting a paradox of gigantic proportions.)

The political struggle between Russia and "the West" may well be of cosmic significance, affecting not only the allocation of world resources (military expenditures alone exceed $1 trillion per year!) and the character of national and international institutions, but even the physical and psychological survival of man himself.

Soviet Ideology and Reality

The conflict began with the Russian Revolution of 1917 when Lenin and his cohorts *rejected the fundamental institution of capitalist society,* private ownership of the means of production (see Chapter 17 and appendix to Chapter 14). Under a socialist (communist) system, "free markets" (guided by individual economic self-interest) are no longer relied upon to determine which goods shall be produced, in what quantities, to be sold at what prices. Under *central planning,* the basic economic decisions reflect the discretionary judgments of government officials as to how resources can best be used (balancing short-run and long-run considerations). Without private property, individuals lose personal control over production and profits, and are stripped of the socioeconomic *power* associated with such control. "Exploitation" ceases. Other hoped-for effects of a socialistic planned economy include high levels of production (using humane methods), stable growth, optimal composition of output, and a distribution of income that provides economic security, opportunity for personal development, and social equity. Such is the socialist "vision."

The challenge of implementing a planned, nonmarket economy consistent with the socialist vision has proved formidable for the Soviet Union (and other socialist countries). Even without private ownership of natural resources and capital, experience shows that individuals (such as Communist Party officials) do wield power; nor does planning necessarily lead to optimal results with respect to the overall level, composition, and distribution of real income. Most importantly, the "side effects" of such a system may taint the social, political, and cultural aspects of community life and damage the individual human spirit. Many who give the Soviet Union high marks for economic performance—a *GNP* that, before Japan's emergence, was second only to that of the United States, and a pattern of income distribution that has virtually eliminated poverty in a nation of 270 million people—nevertheless remain doubtful that communism can generate a high overall *quality of life* (citing the prison camps, widespread alcoholism, economic favoritism, and suppression of civil liberties).

American Capitalism

The American capitalist ideology—strongly individualistic—rests on the argument that "guided capitalism" not only promotes superior *economic* performance but offers sociopolitical side effects that, on balance, are overwhelmingly preferable to those of a planned society. Most prominent is *freedom,* which is promoted in the *economic* sphere by private ownership and decentralized control, in the *political* sphere by such democratic institutions as a two-party system, popular elections, and conscientious regard for civil liberties (as in our constitutional Bill of Rights), and in the *social and cultural* spheres by diversity and free expression.

Few will deny imperfections in America's economic-social-political system, citing macroeconomic instability, poverty, wasteful consumption, concentration of power, and such side effects as crime, violence, drug abuse, personal malaise, etc. (Some people argue that many of these features are actually *virtues* because they demonstrate that our system gives people the freedom to *fail* as well as to reap the "natural" rewards of "success" in the form of wealth, income, and power.) But it hardly needs saying that our system, on balance, is admired and staunchly defended by the vast majority of Americans and their political leaders.

In the context of this chapter, the essential point to be made is that the international economic relations of the United States cannot be judged in the narrow perspectives of profitable trade and/or compassion for the poor nations of the world. Support or criticism of American policy strictly on grounds of "pure economics" or humanitarian concern for the poverty-stricken peoples of Africa and Asia does violence to the multidimensionality and complexity of the field. If we believe in the "cosmic significance" of the East-West ideological conflict, or simply its realpolitik, it behooves us to bear this component in mind as we "define the problem" of international economic relations en route to the formulation of wise policies.

Issues in International Trade

Discussing the plight of the less-developed countries first and the USA-USSR conflict second in this chapter does not necessarily imply that traditional concerns with international trade, investment, and finance are of tertiary importance. Indeed, how well the United States can cope with a wide range of "purely economic" problems will greatly affect not only our economic prosperity but also the standing and influence the United States enjoys vis-a-vis the communist nations and Third World. At mid-decade, these problems include an enormous merchandise trade deficit (amounting to $120 billion in 1984!); a strong and perhaps "overvalued" dollar; erosion of export markets for a great many manufactured goods as well as agricultural products; continuing pressures for import restrictions (costing American consumers $7 billion per year for sugar and dairy products alone, not to mention higher prices for textiles, motor vehicles, and steel); adverse effects of international debt problems suffered by developing countries (e.g., loss of U.S. export markets in the early 1980s as Latin American nations pursued austerity measures); and the worldwide mood of protectionism accompanying the economic recessions of the past decade.

The other side of the coin, in terms of the large current-account deficits and strong dollar (see Chapter 23 on the international balance of payments), is the *disinflationary* effect of lower-priced foreign goods and services, and the *surplus* in the *capital* account that provides funds for private investment and financing of the federal budget deficit. (Americans traveling abroad have learned that a strong dollar means highly favorable foreign exchange rates on such currencies as the French franc, Italian lira, and British pound, the dollar price of the latter dropping from $2.33 in 1980 to $1.20 just four years later.)

How are these problems resolved? Over a period of time, adjustments occur in a nation's balance of payments that tend to correct a disequilibrium—in part through the response of market forces, but also the result of deliberate policy actions. U.S. exports *increase,* for example, as economic recovery gathers momentum in other nations. Correspondingly, U.S. *imports* predictably decline when our economic cycle flattens or begins to turn downward.

In addition to such "normal market forces," government policies may be implemented to provide short-term protection of profits, markets, and jobs—as in the case of motor vehicles, agricultural commodities, textiles, and steel. Increasingly popular are such nontariff barriers as voluntary restraint agreements (VRAs), which can be negotiated without legislative action and are quite flexible in terms of duration and quantity specification. (History teaches us, by the way, that whatever device is used to cope with balance-of-trade problems—tariffs, quotas, VRAs, preferential procurement and/or credit arrangements, direct export subsidies, marketing franchises—they typically have a much longer life than originally intended, and therefore limit freedom of trade in the long run.)

With respect to developing countries, large U.S. trade deficits (along with eased credit arrangements) help those nations meet their international debt obligations and enable them to continue implementing their own development plans.

The Delicate Balance

Recapitulating the main theme of this chapter, the international domain finds a complex interplay of traditional *economic values* (efficiency, growth, profits, jobs, lower consumer prices) confronting such *sociopolitical concerns* as humanitarianism, ideology, and national security. As the world's largest market economy, the United States finds itself in a delicate balance where it must demonstrate to the world that guided capitalism *works* and therefore is an attractive alternative to central planning. Moreover, we must show that an open-market system not only benefits *us* but serves the needs and aspirations of the *developing nations* as well. When the "colossus of the North" (or West) *prospers,* it must not be at the expense of the LDCs. On the other hand, when our $4 trillion economy *malfunctions,* the symptoms of instability— recessionary declines in import demand, inflated prices, high interest rates, protectionism, etc.—must not send out tidal waves that swamp the developing nations (and drive our industrialized allies to acts of desperation). To avoid such harmful effects, institutional adjustments must necessarily be made, both within the U.S. economy and externally, perhaps along the lines of the proposed New International Economic Order.

These imperatives are not mere rhetoric; for if the U.S. economy fails in its international relationships, pragmatic consequences may well trigger a worldwide swing toward cartelization, central planning, and/or widespread international violence. If one of the dramatic facts of contemporary economic life is poverty for billions of people, another is that the less-developed countries are absolutely resolved, one way or another, to overcome this poverty and achieve a satisfactory rate of economic development so their people too can share in the material wellbeing that modern technology makes possible in today's world.

Selected Readings and References

P.R. Gregory and R.C. Stuart, *Comparative Economic Systems* (cited in Chapter 4).

W. Loehr and J.P. Powelson, *The Economics of Development and Distribution.* New York: Harcourt Brace Jovanovich, 1981. (Discusses issues related to the New International Economic Order, as does *Economic Development,* 4th ed., by B. Herrick and C.P. Kindleberger, McGraw-Hill, 1983).

World Bank, *World Development Report 1984.* New York: Oxford University Press, 1984.

Economic Indicators (cited in Chapter 18).

Economic Report of the President 1985 (cited in Chapter 2).

International Financial Statistics (cited in Chapter 23, along with other IMF publications).

Survey of Current Business (cited in Chapter 15).

PART SIX
SOCIAL VALUES AND
INDIVIDUAL WELLBEING

The ideas presented in Chapters 30 and 31 are perhaps the least conventional in the book and potentially the most far-reaching in importance. Chapter 30 is a blend of "positive science" dealing with what *is,* and "normative analysis" addressing what is *good* (i.e., Level 5 on the scale of knowing) and therefore, granting certain premises, what *ought to be.* The discussion reflects economic, philosophical, and psychological considerations that influence people's *value judgments* and *behavior* connected with socioeconomic life. While the analysis does not prescribe specific goals and policies concerning, say, unemployment, inflation, poverty, extreme inequality, *GNP* growth, wasteful consumption, U.S. economic aid for less-developed countries, and power politics, it nevertheless can assist individuals in making their own more responsible judgments about such matters. Moreover, the approach to value analysis developed here can help people avoid valuation pitfalls in areas of life *beyond* the economic. Chapter 31 concludes the book with a definition of economic *progress* formulated in terms of enhancing the overall quality of life not only for "society," but preeminently for *individual* human beings.

One of the secrets of life is to have good side effects.
        —Snoopy (Charles Schulz)

Values, Valuation, and the "Traditional Virtues"

Economics is a normative science, concerned not only with what *is* but also what *ought to be*. *Values* are important considerations that serve as criteria of choice for selecting *goals and policies,* and for *evaluating performance.* *Pitfalls* in dealing with values include failure to consciously identify the criteria being applied in a given situation of goal-setting or performance evaluation, unquestioning adherence to received or relativistic values, a proclivity for single-criterion thinking, and insistence that the ends justify the means.

The effect of affluence to individuals is that they may do what they please. We ought to see what it will please them to do before we risk congratulations!

　　　—(adapted from Edmund Burke, "On Liberty")

But after all, what is goodness? Answer me that, Alexey. Goodness is one thing with me and another with a charwoman, so it's a relative thing. Or isn't it? ... A treacherous question! You won't laugh if I tell you it's kept me awake two nights. I only wonder how people can live and think nothing of it. Vanity!

　　　—Dostoevsky, The Brothers Karamazov

Economics is nothing if it is not a science of value.

　　　—C. E. Ayres

Economic discussion is so laced with references to problems and goals—such as unemployment and inflation, efficiency and growth—that one fact quickly becomes clear. Economists are not content merely to *describe* the economy; they have a penchant for *evaluating* economic performance and suggesting ways to make it *better*. Nor do economists stand alone in this value-toned attitude; politicians and people in general are seldom indifferent to the state of the economy, especially as it affects their own jobs, incomes, and levels of living. This preoccupation with value considerations clearly makes economics a *normative* science, concerned not only with what *is* (the content of "positive" science), but also with what *ought to be*. Valuation and goal-setting, therefore, imply a knowledge of what constitutes "goodness" in the economic process, an ability to distinguish "better" from "worse" in the production and distribution of income. And in terms of the Cardinal Virtues, *prudentia* requires not just "good intentions" but knowledge of reality: "None but the Prudent can be Just, Brave, and Temperate."* To *do* the Good, one must *know* the Good.

The Normative Tradition in Economics

Economists observe the effects of given measures (causes) and seek to discover which measures tend to produce given effects, especially those effects which are more desirable. The question of what constitutes a "good" pattern of resource use—a particular application of what we shall generally refer to as "the value question"—has attracted the attention of economists from the time of Adam Smith (whose own interest in value is not surprising since he was a professor of moral philosophy before he turned to political economy). In the two centuries since *The Wealth of Nations,* various methods have been developed for *(a)* defining "good" performance and *(b)* evaluating actual performance. The neoclassical model of long-run competitive equilibrium (results of which are described in the appendix to Chapter 17) illustrates the former, while such empirical techniques as benefit-cost analysis, PPBS (Planning-Programming-Budgeting System), cost-effectiveness analysis, program evaluation, and policy analysis are examples of the latter.

Without going into details of the various normative methodologies, we want to point out that all evaluative models have *four features* in common. First, they are applied to a *particular entity* (program, policy, or institution). Second, they identify *criteria* to be used as the basis for evaluation. Third, they establish *standards* or levels of performance to which the entity can be compared. And fourth, they utilize *data* for describing the structure, operation, and consequences of the entity, including its benefits, costs, and side effects.

While each of these features is crucial in the evaluation process, the one that we want to focus on in this discussion is *criteria,* the basis on which a program or system is judged to be good, bad, or indifferent. The neoclassical approach to value analysis, for example, uses the criteria of allocative efficiency, productive efficiency, commutative justice, and freedom of choice by consumers and entrepreneurs. On the basis of these particular criteria (by no means the only ones that might have been chosen for evaluating the economy!), neoclassical economists concluded that *the best pattern of resource use for society is that which results from a capitalistic system with purely competitive markets.*

Following the Great Depression, mainstream market economists added the overall level of employment to their list of evaluative criteria, along with economic growth and, by the 1970s, reasonable price-level stability. The newer evaluation models

---

*The author is indebted to E. F. Schumacher, whose book *Small is Beautiful* called attention to the Traditional Virtues, and pointed the way to the works by Joseph Pieper and P. T. Geach cited below.

mentioned above, such as cost-benefit analysis, use monetary payout as the central criterion. Focusing mainly on measured and imputed income flows such as actual and foregone earnings, estimated social benefits, etc., they seek to determine whether a discounted stream of future income is sufficient to warrant a given present-day expenditure.

Values as Criteria of Choice

Now what is the logical connection between economic *goals* (what we would like to achieve), and economic evaluations (appraisals of how well the economy has actually performed)? Both are dependent not only on what happens in the economy, but also on what we *want* to happen. Success, in an important sense, lies in the eye of the beholder. (Consider the case of a "successful" bombing mission on London or Hiroshima.) Goal-setting and evaluation require a vision of what is important, good, desired, or desirable. *Evaluation is always based on evaluative criteria.* Something is good/bad, better/worse in terms of *particular criteria* (and also in comparison to some standard or level of performance of the "criterion variable.") *Goals* (and policies as well) are selected on the basis of *underlying values,* i.e., considerations that are important to us. Thus, there is a logical connection between evaluation and goal-setting; and there is a logical connection between criteria and values. In fact, we can now recognize that values are considerations (ideas, qualities, essentials) that are important to us, and because they are important, we use them as criteria to guide our decisions, choices, and actions. Concisely put, *values are criteria of choice.*

Values are not concrete entities like a trusted friend or a $30,000 sports car, but the essential qualities or ideas they represent. We may admire an honest man because of his honesty, a beautiful painting because of its beauty, and a wealthy family because of their material possessions. We speak of the values of honesty, beauty, wealth, and also freedom, efficiency, compassion, adaptability, cunning, power. Certain of these values are more specialized to economic affairs than others, but given the holistic worldview of this book, few if any lack relevance to economic analysis. Sometimes we refer to "personal values" and "social values," though we know that values can really be held only by *individuals,* not by inanimate objects or abstractions such as society. In any case, one would be suspicious of values that are bad for individuals yet somehow good for society. Social values are perhaps best thought of as personal values that are widely shared by members of the community. Sometimes the criteria that are represented as "social values" are actually the values imputed to society by groups who wield social power.

Values and Value Differences

What do economists (and society in general) know about values? We have already considered what values are and the important role they play in evaluating economic performance as well as providing guidelines for policy. And we noted some familiar values that underlie goals and policies regarding the overall level of economic activity, the composition of production, and the distribution of personal income. These values include efficiency, freedom of choice, full employment, income equity, international balance, et al., *plus* the avoidance of harmful side effects in the social, political, and "human" spheres (the Achilles heel of present-day communist regimes). One of the lessons that economists and other social scientists have learned about values, however, is that not everyone holds the same values or attaches equal importance to the values they do share. Value systems differ among individuals and groups mainly in the respect that some values ranking high on one list often receive a much lower priority on somebody else's list. The familiar efficiency-versus-equity controversy comes to mind. "Thirty million poor people in a $4 trillion-dollar economy is a national disgrace," liberals say; while conservatives argue that "It's better to tolerate poverty than risk killing the goose that lays the golden eggs; and, besides, if people are poor, it is probably their own fault." (Ironically, neither side may really know what causes poverty, whether there is a tradeoff between equality and efficiency, what the "terms of trade" might be, and whether or not the overall benefits are worth the costs.)

Sources of Values

Recognition of such differences raises the questions of (1) how people acquire their values and (2) what attitudes they adopt with respect to the validity of their own and other people's value systems and the tenacity with which they are held. More understanding here perhaps could lead to improvements in the resolution of value differences, and in turn to wiser economic policies and better performance of the economy.

A person's values seem to derive from three major sources: learning, judgment, and human nature. The *"learning"* of values often is the result of *conscious indoctrination* from parents, religious authorities, social and political leaders, etc., and less conscious *subtle indoctrination* from peer groups, schools (including college courses that impart particular economic ideologies), and such media as newspapers and television, among other sources. Willingness to accept the values of significant other people simply because they are *held* by those people is often regarded as a vital part of acculturation.

Indoctrination, however, is not the only way that values are learned. Through *formal and informal education,* we learn "instrumental" values that are tested and verified in cause-and-effect terms, such as the tool behavior discussed in Chapter 7 (i.e., a hammer is good for driving nails because it works). Finally, we learn some of our values quite unconsciously, by a process of "osmosis," or *gradual absorption* over time. Thorstein Veblen's "cultural incidence of the machine process" fits into this category. By growing up in a technological society, we learn that standardization, repetitive behavior, interchangeable parts, clock discipline, etc., are "good." As suggested in Chapter 7, we may not always limit the application of these "value lessons" to appropriate areas of human behavior!

The second major source of a person's values is *judgment* (Level 5 on the scale of knowing), not merely in applying values that are already held but actually establishing them in one's own value system. Because some people deny the possibility or legitimacy of this source, it merits special comment.

While the development of reasoning ability is often cited as an important objective of formal education, many people argue that weighing the evidence and arriving at one's own conclusions (i.e., the scientific method) is a procedure that should be used *only* in the realm of fact (what is), *not* in the field of values (what ought to be). This attitude serves to block inquiry on the most crucial value issues of our time, answers to which, in an era of nuclear weapons, literally become a matter of life or death. The traditional view that the world of value is fundamentally different from the world of fact, and therefore unresponsive to rational-empirical inquiry, seems to be changing, however. More and more of today's leading scientists, humbled by such discoveries as "the uncertainty principle," are far less inclined to view fact and value as totally separate realms.

With regard to the third major source of values, *human nature,* it is Veblen again who provides suggestive hypotheses within the tradition of American economic thought. In his view, values derive not only from indoctrination ("ceremonialism") and instrumental learning ("technology") but from certain predispositions that are part of man's inherited psychological makeup. He cites "the instinct of workmanship" (a basic human propensity directed toward the efficient completion of a task), the "instinct of idle curiosity" (impelling man to discover tasks that are worthwhile to undertake); and a "parental bent" (urging people to strive to improve the world for the benefit of future generations). Certain other "instincts," and some complex processes of "contamination," are shown to have less benign effects on human values and behavior.

What makes it especially interesting to reexamine Veblen today is the support that his ideas get from modern depth psychologists such as C. G. Jung, whose general theory of archetypes encompasses and clarifies Veblen's persistently articulated ideas. The important role that "human nature" plays in the economic process has never been doubted. But the particular character of human nature, or the "no-contents" hypothesis of tabula rasa (i.e., that babies are born with blank psychic slates) are typically assumed as "given premises" by economists of the various schools rather than questioned and examined in light of recent evidence. Examples are the *hedonistic individualism* of classical/neoclassical economics and the "plastic man" *behaviorism* of neoinstitutionalism.

Differing conceptions of human nature predictably lead to quite different explanations and valuations concerning the economic process. The view that a congeries of psychological instincts and archetypes may exert powerful influences on human valuations and behavior, as implied by Veblen and Jung, seems a more enlightened idea of human nature than the engagingly simple notions of hedonistic individualism or hard-line behaviorism—and implies quite different strategies for dealing with value issues. Prominent among the innate psychological propensities and dynamics that appear to shape value behavior are (1) "participation mystique," or the herd instinct, which when unconsciously acted out make individuals vulnerable to fads, mass movements and other collectivized patterns of conduct; (2) "enantiodromia," the tendency of extreme attitudes and energy flows to swing to their opposites; and (3) contamination of natural, healthy predispositions through contact with distortional influences (as Veblen emphasized in his analysis of the business system).

The "Validity" of Values

Understanding where values come from and how they are transmitted (and sometimes contaminated) carries provocative implications for anyone interested in shaping social policy. Still remaining, however, is the biggest question of all: What do we know about the *validity* of particular values and value systems? Is it simply a matter of "might makes right," or are there guidelines for discovering and verifying not merely what is *desired* by whom, but what is *desirable* for the individual and society?

In addressing the question of "validity" of particular values, some people argue that values are *absolute;* certain criteria of choice are valid for all people at all times.

Others claim that values are *relative;* particular criteria may be "right" for Group X in Year N, while other criteria are equally "right" for the same group at another time in history, or for Group Y across the ocean. The litmus test in the view of ethical relativists is whether particular values are *accepted* by the group itself. What *is* is "good." Validation becomes a matter of current practice and statistics. If most taxpayers cheat on their taxes, it's OK for Mr. Z to cheat on his own taxes. If consumers want to spend their money on X-rated movies or designer jeans, the market ought to respond to these expressed values. If the members of a democratic society (or their elected representatives) prefer nuclear weapons to improved mass-transit or pollution-control systems, the economy ought to give them what they desire, without a searching examination of whether those particular uses of society's productive wherewithal can be justified as desirable. In effect, surveys and opinion polls (such as the Kinsey Reports) tell us what constitutes goodness. But an obvious characteristic of this approach, regardless of whether the wants are expressed through the market or governmental mechanisms, is its own circularity: "I want it because I want it."

An alternative to absolutism and relativism is the *instrumental* orientation to value (not to be confused with hedonistic utilitarianism). It begins by recognizing that some values that are highly relevant to economic policy—such as freedom, honesty, and compassion—may indeed be absolute (in the sense of being innate human propensities). Nor can the existence and force of relativistic values be ignored as "observable empirical data." On the other hand, instrumentalism holds that no values should be accepted unquestioningly. And the test of any value lies in its *total consequences*—immediate and longer term, material and intangible, intended and unintended. Values are "good" if they are good-for the individual and good-for the community of individuals, if their use results in desirable human consequences in terms of a complex variety of considerations. Among these are good health, development of productive intelligence, and progress towards fulfillment of individual human potentiality. Individuals and societies that direct their actions in accordance with a balanced blend of such values seem far more likely to succeed in promoting human wellbeing than those which rely on such single-minded pursuits as maximizing "consumer satisfaction" or production, promoting technological advance, or perpetuating a particular politico-economic system.

Pitfalls in Valuing

The instrumental approach avoids certain *pitfalls to valuing* that have blocked social progress within the United States and around the world. One such pitfall is the *implicitness* of value criteria, a failure to consciously identify the particular criteria being applied in a given situation of goal-setting or performance evaluation. A second pitfall is *unreflective adherence* to indoctrinated or relativistic values (such as the automatic assumption that the market mechanism allocates resources and distributes income in the best of all possible ways (or "it's OK because everybody's doing it")); "knee-jerk" valuing in effect refuses to consider value issues on the basis of their merits and possible demerits.

A third error is "tunnel vision," *reliance on a single criterion* for evaluative judgment and the systematic overlooking of "side effects." So often in discussion of economic policy we hear that equity is the only thing that matters, or incentives (because they are vital for efficiency), or control of inflation, or indeed whatever *one* consideration happens to dominate collective thinking at the particular time. (But like the weather in Kansas, if you don't like it just wait 10 minutes; it will surely change.) Hall-of-Fame football coach Vince Lombardi expressed this attitude memorably with his dictum: "Winning isn't the most important thing; it's the *only* thing." In our age of narrow specialization we perhaps find it difficult to "chew bubble gum and walk a straight line at the same time." An all-too-common example of tunnel vision (contaminated by "me-ism") is the particular group of workers who threaten to strike unless their money wages rise by, say, 5% on grounds that the expected rate of inflation is 5%. The only effect of the pay hike that they see, or consider relevant, is protection of their own real income. What they prefer to ignore are the "side effects" of the strike and/or pay increase on the perpetuation of inflation.

A fourth pitfall to responsible valuing is the attempt to defend obviously indefensible behavior on grounds that *"the ends justify the means."* The flaw in this approach becomes apparent when one recognizes that ends and means are not qualitatively distinct but exist on a continuum. (Recall from Chapter 5 the observation of C. E. Ayres that "There are no ends, only means"; and Ferdinand LaSalle's verse on the interdependence of "paths and ends.") Once again it is the tunnel vision of ignoring "side effects" that creates the illusion that means and ends are distinct entities; only certain narrow "ends-in-view" are acknowledged.

This combination of unconsciousness, unreflective adherence to given values, tunnel vision, and the insistence that the ends justify the means serves to set group against group in an endless power struggle (as the rise of the PACs and single-interest lobbies makes so clear). The result is a sordid game of musical chairs—one group gaining temporarily at the expense of others—with degenerating political ethics and stunted social progress as costly side effects.

Recapitulation on Value Analysis

In our next and concluding chapter, we consider the value dimensions of economic progress and improvements in the overall quality of life. Before doing so, however, let us summarize what this chapter has said about values, and suggest some implications for individual behavior. First, *values are important* because they influence choices and courses of action, with significant consequences for the individual and the society in which he lives. Second, *value judgments are as good as the reasons and evidence that support them* and as weak as the evidence that supports alternative views. While everyone has a right to his own values, the right carries a responsibility to ensure that one's values are founded on something more humanly valid than a Pavlovian conditioned response. We suggest that, in our age of science and interdependence, there is a *dual human imperative:* to strive to know not only what *is,* but also what *ought to be.* (The great lesson of the "thinking robot" may be to remind man that his real uniqueness lies not in his ability to reason but in his moral consciousness and capacity to make value judgments.) Third, *the goodness of anything must be judged by its total consequences,* hence on the basis of *multiple criteria*—at least until man is wise enough to discover the concert of values that reduces the "totum bonum" to one all-encompassing criterion. Fourth and last, as we endeavor to fulfill the "dual human imperative," *we should use all of the intelligence available to us.* As a practical matter, this includes applying the opportunity-cost principle explained in Chapter 11 and, to the extent possible, the method of reasoning described in Chapter 16. If each of us will consciously weigh the tradeoffs and consider the full range of consequences involved in alternative courses of action, we stand a better chance of arriving at value judgments that meet the test of responsibility both to self and society.

Addendum on the "Traditional Virtues"

In the opening paragraph of this chapter, reference was made to the Traditional Virtues that have played so prominent a role in the intellectual and moral life of Western man. The virtues are seven in number: Faith, Hope, and Charity (the "theological" virtues); and Prudence, Justice, Courage, and Temperance (the "natural" virtues, or Four Cardinal Virtues). As Josef Pieper persuasively argues, *prudentia* (which, he points out, does not quite translate into the modern meaning of "prudence") is the mother of all the other Cardinal Virtues in that one cannot, for example, behave in a manner that effectively promotes Justice unless one understands reality: "what things are like and what their situation is." Similarly, fearlessness or martydom in an ignoble cause is hardly expressive of the virtue of Courage. Recalling John Gardner's quip that "To *do* something, you have to *know* something," we expand that statement to read: "To do something *worthwhile*, you have to know what *is* worthwhile and have the *skill* and *commitment* to follow through." Good intentions are insufficient.

Pieper makes a strong case for economic understanding *(prudentia economica)* when he writes: "Realization of the good presupposes that our actions are appropriate to the real situation, that is to the concrete realities which form the 'environment' of a concrete human action." People who are economically illiterate are not well qualified to dictate the restructuring of the economic system. In the context of specific problems examined in this book, it is hardly prudent, and therefore hardly virtuous, to advocate eliminating income poverty without acknowledging the need for middle-income families to accept higher taxes; to support government job programs for full employment without dealing with the "side effects" of inflation and inequity; to favor reducing another group's economic power without yielding any of one's own; and to call for debt relief for the developing countries without facing the issue of who will bear the burden of the subsidy. Espousal of such causes may project an image of Justice and Courage, but the image is superficial. As for Temperance, the massive American appetite for goods and services is so thoroughly institutionalized that efforts to retrench would be labeled unpatriotic (especially by the advertising industry).

The Traditional Virtues are also relevant, again in the context of the economic process, when considering *motivation* to *do* what is worthwhile once people have made up their minds what the Good entails. Virtues are not quite the same thing as values; rather than being criteria of choice, virtues are attributes of individuals— human strengths that guide and motivate one toward "right conduct." P. T. Geach argues that man *needs* these virtues, and therefore should strive to develop them, not as a social duty but in order to "attain ends proper to man." It takes Prudence to discover authentic values (in contrast to "false" values), and it takes Justice, Courage, and Temperance to *realize* those values in the concrete setting of the actual world.

Selected Readings and References

C.E. Ayres, *Toward a Reasonable Society: The Values of Industrial Civilization* (cited in Chapter 5).

Kenneth E. Boulding, "Economics as a Moral Science" (cited in Chapter 17).

J. Bronowski, *Science and Human Values,* Rev. ed. New York: Harper & Row, 1965.

Robert L. Darcy, "Economic Education, Human Values, and the Quality of Life," Chapter 10 in *Humanistic Frontiers in American Education.* Edited by Roy P. Fairfield. Englewood Cliffs, NJ: Prentice-Hall, 1971.

Robert L. Darcy, *Vocational Education Outcomes: Perspective for Evaluation.* Columbus: National Center for Research in Vocational Education at Ohio State University, 1979. (Also see R.L. Darcy, "Value Issues in Program Evaluation," *Journal of Economic Issues,* Vol. XV, No. 2, June 1981.)

P.T. Geach, *The Virtues.* London: Cambridge University Press, 1977.

C.G. Jung, *The Undiscovered Self* (cited in Chapter 2).

C.G. Jung, *Modern Man in Search of a Soul* (cited in Chapter 14).

C.G. Jung, *Two Essays in Analytical Psychology.* Princeton/Bollingen paperback: Princeton University Press, 1972 (original copyright 1953).

Josef Pieper, *The Four Cardinal Virtues: Prudence, Justice, Fortitude, Temperance.* New York: Harcourt, Brace and World, 1965.

Thorstein Veblen, *The Theory of Business Enterprise* (cited in Chapter 7) and *The Instinct of Workmanship* (cited in Chapter 8).

H.G. Wells, "The Country of the Blind," from *The Time Machine and Other Stories,* in *The Complete Short Stories of H.G. Wells.* New York: St. Martin's Press, 1971. (On the theme of ethical relativism.)

Edward C. Whitmont, *The Symbolic Quest: Basic Concepts of Analytical Psychology.* New York: Putnam's, 1969 (paperback ed. 1978, Princeton University Press).

31

Growth, Development, and Progress: Perspectives on Improving the Quality of Life

Economic *growth* is defined in strict quantitative terms as an increase in production. *Development* is growth plus the transformation of technology and institutions. *Progress* implies an overall improvement in material wellbeing. The economy's performance contributes to a higher *quality of life* not by growth alone but also by bettering the conditions of work, production, consumption, the environment, and other facets of economic life. Strategies for improving the quality of life must recognize the key role of *individual transformation* along with *institutional adjustments*. Higher levels of consciousness and the impulse to personal fulfillment can help to humanize the economic system and encourage changes in the distribution of income, wealth, and power that will benefit rich and poor alike.

The machine process pervades modern life; its dominance is seen in . . . the reduction of all manner of things, purposes and acts, necessities, conveniences, and amenities of life, to standard units. The cultural incidence of the machine process [entails] a relative neglect and disparagement of . . . intellectual faculties [which do not run on the lines of] regularity of sequence and mechanical precision.
—Thorstein Veblen

Apart from agglomerations of huge masses of people, in which the individual disappears anyway, one of the chief factors responsible for mass-mindedness is scientific rationalism, which robs the individual of his foundations and his dignity. As a social unit he has lost his individuality and become a mere abstract number in the bureau of statistics . . . [We become] fascinated and overawed by statistical truths and large numbers, and are daily apprised of the nullity and futility of the individual personality.
—C. G. Jung

The most important economic problem in any age is to know what we want, to define useful and worthy ends, and to balance our efforts among them in due proportion.
    —Moses Abramovitz

We have met the enemy, and "they" is us.
    —Pogo (Walt Kelly)

There is no question in anyone's mind that the United States has experienced economic *growth* during the 20th century. The long-term increases in output and expanded availability of goods and services are readily apparent; *GNP* statistics reported earlier support this observation. In like manner, we can agree that the American economy has *developed* in the sense that we not only have more goods but obviously have undergone a dramatic cultural *transformation*—in technology, institutions, and lifestyles. (During the course of this growth and development, *population* has increased terrifically in the most literal sense of the word!)

What we are not quite so sure about is whether or to what extent we have experienced economic *progress,* i.e., whether being "richer" and "smarter" has made us better off. This is the central question to be considered in this final chapter. The discussion will be philosophical in spirit and avowedly more suggestive than definitive. (Perhaps a Surgeon General's warning is appropriate here: "What follows may be harmful to your peace of mind—if it is based on the unquestioning acceptance of collective thinking!)

More, Different, Better

When the issue was introduced in Chapter 24, economic growth was treated essentially in quantitative terms while discussion of the more qualitative concepts of "development" and "progress" was explicitly reserved for the valuational analysis of Part Six. Now, to distinguish clearly among the three concepts, we shall define growth as *increased production,* development as *growth-plus-change* (in technology and institutions), and progress as an overall *improvement* in material wellbeing— explicitly defined in terms of *responsible value judgments.* In simplest terms, growth is "more"; development is "different"; and progress is "better." Improving the overall *quality of life* means creating better conditions for individual human beings in all aspects of their lives, noneconomic as well as economic.

Defining Economic Progress

This concept of economic progress requires some elaboration. For economic growth and change to make people better off, it is not enough that they simply have larger quantities of goods and services available to consume. Human beings are surely more than "eternal sucklers," to use Erich Fromm's rather harsh description, or "lightning calculators of pleasure and pain" in Veblen's terms. Even within the limits of their *economic* functions, individuals are also workers, citizens, and sometimes entrepreneurs. Genuine economic progress therefore requires not just increased production but improvements in the *conditions* and *processes* of production, consumption, and general economic life. Moreover, the evaluational framework employed in judging the extent to which progress is occurring must include criteria reflective of *individual* wellbeing along with conventional "social indicators." (Contrary to certain assumptions of neoclassical theory, we do not cease being human beings during our 8-hour work shift, nor are we homogenous "units" to be allocated as interchangeable parts in the production process.) Increasingly, as people become more individuated, the economic system must respect individual differences in personal characteristics and potentialities rather than casting people in the single mold of what the machine "prefers." As Schumacher suggests with the very meaningful subtitle to his book *Small Is Beautiful,* we need to structure the economic process "as if people mattered." (Under the present system, in terms of Jungian typology, machines seem to "demand" extraverted sensation-thinking types; and therefore these are the kinds of "individuals" that our society and its educational institutions strive to "supply.")

Apart from the economic domain, beyond physical survival and hedonistic gratification, human beings have almost limitless needs and potentialities. Economic progress can make important contributions to improving the *overall quality of life,* but this desideratum also requires advances in areas that *transcend* material wellbeing, including, for example, the development of a social climate less hostile to individuality, personal growth, and transformation. Recalling once again the popular Lombardi maxim that "Winning is the *only* thing," too many Americans apparently have learned that "getting and spending" are the only thing. It is a false lesson that impoverishes the learner as well as the community with which he interacts.

Returning for a further comment on the basic *logic* of the concept of economic progress, it might seem that the process necessarily entails growth of output along with improvements in material knowledge and social structure. At various times and places in human history, this has doubtless been the pattern; particular combinations of "more" and "different" have indeed met the test of "better." But it is also logically possible that once a relatively high level of living has been attained, progress no longer requires increased income but "merely" a modified techno-institutional environment reflecting human attitudes that give priority to the overall quality of life. (Of course it is also conceivable that progress could stem from increased income alone, without technological and institutional change, but this is almost a contradiction in terms and seems quite inconsistent with the dynamic nature of the world as we know it.)

What all these remarks lead to is the suggestion that in the America of the 1980s (and elsewhere around the world as the second millennium of the Christian era draws to a close) it is by no means obvious that contemporary circumstances and trends qualify as unabashed progress. At the same time, it is hard to resist being fascinated by the powerful forces whirling around us, and even appreciative of the opportunity that this remarkable period offers for gaining insight into the human experience. If we learn our lessons well, that knowledge conceivably might reassure us that human evolution is indeed moving along favorable lines, or, alternatively, could alert us that we need to change directions, perhaps even radically.

Removing the "Blinders"

Among the themes receiving special attention in this book have been (1) the powerful and multifaceted influence of dynamic *technology* on human culture; (2) the continuing need for *institutional adjustments* to promote individual wellbeing in our dangerously collectivized society; (3) the pervasiveness of *value issues* in socio-economic-political life and critical need for progress in this sphere of knowledge (to match our vigorous if undisciplined advances in materialistic science); and (4) the need for a higher level of *personal consciousness* about the nature and needs of the individual human being as the *container of life, locus of value,* and both *agent* and *beneficiary* of progress toward a higher quality of being.

Such consciousness requires that we remove our "blinders" and acknowledge not only the materialistic and power-oriented goals of economic life but also the unintended *side effects,* or "spillovers," from the activities of working, earning, fulfilling civic duties, and pursuing the hedonistic pleasures of mass consumption. More destructive perhaps than any other aspect of personal conduct is the *narrowness of vision* that afflicts so many individuals in our machine-dominated, mass-minded, over-specialized, and commercialistic culture. ("If your eye is sound," according to the Gospel, "your whole body will be full of light; but if your eye is not sound, your body is full of darkness.")

Depth psychologists like C. G. Jung remind us that the one-sidedness and overvaluation of the rationalist-materialist attitude can manifest itself not only in the widely acknowledged malaise of modern man but also in such specific pathologies as personal violence, crime, political corruption, alcoholism, drug abuse, epidemic obesity, sexual promiscuity, child abuse, pornography, mental illness, abominable personal hygiene, suicides, rampant tax avoidance, compulsive shoplifting, family disintegration, illegitimacy, child abduction and flight, TV addiction, cults, organized violence, vindictive and avaricious litigation, unending wars, revolutions, terrorism, moral nihilism, and countless other perversities that titillate tabloid readers and viewers of the evening TV news. It is hardly reassuring to ponder the psychic health of a society whose combined annual expenditures for military purposes and health care approach $1 trillion per year!*

Strategies for Improving the Quality of Life

What strategies suggest themselves for converting economic growth and development to genuine *progress* and, most importantly, for improving the overall quality of human life?

We can begin with certain premises. First is the certainty of change, a phenomenon that apparently is inherent in nature and historically has manifested itself in the evolution of human knowledge, including *science and technology.* Correspondingly there is an imperative for *continuous institutional adjustment,* i.e., the discretionary restructuring of social arrangements aimed at meeting mankind's material needs while at the same time conducing to human progress in other areas of human potential, including spiritual growth. Institutional adjustment , in other words, must be guided not by a single value criterion—such as the increased production of goods and services, or even the advance of materialistic knowledge—but by a panoply of emerging values expressive of the *totality of human capability and needs.* In the

---

*In *The Symbolic Quest,* Edward C. Whitmont offers an explanation of "the feeling of meaningless existence which lurks everywhere today as the result of our positivistic outlook and education." He identifies what he terms our "pseudo-religion of material prosperity, monetary greed, and sexual thrills" as the "neurosis of our time," warning that the "primitive mythologization of secular values...[creates a] threat of collective no less than individual psychosis" (p. 102).

context of this book, and especially the valuational analysis presented in Chapter 30, the key strategy for economic progress is precisely what Professor Moses Abramovitz identified in an essay written many years before he was honored with the presidency of the American Economic Association, namely that the *most important economic problem of our time is to "define useful and worthy ends, and to balance our efforts among them in due proportion."*

Progress in *knowing the good*—advancing our knowledge in the broad universe of values—is necessary but not sufficient, however. Equally crucial is the impulse to action, the problem of *motivation*. It is not enough to define worthy ends; one must *strive to realize the Good.* The word "one" is chosen advisedly. The problems of value and institutional adjustment cannot be resolved solely by a strategy of collective power channeled toward social reform, whether blatantly coercive or more subtly manipulative. (Our "social Geiger counters" are still detecting fallout from the pragmatically successful power strategies of the 1920s, 1930s, and 1960s.) "Social reform" alone will not ensure socioeconomic progress, particularly when it entails imposing one's will on other people; *individuals* must also transform themselves and *willingly* strive for beneficial changes in the social environment (as in themselves).

In this context there seems to be, as the 20th century approaches its close, a constellation of forces expressing a teleological impulse for growth and transformation (popularized by such themes as the coming "Age of Aquarius" and finding profound expression in C. G. Jung's concepts of individuation and evolving consciousness). Unless one's nose is stuck obsessively to the grindstone of the workaday world it is impossible to overlook the power of such forces at work in American society today—by no means all benign! (The human soul reacts in diverse ways to stimuli bombarding it from inside and out.)

The challenge to each individual, then, is to ponder the "ends proper to man," and strive to develop in one's own self the personal attributes required as "ways and means" for progressing toward those ends. It should not be surprising to discover that they include the Traditional Virtues alluded to in Chapter 30, as well as the self-understanding emphasized by depth psychology.

Full recognition of the dynamic character, enormous power, and amoral nature of materialistic knowledge may place people in awe but will hardly lead to demands for a moratorium on technological progress. Predictably the recognition that technology is *not* a "benevolent god," however, will call for abandonment of the "invisible-hand" orientation which for two centuries has helped legitimize whatever technological innovations that profit or power happened to inspire. In its place must come a more *discretionary* economy in which responsible value judgments play an expanded role. Increased awareness of the *total effects* of instability, poverty and extreme inequality, concentration of power, and our other economic problems—on the *individual* as well as the community—can lead, for example, not only to reasonable demands by the have-nots but, more importantly, to the willing relinquishment of excesses by the *privileged.*

There will be no quick cure-alls for our nation's economic problems, and much less the world's. Man's evolution has a long way yet to go. But the *absolute* and *relative* affluence of the overall U.S. economy today places the American people in a favorable position to adopt enlightened policies in pursuit of a higher quality of life for rich and poor alike. What is required is a surge of commitment from increasingly conscious and caring individuals.

Selected Readings and References

Moses Abramovitz, "Economic Goals and Social Welfare in the Next Generation," in *Problems of U.S. Economic Development,* Vol. I. New York: Committee for Economic Development, 1958.

Erich Fromm, "Man in Capitalistic Society," Chapter 5 in *The Sane Society.* New York: Holt Rinehart & Winston, 1955. (Also see *The Art of Loving,* New York: Harper & Row, 1956.)

John S. Gambs, *Beyond Supply and Demand* (cited in Chapter 8).

David Hamilton, *Evolutionary Economics: A Study of Change in Economic Thought.* Albuquerque: University of New Mexico Press, 1970.

Robert L. Heilbroner, *An Inquiry into the Human Prospect.* New York: W. W. Norton, 1980.

C.G. Jung, *The Undiscovered Self* (cited in Chapter 2).

C.G. Jung, *Modern Man in Search of a Soul* (cited in Chapter 14).

C.G. Jung, *Two Essays in Analytical Psychology* (cited in Chapter 30).

W. Arthur Lewis, *The Theory of Economic Growth* (cited in Chapter 24).

S.B. Linder, *The Harried Leisure Class.* New York: Columbia University Press, 1970.

M. Scott Peck, *People of the Lie: The Hope for Healing Human Evil* (cited in Chapter 28).

E.F. Schumacher, *Small is Beautiful: Economics as if People Mattered* (cited in Appendix to Chapter 14).

Marc Tool, *The Discretionary Economy* (cited in Chapter 8).

Thorstein Veblen, "The Cultural Incidence of the Machine Process." (cited in Chapter 7).

Thorstein Veblen, *The Instinct of Workmanship* (cited in Chapter 8)

Edward C. Whitmont, *The Symbolic Quest: Basic Concepts of Analytical Psychology* (cited in Chapter 30).

Readings and References

Angle, Elizabeth W. *Keys for Business Forecasting,* 5th ed. Richmond, VA: Federal Reserve Bank of Richmond, 1980.

Abramovitz, Moses. "Economic Goals and Social Welfare in the Next Generation," in *Problems of U.S. Economic Development,* Vol. I. New York: Committee for Economic Development, 1958.

Ayres, C.E. *The Industrial Economy.* Boston: Houghton Mifflin, 1952.

———. *The Theory of Economic Progress,* 3d ed. Kalamazoo: New Issues Press at Western Michigan University, 1978 (originally published in 1944 by University of North Carolina Press).

———. *Toward A Reasonable Society: The Values of Industrial Civilization.* Austin: University of Texas, 1961.

Boulding, Kenneth E. *Economic Analysis,* 4th ed. (Vol. I, *Microeconomic;* Vol. II, *Macroeconomics).* New York: Harper & Row, 1966.

———. *Economics as a Science.* New York: McGraw-Hill, 1970.

———. *The Meaning of the 20th Century* (The Great Transition). New York: Harper & Row, 1965.

Bronowksi, J. *Science and Human Values,* Rev. ed. New York: Harper & Row, 1965.

Browning, E.K. and J.M. Browning. *Public Finance and the Price System,* 2d ed. New York: Macmillan, 1983.

Browning, E.K. and W.R. Johnson. *The Distribution of the Tax Burden.* Washington: American Enterprise Institute for Public Policy Research, 1979.

Bury, J.B. *The Idea of Progress.* New York: Dover, 1955 (originally published in 1932 by Macmillan).

Caves, R.E. and R.W. Jones. *World Trade and Payments,* 3d ed. Boston: Little Brown, 1981.

Committee for Economic Development. *Productivity Policy: Key to the Nation's Economic Future* (A Statement on National Policy). New York: Committee for Economic Development, April 1983.

Commons, John R. et al. *History of Labor in the United States.* New York: Macmillan, 1918.

Darcy, Robert L. "Economic Education, Human Values, and the Quality of Life," Chapter 10 in *Humanistic Frontiers in American Education* (see Fairfield).

————. *First Steps Toward Economic Understanding.* Athens: Ohio Council on Economic Education at Ohio University, 1966.

————. "The Nature of Economic Enterprise," Chapter 5 in *Vocational Guidance and Human Development* (see Herr).

————. "Value Issues in Program Evaluation," *Journal of Economic Issues* (Vol. XV, No. 2) June 1981.

————. *Vocational Education Outcomes: Perspective for Evaluation.* Columbus: National Center for Research in Vocational Education at Ohio State University, 1979.

Darcy, R.L. and P.E. Powell. *Manpower and Economic Education.* Denver: Love, 1973.

————. "What All Workers Should Know About Economics," Chapter 11 in *Vocational Education and the Nation's Economy* (see Meyer).

Denison, Edward F. *The Sources of Economic Growth in the United States and the Alternatives Before Us* (Supplementary Paper No. 13). New York: Committee for Economic Development, January 1962.

————. *Why Growth Rates Differ.* Washington: Brookings, 1967.

————. *Accounting for U.S. Economic Growth 1929-1969.* Washington: Brookings, 1974.

————. *Accounting for Slower Economic Growth: The United States in the 1970s.* Washington: Brookings, 1979.

Economic Education in the Schools (Report of the National Task Force on Economic Education). New York: Committee for Economic Development, 1961.

Fabricant, Solomon. *A Primer on Productivity.* New York: Random House, 1969.

Facts and Figures on Government Finance, 22d biennial ed. Washington: Tax Foundation, 1983.

Fairfield, Roy P. (editor). *Humanistic Frontiers in American Education.* Englewood Cliffs, NJ: Prentice-Hall, 1971.

Ferman, Louis A. et al. (editors). *Poverty in America,* Rev. ed. Ann Arbor: University of Michigan Press, 1968.

Foster, J. Fagg. "The Papers of J. Fagg Foster" (edited by Baldwin Ranson), *Journal of Economic Issues* (Vol. XV, No. 4) December 1981.

Friedman, Milton. *Capitalism and Freedom.* Chicago: University of Chicago Press, 1962.

Friedman, M. and R. Friedman. *Free to Choose.* New York: Harcourt Brace Jovanovich, 1979.

Fromm, Erich. *The Art of Loving.* New York: Harper & Row, 1956.

————. *The Sane Society.* New York: Holt Rinehart & Winston, 1955.

Galbraith, John Kenneth. *The New Industrial State.* Boston: Houghton Mifflin, 1967.

Galbraith, J.K. and N. Salinger. *Almost Everyone's Guide to Economics.* Boston: Houghton Mifflin, 1978 (Bantam paperback, 1979).

Gambs, John S. *Beyond Supply and Demand: A Reappraisal of Institutional Economics.* New York: Columbia University Press, 1946.

————. *Man, Money, and Goods.* New York: Columbia University Press, 1952.

Gambs, J.S. and J.B. Komisar. *Economics and Man,* 3d ed. Homewood, IL: Irwin, 1968.

Geach, P.T. *The Virtues.* London: Cambridge University Press, 1977.

Goode, Richard. *The Individual Income Tax,* Rev. ed. Washington: Brookings, 1976.

Gregory, P.R. and R.C. Stuart. *Comparative Economic Systems,* 2d ed. Boston: Houghton Mifflin, 1985.

Gwartney, J.D. and R. Stroup. *Economics,* 3d ed. New York: Academic Press, 1982.

Hamilton, David. *Evolutionary Economics: A Study of Change in Economic Thought.* Albuquerque: University of New Mexico Press, 1970 (essentially a reissue of *Newtonian Classicism and Darwinian Institutionalism,* 1953, same publisher).

Heilbroner, Robert L. *An Inquiry into the Human Prospect.* New York: W.W. Norton, 1980.

————. *The Making of Economic Society,* 6th ed. Englewood Cliffs, NJ: Prentice-Hall, 1980.

————. *The Worldly Philosophers,* 5th ed. New York: Simon & Schuster, 1980.

Heilbroner, R.L. and A. Singer. *The Economic Transformation of America: 1600 to the Present,* 2d ed. New York: Harcourt Brace Jovanovich, 1984.

Herr, Edwin L. (editor). *Vocational Guidance and Human Development.* Boston: Houghton Mifflin, 1974.

Herrick, B. and C.P. Kindleberger. *Economic Development,* 4th ed. New York: McGraw-Hill, 1983.

Hession, C.H. and H. Sardy. *Ascent to Affluence: A History of American Economic Development.* Boston: Allyn & Bacon, 1969.

Huff, Darrell. *How to Lie with Statistics.* New York: W.W. Norton, 1954.

Information Please Almanac, 38th ed. Boston: Houghton Mifflin, 1985.

International Monetary Fund. *World Economic Outlook; International Financial Statistics Yearbook; Balance of Payments Statistics Yearbook; Direction of Trade Statistics Yearbook; Government Finance Statistics Yearbook.* Washington, DC: International Monetary Fund, annual publications.

Josephson, Matthew. *The Money Lords* (The Great Finance Capitalists, 1925-1950). New York: Weybright & Talley, 1972.

―――. *The Robber Barons* (The Great American Capitalists, 1861-1901). New York: Harcourt Brace, 1934.

Jung, Carl Gustav. "The Art of Living" in *C.G. Jung Speaking* (see McGuire and Hull).

―――. *Modern Man in Search of a Soul.* New York: Harcourt Brace Jovanovich (first published 1933).

―――. *Two Essays in Analytical Psychology.* Princeton, NJ: Princeton/Bollingen paperback by Princeton University Press, 1972 (original copyright 1953).

―――. *The Undiscovered Self.* New York: Mentor, 1957.

Keynes, John Maynard. *The General Theory of Employment, Interest, and Money.* New York: Harcourt Brace, 1936.

Kuznets, Simon. "The Pattern of U.S. Economic Growth" in *The Goal of Economic Growth* (see Phelps).

Landsberg, Hans H. *Natural Resources for U.S. Growth* (A Look Ahead to the Year 2000). Baltimore: John Hopkins, 1964 (published for Resources for the Future, Washington, D.C.).

Lerner, Max (editor). *The Portable Veblen.* New York: Viking, 1958.

Lewis, W. Arthur. *The Theory of Economic Growth.* Homewood, IL: Irwin, 1955.

Linder, S.B. *The Harried Leisure Class.* New York: Columbia University Press, 1970.

Lipsey, R.G. and P.O. Steiner, *Economics,* 7th ed. New York: Harper & Row, 1983.

Loehr W. and J.P. Powelson. *The Economics of Development and Distribution.* New York: Harcourt Brace Jovanovich, 1981.

Lundberg, Ferdinand. *The Rich and the Super-Rich: A Study in the Power of Money Today.* New York: Lyle Stuart, 1968.

Mansfield, Edwin. *Economics,* 4th ed. New York: W.W. Norton, 1983.

―――. *The Economics of Technological Change.* New York: W.W. Norton, 1968.

Marshall, Alfred. *Principles of Economics,* 8th ed. New York: Macmillan, 1949 (1st edition, 1890).

Marx, Karl. *Capital* (A Critique of Political Economy). New York: Modern Library, no date (Vol. I of *Das Kapital* first published 1867).

Marx, K. and F. Engels. *The Communist Manifesto.* (Numerous editions; first published 1848).

McConnell, Campbell R. *Economics,* 9th ed. New York: McGraw-Hill, 1984.

McGuire, W. and R.F.C. Hull (editors). *C.G. Jung Speaking.* Princeton, NJ: Princeton University Press, 1977.

Means, Gardiner C. *The Corporate Revolution in America* (Economic Reality versus Economic Theory). New York: Collier, 1964.

Meyer, Warren G. (editor). *Vocational Education and the Nation's Economy.* Washington: American Vocational Association, 1977.

Mishan, Ezra J. "The Costs of Economic Growth" in *The Goal of Economic Growth* (see Phelps).

Mitchell, Wesley Clair. *Business Cycles and their Causes.* Berkeley: University of California Press, 1941 (originally published as Part III of *Business Cycles,* 1913).

Moore, Geoffrey H. *Business Cycles, Inflation, and Forecasting,* 2d ed. Cambridge, MA: Ballinger, 1980 (published for the National Bureau of Economic Research).

Mumford, Lewis. *The Myth of the Machine,* Vol. II *The Pentagon of Power.* New York: Harcourt Brace Jovanovich, 1964 (Vol. I, *Technics and Civilization* published in 1934).

Murray, George. *The Legacy of Al Capone.* New York: Putnam's, 1975.

Musgrave, R.A. and P.B. Musgrave. *Public Finance in Theory and Practice,* 3d ed. New York: McGraw-Hill, 1980.

Myrdal, Gunnar. *Asian Drama: An Inquiry into the Poverty of Nations.* New York: Twentieth Century Fund, 1968.

Noonan, John T. *Bribes.* New York: Macmillan, 1985.

Okun, Arthur M. *Equality and Efficiency: The Big Tradeoff.* Washington: Brookings, 1975.

Pechman, Joseph A. *Who Paid the Taxes: 1966-1985.* Washington: Brookings, 1985.

Peck, M. Scott. *People of the Lie: The Hope for Healing Human Evil.* New York: Simon & Schuster, 1983.

Peterson, Rodney D. "Business Cycles: Recessions and Depressions," *Colorado Economic Issues* (Vol. 5, No. 5) January 1981.

Phelps, Edmund S. (editor). *The Goal of Economic Growth,* Rev. ed. New York: Norton, 1969.

Pieper, Josef. *The Four Cardinal Virtues: Prudence, Justice, Fortitude, Temperance.* New York: Harcourt, Brace & World, 1965 (paperback edition, University of Notre Dame Press, 1966).

Polanyi, Karl. *The Great Transformation.* Boston: Beacon, 1957 (originally published in 1944 by Rinehart).

Reich, Robert B. *The Next American Frontier.* New York: Times Books, 1983.

Robinson, M.A., H. Morton, and J. Calderwood. *An Introduction to Economic Reasoning.* Washington: Brookings, 1956 (also subsequent editions).

Ross, Arthur M. "The Use and Misuse of Statistics," *Washington Post,* June 30, 1968.

Samuelson, P.A. and W.D. Nordhaus, *Economics,* 12th ed. New York: McGraw-Hill, 1985.

Saunders, Phillip et al. *Master Curriculum Guide in Economics: A Framework for Teaching the Basic Concepts,* 2d ed. New York: Joint Council on Economic Education, 1984.

Schnapper, M.B. *American Labor* (A Pictorial Social History). Washington: Public Affairs Press, 1972.

Schumacher, E.F. *Small Is Beautiful: Economics as if People Mattered.* New York: Harper & Row, 1973.

Schumpeter, Joseph A. *History of Economic Analysis.* New York: Oxford University Press, 1954.

Shaw, George Bernard. *The Intelligent Woman's Guide to Socialism, Capitalism, Sovietism, and Fascism.* New York: Penguin, 1937 (1st ed. published in 1928).

Smith, Adam. *The Wealth of Nations.* New York: Modern Library, 1937 (originally published in 1776 as *An Inquiry into the Nature and Causes of the Wealth of Nations).*

Somers, Gerald G. (editor). *Collective Bargaining: Contemporary American Experience.* Madison, WI: Industrial Relations Research Association, 1980.

Spencer, Milton H. *Contemporary Economics,* 5th ed. New York: Worth, 1983.

Stern, P.M. and G. deVincent. *The Shame of A Nation.* New York: Ivan Obelensky, 1965.

Studenski, P. and H.E. Kroos. *Financial History of the United States,* 2d ed. New York: McGraw-Hill, 1963.

Sweezy, Paul M. *The Theory of Capitalist Development.* New York: Oxford University Press, 1942.

Taft, Philip. *Organized Labor in American History.* New York: Harper & Row, 1964.

Terkel, Studs. *Working.* New York: Random House/Pantheon, 1972.

Thurow, Lester C. *The Zero-Sum Society* (Distribution and the Possibilities for Economic Change). New York: Basic Books, 1980.

Tool, Marc R. *The Discretionary Economy.* Santa Monica, CA: Goodyear, 1979.

Toynbee, Arnold. *The Industrial Revolution.* Boston: Beacon, 1956 (first published in 1884 as *Lectures on the Industrial Revolution in England).*

Twain, Mark. "Sixth-Century Political Economy," Chapter 33 in *A Connecticut Yankee in King Arthur's Court.* Various editions.

Veblen, Thorstein. *The Engineers and the Price System.* New York: Viking, 1921.
––––. *The Instinct of Workmanship and the State of the Industrial Arts.* New York: Macmillan, 1914 (paperback edition by Norton, 1964).
––––. *The Portable Veblen* (see Lerner).
––––. *The Theory of Business Enterprise.* New York: Scribner's, 1904 (paperback edition by Mentor, 1958).
––––. *The Theory of the Leisure Class* (An Economic Study of Institutions). New York: Macmillan, 1899 (Modern Library edition, 1934, and various paperbacks).
Wells, H.G. "The Country of the Blind," from *The Time Machine and Other Stories* in *The Complete Short Stories of H.G. Wells.* New York: St. Martin's, 1971.
Whitmont, Edward C. *The Symbolic Quest: Basic Concepts of Analytical Psychology.* New York: Putnam's, 1969 (paperback edition by Princeton University Press, 1978).
Wilson, Mitchell. *American Science and Invention* (A Pictorial History). New York: Bonanza Books, 1960.
World Bank. *World Development Report 1984.* New York: Oxford University Press (for the World Bank), 1984 (published annually).

Periodicals

AFL-CIO News (weekly newspaper, with monthly "American Federationist" supplement)
American Economic Review (quarterly)
Forbes (biweekly magazine with annual special issue, "The Forbes 400: The 400 Richest People in America")
Fortune (biweekly magazine, with annual feature, "The Fortune 500: The Largest U.S. Industrial Corporations" and similar listings)
International Financial Statistics (monthly publication of the International Monetary Fund; also other IMF statistical series)
Journal of Economic Issues (quarterly)
Journal of Economic Literature (quarterly)
Monthly Review (monthly)
Public Citizen (quarterly)
Review of Institutional Thought (annual)
Review of Radical Political Economics (quarterly)
Wall Street Journal (daily newspaper)

U.S. Government Periodicals and Documents

Business Conditions Digest (monthly). Bureau of Economic Analysis, Department of Commerce.
Current Population Reports. Bureau of the Census.
    Consumer Income, Series P-60, No. 145, "Money Income and Poverty Status of Families and Persons in the United States: 1983" (Advance Data from the March 1984 Current Population Survey), August 1984.
    Household Economic Studies, Series P-70, No. 1, "Economic Characteristics of Households in the United States: Third Quarter 1983" with Average Monthly Data from the Survey of Income and Program Participation, September 1984.
Economic Indicators (monthly). Prepared for the Joint Economic Committee by the Council of Economic Advisers.
Economic Report of the President (yearly). Together with the Annual Report of the Council of Economic Advisers. Executive Office of the President.
Employment and Earnings (monthly). Bureau of Labor Statistics, Department of Labor.
Employment and Training Report of the President (yearly; discontinued after 1982 edition). Employment and Training Administration, Department of Labor.

Federal Reserve Bulletin (monthly). Board of Governors of the Federal Reserve System.

Federal Reserve System: Purposes and Functions. Board of Governors of the Federal Reserve System, 1974.

Governmental Finances in 1982-83 (GF83 No. 5, Government Finances). Bureau of the Census, Department of Commerce, October 1984 (annual series).

Handbook of Labor Statistics (yearly). Bureau of Labor Statistics, Department of Labor.

Historical Statistics of the United States, Colonial Times to 1970. Bureau of the Census, Department of Commerce, 1976.

Monthly Labor Review (monthly). Bureau of Labor Statistics, Department of Labor.

Report of the Joint Economic Committee on the Economic Report of the President (yearly). Joint Economic Committee, Congress.

Statistical Abstract of the United States: National Data Book and Guide to Sources (yearly). Bureau of the Census, Department of Commerce.

Survey of Current Business (monthly). Bureau of Economic Analysis, Department of Commerce.

Technology and the American Economy. Report of the National Commission on Technology, Automation, and Economic Progress, 1966.

Time of Change: 1983 Handbook on Women Workers. Bulletin 298. Women's Bureau, Department of Labor, 1984.

Your Federal Income Tax: For Individuals (yearly). Publication 17 (revised annually). Internal Revenue Service, Department of the Treasury.

Index

About the Author

Robert L. Darcy earned his B.A. from Knox College, M.A. from Indiana University, and Ph.D. from the University of Colorado—all in economics. During a 25-year academic career he held senior faculty positions at Ohio State University, Colorado State University, and Ohio University. Dr. Darcy has served as economic consultant and manpower specialist for the Department of the Treasury, Agency for International Development, the World Bank, Department of Labor, Joint Council on Economic Education, and numerous other organizations in the United States and abroad. His publications include more than 50 articles, contributions to books, research reports, and an earlier book *Manpower and Economic Education* co-authored with Phillip E. Powell. As an independent economist, Dr. Darcy currently devotes his energies to study, teaching, consulting, and writing.